THE POWER GAME

THE HISTORY OF FORMULA 1 AND THE WORLD CHAMPIONSHIP

THE POWER GAME

THE HISTORY OF **FORMULA 1** AND THE WORLD CHAMPIONSHIP

IVAN RENDALL

CASSELL&CO

World Champion
1996: Damon Hill
at Silverstone with
Jordan team-mate
Ralf Schumacher
and guests, 1998.

Contents

Fashion slaves: Diana, Princess of Wales and Prince Harry meet Flavio Briatore of Benetton's Formula 1 team at the 1994 British Grand Prix.

INTRODUCTION

The presence of Diana, Princess of Wales, at Silverstone for the 1994 British Grand Prix gave a huge boost to the new nineties image of Formula 1, endorsing the Fédération Internationale de l'Automobile (FIA) World Championship not only as a great sporting event, but as a rich, glamorous and exciting slice of global popular culture. Her visit was another milestone on motor racing's long march from its origins in the oily shadows of the sporting and social calendar into the bright, new uplands of Cool Britannia. Closer to Wembley than Henley or Ascot, Silverstone is a place for baseball caps and tee-shirts rather than top hats and tails. It is a watering hole for the new rich of New Britain where the royal party mingled in the hospitality tents with the stars of Formula 1 and top people from all points of the celebrity compass: football, pop music, the movies and television.

This smell of New Britain made Silverstone attractive to politicians too, particularly those who wanted to be part of a new, more informal world. In 1995, the deputy leader of the Labour Party, John Prescott, attended the British Grand Prix as the guest of the RAC. In 1996 seven members of parliament attended, among them the Rt Hon Tony Blair MP, Leader of the Opposition. Blair, his wife Cherie and their three children were the guests of the FIA, the sport's governing body. Their host was David Ward, a former Labour Party researcher and campaign organizer, now working as a lobbyist for the FIA. That day the Blairs met Bernard Charles Ecclestone, the undisputed boss of Formula 1, the most powerful man in the World Championship for the last twenty years.

This meeting would have unforseen consequences for Formula 1 and for British politics. Just four months before the General Election, Ecclestone made a secret donation of £1m to the Labour Party, a huge donation by any standards. Only a handful of people in the Party knew about it and had it been public, there would undoubtedly have been comment.

Bernie Ecclestone is something of an enigma.

Now seventy years old, he has been involved in motor racing for fifty years, briefly as a driver, then as a team owner and more recently as head of the Formula 1 family. He is an original South London wheeler-dealer, a used motorcycle and car salesman whose business career included forays into car auctions, property and finance in the 1960s. He is small at 5 ft 3 inches, with darting eyes, an acute awareness of his surroundings and an aura of nervous energy waiting to burst into action. He speaks sparingly, usually in short, rather abrupt sentences, giving little away. In every other sense Ecclestone is a very big man, with a rare combination of high intelligence, shrewdness and boldness supporting a fierce reputation as a negotiator, somebody who lives for the deal. He is feared for the directness of his 'take it or leave it' style, and feared for his instinctive ability to achieve his ends using the personal power that comes with extreme wealth.

He is very rich, with a business empire that reaches beyond Formula 1 into television and property; in the year he met Tony Blair, Ecclestone bought Biggin Hill airfield to house his collection of executive jets and classic racing cars. The bulk of his wealth comes from the commercial structure of Formula 1 which he invented and controls, particularly the many channels of commercial exploitation which flow into Ecclestone family trusts and companies, the most important of which is Formula One Holdings Ltd. His salary in 1996 was £54m. The *Sunday Times* Rich List, a schedule of the thousand richest people in Britain, ranked him 58th in 1997, equal with Lord Forte at £275m. In 1998 he had risen to sixth place, with £1.5bn, just below the Duke of Westminster, putting him among the 500 richest people in the world. In 1999 his ranking slipped to 20th with a mere £900m, the decline due almost entirely to the events which unfolded in 1997.

He is also very powerful. His power base is twofold: he is president of the Formula One Constructors' Association (FOCA), the body which represents the Formula 1 teams, and he is a vice president of the FIA, with which he has a strong, some would say too strong, commercial relationship. Ecclestone is chief executive of Formula 1 in all but name. He is at the hub of a complex web of companies, contracts and personal contacts which control the fees paid by circuit owners to stage Grands Prix (around $10m a race), and from track-side advertising, hospitality and sponsorship worth around $50m a year. This is handled by a Swiss-based Ecclestone company, Allsport Management, run by a close business colleague, Paddy McNally. The biggest money spinner is television: the seventeen Grands Prix are covered by national broadcasters in their respective countries then sold, via Ecclestone's companies, to around 130 broadcasters worldwide, creating revenues put at £200m a year. Race coverage reaches some 5.5 billion viewers a year and with news and feature coverage, the figure rises to over fifty billion viewers worldwide, making it extraordinarily attractive to sponsors, particularly tobacco companies. To exploit that interest, Ecclestone has invested a reported $150m to create his own digital television channel which covers each Grand Prix, giving the viewer five different perspectives of the race on a pay-per-view basis.

The commercial heart of the World Championship is Ecclestone's London base near Hyde Park. From there it spreads out into the Home Counties and the Thames Valley where most of the top Formula 1 teams are based. Southern England is home to a large number of specialist, high-tech manufacturing businesses which have fostered racing car development and manufacture, creating an industry and one of the British success stories of the last thirty years. It is worth £2bn a year in foreign exchange and employs thousands making electronic components and engines which go around the world, and building whole cars for other international formulae, including Indy Car racing in the US.

Ecclestone rules this brash, modern industry in the manner of a stern *pater familias*, leading a small group of people, many of whom have known each other for decades and all of whom have benefitted from the huge wealth generated by television and tobacco sponsorship. Further down the *Sunday Times* list are some long-time colleagues: Sir Frank Williams, Patrick Head, technical director at Williams Grand Prix Engineering, Ron Dennis of McLaren, Paddy McNally, Tom Walkinshaw of Arrows, Jackie Stewart, Eddie Jordan and Dave Richards of ProDrive.

Bernie Ecclestone is one of Britain's great entrepreneurs, on a par with Richard Branson of Virgin and Anne Gloag of Stagecoach, yet he has virtually no public profile or public recognition. He rarely gives interviews; his family does not appear in *Hello* magazine, he is not in *Who's Who*, nor *Debrett's People of Today*, and he has never appeared on any honours list. Ecclestone is by nature and business inclination a secretive person, that is his style. He is custodian of the commercial relationship between FOCA and the Formula 1 teams, particularly the arrangements for the distribution of television income which is enshrined in a series of documents, the Concorde Agreements, the contents of which are secret. The first of these was signed in 1981 when Ecclestone established his power base by wrenching control of Formula 1's finances from the governing body, the FIA.

Ecclestone had kept most of the details of the commercial side of Formula 1 secret for over two decades, but in 1997 they started to leak out when he had to allow public scrutiny of this private world as he prepared to float his businesses on the stock market. The prospects looked bright and when the first leaks of his plans came in March 1997, there was immediate interest. Salomon Brothers had been appointed to handle the flotation and although Ecclestone kept the details secret, speculation about the likely composition of the board of the new company appeared. Estimates of the value of the float varied between £1.5bn and £2.5bn with half the shares to be sold, making Ecclestone a billionaire. He was to keep 30 percent of the shares for himself with 10 percent going to the FIA and the remaining 10 percent going to the FOCA teams and other colleagues. Ecclestone said, 'we are restructuring the way the businesses will be run, away from its entrepreneurial basis towards a more transparent business'.

The flotation was based on three sources of income: the fees paid by track owners; trackside hospitality and advertising; and crucially, television revenues. The latter, it then emerged, were covered by another secret and highly lucrative contract between the FIA and Formula One Holdings granting Ecclestone's company the exclusive rights to televise Grands Prix from 1995 to 2010. This lack of transparency, the suddenness of the revelation of a deal between Ecclestone's company, Formula One Holdings, and the FIA, of which he was a vice president, senate and council member, and on the Formula 1 Commission, sent ripples of uncertainty through the top echelons of Formula 1. It caused at least one major row between Ecclestone and several team bosses. Ecclestone was president of FOCA, in which capacity he represented the teams; FOCA members believed that they owned the television rights which were passed on to the FIA, which in turn were passed on to Formula One Holdings to exploit, sharing in the revenues through the Concorde Agreement. The team bosses were furious when they discovered that the rights had been vested directly in the FIA and passed on in this way. Three team bosses refused to sign a new Concorde Agreement which was due from 1997.

The contract had also come to the attention of the European Union commissioner for competition, Karel van Miert. He had begun investigating the power of the FIA and Ecclestone's companies in motor racing in 1996 when the FIA changed its rules, claiming to own the television rights to any race held under its name, then passed the rights on to Formula One Holdings to exploit. Under the new FIA rules, the promoters of a European GT car and a truck racing championship immediately ran into problems televising their races unless Formula One Holdings was involved. They both went to court and while the GT promoters settled with Ecclestone out of court, the truck racers won in a German court, following which the FIA cancelled their championship, although it later continued in modified form. These two incidents, and the apparently anti-competitive arrangements between the FIA and Formula One Holdings, which could be used to favour Formula 1, triggered a formal EU investigation into the legality of the contract under its competition rules.

When New Labour won the General Election on 1 May 1997, Tony Blair became Prime Minister of a government committed to a new agenda in British politics, politics free from the sleaze associated with the defeated Tories. It also included a manifesto commitment to ban tobacco advertising, a policy in tune with plans by the EU to ban tobacco sponsorship of sport. Three weeks later, on 19 May, the Secretary of State for Health, Frank Dobson, announced that the government would introduce legislation to ban tobacco advertising and sponsorship, reiterating that he did not want to harm any sport and that the government would help find alternatives. It was a policy completely inimical to the interests of Formula 1 with its heavy reliance on tobacco sponsorship. The following day, after consultation with Health Department officials, David Mills, a solicitor and husband of Public Health Minister, Tessa Jowell, resigned as a director of the Benetton Formula 1 team to which he was also legal advisor.

Ecclestone responded to this news a week later from Barcelona where he was presiding over the Spanish Grand Prix. He announced that legislation ending tobacco sponsorship could cause the cancellation of up to eight European Grands Prix, pointing out rather ominously that all contracts with circuits contained a clause which cancelled

Ringmaster and maestro: Bernie Ecclestone, Formula 1 powerbroker and Michael Schumacher, 1990s star driver, play to the cameras.

them automatically if any restrictions were placed on the sport's promotional activities. Ecclestone was using the political power of Formula 1 to dabble in national, European and international politics. Prime ministers and presidents of countries with Grands Prix were acutely conscious of the prestige, popularity and national pride associated with having a national Grand Prix and were keen to hang on to them. Other national leaders, particularly those in the Far East, were equally keen to acquire a national Grand Prix for the same reasons. Ecclestone's statement amounted to a threat to start dismantling Grand Prix racing in Europe and move it to the Pacific Rim where there was a huge appetite for it, plenty of money to back it and a much more relaxed attitude to tobacco sponsorship and advertising. He also made a specific reference to the British Grand Prix, skilfully using not only national pride, but adding the thought that Britain could lose as many as 50,000 jobs which depended on Formula 1.

It was clear to the British government that it was going to have difficulties with Formula 1. Tessa Jowell made a speech in May signalling support for the EU Directive on tobacco sponsorship of sport, admitting that there would be practical problems. She also met with David Ward, the one-time Labour Party colleague, now working for the FIA. Frank Dobson, who was involved in discussions with Brussels over the Directive, minuted Blair on 29 May, seeking the Prime Minister's support for a tough line but saying that sport, and particularly Formula 1, would be an issue.

At the same time as the politics of tobacco sponsorship were stealing the pre-race headlines at the Spanish Grand Prix, in the plush seclusion of the hospitality enclosures the VIP guest list in Barcelona included a group of City financial analysts. They were there to see what a thriving business the World Championship was and to understand how the tobacco sponsorship issue could be countered. They were also there to see Ecclestone's digital television system in operation.

The flotation was reported to be based on forecasts of £600m a year from television five years down the line, three times the 1997 forecast, and much of that increase was to come from digital coverage. The operation the analysts saw was impressive: two jumbo jets to carry twenty identical Renault vans full of equipment, parked at the circuit in order of their consecutive British number plates. The system broadcasts its pay-per-view service to Germany, Italy and France, with pictures from on-board cameras on all the cars in the race compared with just one for terrestrial viewers. The system is destined for Britain as well, but details of how many subscribers it has are a closely guarded secret; despite optimistic forecasts for the future, it is now an open secret that subscriptions have not been up to expectations.

What was not public at Barcelona was the continuing row between Ecclestone and three of his long-time colleagues, Frank Williams, Ron Dennis and Ken Tyrell, who had still not signed the new Concorde Agreement to run from 1997 to 2001. They confronted Ecclestone, demanding a bigger share of the television revenue. The Concorde Agreement was crucial to the flotation because the teams provide the show, and without the top two, Williams and McLaren, the flotation would be dead in the water.

On 6 June, Tessa Jowell met ministerial colleagues from other EU countries and supported the Directive on banning tobacco sponsorship, again warning that there would be problems with Formula 1. Her boss, Frank Dobson then set out his policy for supporting the Directive in a memo to the Prime Minister on 17 July which is supposed to have outlined a number of options ranging from an outright ban to some form of exemption for Formula 1.

The 1997 British Grand Prix was the first time the race had been covered by ITV under a £70m, five-year deal, which had wrenched coverage away from the BBC. There had been indications that July would see Formula One Holdings floated,

possibly even using the British Grand Prix as a backdrop, but later that month, the plans began to falter. There was also uncertainty over what was to be floated. Ecclestone was furious at the leaks and the delay, but he put a brave face on it, insisting that while the flotation was his preferred option, he had thought of 'calling it off entirely', but he was also keeping an 'open mind' about other options. The real problem was that the two contracts which were fundamental to the success of the flotation were both in a state of uncertainty: the 15-year exclusive television contract was being investigated by the EU Competition Commission as potentially anti-competitive; and the Concorde Agreement was mired in dispute with his Formula 1 colleagues.

Another, more general, uncertainty was the future of tobacco sponsorship. In August, the government announced that existing contracts for

sports sponsorship would be allowed to run their course as a result of pressure brought to bear by the tobacco industry. Ecclestone wanted more, and to help him in this battle was Max Mosley, the president of the FIA, who was about to be elected for a second five-year term. Mosley, the son of Britain's wartime fascist leader Sir Oswald Mosley, is a lawyer and has been a close colleague of Ecclestone's since the 1970s when both men ran Formula 1 teams, March and Brabham.

The pace of events quickened. On 23 September, David Ward and Max Mosley met Tessa Jowell and Tony Banks, the Sports Minister. On 26 September the FIA released the provisional calendar for 1998 which showed no French Grand Prix because of a dispute between Ecclestone and the French TV networks, a reminder of the political pressure which could be brought to bear at a national level. On 28 September, the day of the Luxemburg Grand Prix at the Nurburgring, Mosley and Ecclestone met Chancellor Helmut Kohl of Germany to put the case against banning tobacco sponsorship.

On 10 October, the weekend of the Japanese Grand Prix, there were threats of legal action between the FIA and some of the teams which had signed the new Concorde Agreement and were concerned that they had signed away too much. Ecclestone responded through the *Sunday Times* with the comment: 'They think they've got me by the balls, but let me tell you, their hands aren't big enough. Under no circumstances will they get any free equity or a position on the board'.

Four days later Frank Dobson minuted Tony Blair and the whole Cabinet suggesting that Formula 1 would need a longer transitional period than other sports to replace the £100m it received in sponsorship from the tobacco industry and to protect the 8000 jobs it in fact estimated were directly reliant on Formula 1 in Britain. Two days later, on 16 October, Max Mosley, Bernie Ecclestone and David Ward met the Prime Minister at Downing Street. According to notes of the meeting made public later, Mosley opened by saying that the EU Directive made no sense, that if Formula 1 moved out of Europe, there would be more tobacco sponsorship shown on TV coverage of motor racing, not less. He said that he had seen Tessa Jowell but he was not sure if she understood. Tony Blair responded that he did not need persuading of the basic case, but that he was also in favour of the ban. Blair's private secretary asked if alternative sponsors could not be found, for example, car manufacturers; Ecclestone replied that they simply did not have the resources. Ecclestone also said that he had met both Chancellor Kohl of Germany and Prime Minister Prodi of Italy and that they saw the problem and he could not understand why they were arguing for the Directive. The meeting ended with Blair saying they would think about what had been said.

On 20 October Helmut Kohl visited Britain and discussed the EU Directive on tobacco sponsorship with Tony Blair. Kohl was anxious that Formula 1 not be abandoned in a German election year and reports of the meeting hinted at a political trade off: Blair's public support of Formula 1 for Kohl's support in the composition of the committee overseeing the European Bank.

In early November it emerged that Tessa Jowell had written to the EU Commission asking that Formula 1 be exempt from the Directive. When the news reached the anti-smoking lobby, there was an outcry in the press and in parliament, triggering two weeks of frenzied speculation about the relationship between New Labour and Formula 1. On 6 November the news that Tessa Jowell's husband, David Mills, had been an advisor to, and non-executive director of Benetton until he resigned in May, caused a stir, but it was nothing compared to the rumours which swirled around Westminster speculating that Bernie Ecclestone had made a donation to the Labour Party. Ecclestone's solicitors initially appeared to deny the rumours but the speculation continued, putting the Labour Party's famously skilful spin doctors under real pressure for the first time.

The pressure mounted and on 7 November Tom Sawyer, the General Secretary of the Labour Party, wrote to Sir Patrick Neill, Chairman of the Committee on Standards in Public Life, to ask for advice. Meanwhile, the Labour Party prevaricated. On 8 November it issued a statement pointing out that any donation over £5000 would be made public at the time of the Party Conference – nearly a year away – and that until then it was a matter for the donor to make public any donation.

The 9 November edition of the *Sunday Telegraph* reported that Ecclestone was a donor, but did not reveal the amount. It also reported that when Ecclestone's solicitors were asked if the denial included any contribution to blind trusts, they responded by saying that Ecclestone was 'not prepared to enter into a dialogue'. Later the same

A day to remember: 11 November 1997, the day Ecclestone's £1m donation to New Labour was revealed, and Schumacher was let off the hook.

day Tony Blair was pressed to reveal whether Max Mosley had made donations to the Labour Party. It emerged that Mosley was a member of a club, each of whom contributed over £1000 each a year to the Party for a number of years. The weekend was rounded off with general denials that there was any link between any donation and any government decisions, and this was linked in turn to a call for an overhaul of the funding of political parties.

The next day, 10 November, Sir Patrick Neil advised Tom Sawyer that the donation should be returned. News started to circulate, although the amount was still kept secret, Party spokesmen repeating that they could not reveal the size of the donation without Ecclestone's permission. The following day Ecclestone's solicitors announced that the donation had been £1m. Downing Street confirmed it the same day, adding that the money would be returned.

The press had a field day. It was the first blemish on the clean image upon which New Labour had been elected and on which it had promised to govern. Ecclestone continued to deny that his donation had anything to do with tobacco sponsorship.

The problem was that Formula 1 had been given special treatment and now other sports from rugby and cricket to snooker and darts wanted meetings with the Prime Minister. Blair knew about the donation before the meeting on 16 October, but his spokesman denied any link between Ecclestone's generosity and the reversal of the government's policy on tobacco and Formula 1, saying that it had never 'entered the Prime Minister's mind'.

As if one controversy was not enough, by an ironic twist, on the same day that he confirmed the size of his donation, Ecclestone, the FIA and the World Championship were the subject of more attention from the press, thrusting Bernie Ecclestone into more unwelcome limelight. Michael Schumacher had appeared before the World Motor Sports Council following an incident in the European Grand Prix at Jerez in Spain. He had collided with Jacques Villeneuve in what many saw as an attempt to take them both out of the race which would have left Schumacher World Champion. It was a serious charge. Instead of a ban or racing penalty for the following season, the World Council handed down a paltry penalty. There was outrage inside and outside the sport that Schumacher, because of his powerful supporters, appeared to be beyond the reach of the regulations. Max Mosley defended the decision but it left a very nasty taste. It was clear that Formula 1 was a business first, and a sport second.

The way that Formula 1 conducted its business became embroiled with the donation controversy which continued to swirl round Westminster. It was a golden opportunity for the Conservatives and William Hague landed several good punches on Blair, claiming that unless he gave way on other sports, he would be 'strangling the life out of working-class sport'.

For the first time as Prime Minister, Tony Blair looked rattled. He denied that Ecclestone's £1m donation had influenced decisions over tobacco advertising, saying 'there was never any favour sought or given, absolutely not'. Some Labour MPs were shocked at the size of the donation and those on the left expressed astonishment: Ken Livingstone MP, said he was 'stunned' and had assumed that big donations meant £15–20,000, not £1m; Diane Abbot MP, pointed out that the NEC Finance Panel, on which she sat, was not told the identity of big donors, nor how much they had donated, and added 'we need to be very, very careful'. Martin Bell MP, elected on a specifically anti-sleaze ticket, called it 'influence for cash'.

Tony Blair made an unprecedented appearance on the BBC's 16 November edition of the current affairs programme *On The Record*, and defended himself against accusations of sleaze. He said he was 'sorry' for the 'dribs and drabs' of information which had come out about the relationship between Labour and Ecclestone and that he took 'full responsibility' for 'presentational' mistakes.

The television appearance did the trick and after a nasty ten days, the controversy began to subside.

The EU Commission responded to Tessa Jowell's letter with condemnation of the British cave-in and in December there was a long and noisy debate behind closed doors in Brussels. The result was that the EU agreed to ban tobacco sponsorship of sport, but Britain held out for, and got, a suspension of the ban for Formula 1 until 2006. Ecclestone had most of what he wanted.

The biggest loser in all of this was the Labour Party which had suffered the first scratches on its shining image. In the course of the debate, the argument that Britain would lose thousands of high-tech jobs, which the government had apparently accepted, was shown to be unwarranted. The reality was, that like the computer industry in Silicon Valley in California, the Thames Valley home of Formula 1 was an intricate and solid network of individual and corporate relationships between dozens of small businesses and individuals built up over decades; such an industry could not be moved suddenly to Asia. Even if the Pacific Rim had been able to take up the slack if European Grands Prix were cancelled, the collapse of the currencies and the damage to the economies in the Far East which followed shortly after this, dented the argument. There was always the prospect that if Formula 1 went East, a rival series would arise in Europe. But the killer argument was that the non-tobacco sponsors, particularly the engine, oil, fuel and accessory sponsors, and the manufacturers, would not be happy to see Grand Prix racing moved out of its traditional heartland in Europe, with its huge and dedicated base of loyal fans, simply to satisfy the demands of tobacco, an industry which some of them were finding an uncomfortable bedfellow. Would the fanatical tribe of Italian fans, the *tifosi*, used to two Grands Prix a year, be happy with one race every three years? Probably not, and without them there would be no more Ferrari, the mystique of which is one of Formula 1's great attractions.

On reflection, Ecclestone's threats, backed by Mosley, looked weak and more like well-pitched scaremongering. Whatever spin was put on it, New Labour had been bluffed into accepting the arguments, bluffed into a dramatic policy U-turn for which it paid a high political price. To cap it all, on 19 March 1998 the Commissioner for Standards rebuked Tony Blair for not declaring the hospitality extended to him and his family at the British Grand Prix in 1996.

Bernie Ecclestone had challenged the British Government and the EU and won. He had secured a lengthy extension of the existing arrangements, and the tobacco money would continue to flow for a further nine years at least. And he got his £1m back. History will show the true effect of the events of 1997 on Formula 1 but it seems that the year represented a peak in the growth and extravagance of the sport, and in Ecclestone's power and ability to control events. Whatever his successes, the long-term effect of the failed flotation in July and the scandal over the £1m donation to Labour in November, turned Ecclestone into a very public man, exposed to scrutiny. The tobacco sponsorship issue had tainted Formula 1 and the World Championship with a whiff of sleaze, something it was not used to. It appears to have weakened Ecclestone. He had successfully put off the tobacco ban, but the 15-year contract with the FIA for exclusive television coverage of Formula 1 remained under investigation by the EU and the flotation of his interests in Formula 1 was reliant on it not being declared illegal by the European Commission which would take time to deliberate.

Mosley wrote to Karel van Miert asking for a letter of comfort to indicate that the contracts between Formula One Holdings and the FIA were lawful and not anti-competitive. Mosley gave the commissioner two weeks to reply, adding that if the EU refused, ways of addressing the problem could include the FIA moving its headquarters and that of Ecclestone's companies out of the jurisdiction of the EC, and also limiting the number of Grands

Prix in Europe, the same threat that had been used in the tobacco row. No letter of comfort was forthcoming.

In September, instead of floating Formula One Holdings, Ecclestone decided to raise the money using the Eurobond market. On 19 November 1998, his advisors issued a prospectus for $2bn worth of bonds. The bond was largely based on the value of the television contracts and if the EC found against them, that value could be affected. The battle of wills between Bernie Ecclestone and Karel van Miert continued into 1999, surviving the mass resignation of the whole EU Commission. As part of the process the FIA moved its headquarters from Paris, the city where motor racing had started and where successive governing bodies had administered it for over a century, to Geneva in Switzerland, outside the jurisdiction of the EU.

In May 1999, a reduced version of what had become known as the 'Bernie bond' was issued. It was valued at $1.4bn (£880m), underwritten by Morgan Stanley Dean Witter and Westdeutsche Landesbank, the money going to Ecclestone's companies, and secured against the revenues from the television rights vested in Formula One Holdings under its contract with the FIA. A condition of the issue was that Ecclestone had to establish a 'comfort fund', reportedly £255m, in part because the EU investigation into the legality of the contract was still pending.

In late June, Ecclestone went into hospital for a heart bypass operation, then on 30 June 1999, the *Financial Times* published the initial conclusions of the report by the European Commission into the television contract, concluding that it did break EU competition law. The FIA and Ecclestone had until autumn 1999 to appeal against the report, but if its findings are upheld, then the contracts will have to be renegotiated, or the FIA and Ecclestone could face fines of up to 10 percent of turnover.

The uncertainty over television contracts and the politics of tobacco continue to frustrate Ecclestone but it has done nothing to dampen the enthusiasm of sponsors eager to be associated with Formula 1. The World Championship is a powerful global promotional tool, a hugely effective platform for increasing sales of products as diverse as cigarettes, cars, ballpoint pens, financial services, magazines, airlines, computers and computer games, jewellery, fruit drinks, mens' fashion, international telecommunications and an even longer list of motor accessories.

Formula 1's prestige is undiminished, but the structure for that success was created by Bernie Ecclestone. The events of 1997–9, and the prospect of his departure, have created a flurry of interest, not just among sponsors, but also among long-term investors. Benetton's Formula 1 team has been run as part of its clothing empire since 1986, creating the model for investing directly. British American Tobacco bought Ken Tyrell's team outright in 1998 and plans to invest a further £200m. In 1999 Eddie Jordan sold 50 percent of his team to Warburg Pincus, a private US equity fund, and Tom Walkinshaw sold a controlling interest in Arrows to a private equity consortium led by Morgan Grenfell for £77m.

Morgan Grenfell Private Equity (MGPE), a venture capital subsidiary of Deutsche Bank, decided to move even further into Formula 1, opening up secret discussions with Bernie Ecclestone for a stake in Formula One Holdings. In September 1999, *Sunday Business*, the paper which broke the original story of Ecclestone's plans to float in 1997, reported that he was close to a deal to sell half his interests. The following month a deal was announced between MGPE and Ecclestone in which the bank paid $325m for $12\frac{1}{2}$ per cent of the business with an option on a further $37\frac{1}{2}$ per cent for which it would then seek other investors, valuing the whole business at $2.6bn. The bank had clearly decided that even if the EU eventually does rule against the television contracts, as a business, Formula 1 still has great value and even greater potential for growth. The strategy for the future is clear; with serious investors on board, and City people closely involved in managing the business, the prospect of a trade sale, or Ecclestone's dream of flotation, possibly in two or three years' time, is now a more realistic prospect than two years ago.

The sale signalled great changes ahead for the World Championship, and not just in the way Ecclestone is replaced. Formula 1 is going through a revolution every bit as great as the technical revolution of the 1950s, and the commerical revolution of the 1970s, the latter brought about almost entirely by Bernie Ecclestone. As the bankers move in, so too are the major motor manufacturers. They are returning to Formula 1 as part of a process of global rationalization which will probably see just six major names at the top in a few years time. They see the World Championship playing a leading part in projecting selected brand names on a global scale, and their investment makes the whole all the more exciting for other investors.

The manufacturers may take a stake in Ecclestone's evolving business, but their first interest is via the teams, the performers in the global spectacle, who currently occupy the high ground in Formula 1. In 1999, Ford paid £50m for the whole of the Stewart team and announced it will change the name to Jaguar, another of its subsidiaries, in 2000. Stewart rewarded the US giant with its first victory at the Nurburgring in the European Grand Prix. Daimler-Chrysler, which owns Mercedes, is widely reported to be negotiating for 50 per cent of McLaren, the combination which won both the 1998 and 1999 championships. The other great team of the 1980s and 1990s, Williams, has an engine deal with BMW valued at £40m a year for five years, starting in 2000, and until 1999 Honda, which was planning to return with its own works team in 2000 by investing $600m over five years, opted instead to return via its traditional role as engine supplier to BAR, owned by the British American Tobacco, and Jordan, a team which has shown huge promise in 1999, started by former banker Eddie Jordan.

Amid all the heightened speculation about the future, and despite heart surgery, Bernie Ecclestone headed towards the exit with that almost invisible sense of purpose which is his hallmark. In 1999, he continued to play his quiet but crucial role as impressario on race weekends, presiding over one of the most spectacular, ragged and controversial Championships for many years. The season ended in victory for McLaren in the Driver's title and Ferrari in the Constructors' title, but only after both Ferraris were disqualified in Malaysia for illegally shaped barge boards. This made Mika Hakinnen World Champion in Malaysia, a result dubbed as 'nonsense' by Ecclestone and overturned by the FIA before Hakinnen's victory in the final race of the season in Japan. The audience had a treat but for many close to Formula 1, it was another triumph for internecine politics, television contracts and box office over fairness, sportsmanship and the rule book. To understand it is to understand that Formula 1 is different from other sports; it is a tiny, very rich club for tough men, all of whom know the score, and Bernie Ecclestone is one of the richest and toughest. For those who understand but do not accept this, it was another step towards ever-greater commerciality, reinforcing Formula 1's drift from a sport to one of the jewels in the crown of global popular culture.

After 25 years under Ecclestone's control, with his family of team owners growing rich on the proceeds, the entrpreneurial phase of the World Championship is drawing to an end. An elaborate negotiation is going on over who will own and run Formula 1 in the future. Big business and serious money are moving in, and as they do, Formula 1 is moving towards a more corporate future. The problem is that much of its current popularity and success is based on the sharp wits and wisdom of one man and the real question is, can it survive in a form its supporters recognize without Ecclestone's rare talents and his raw, secretive, entrepreneurial spirit.

Epic proportions: The 13-litre Renault in which
François Szisz won the first Grand Prix in 1906,
held over 2 days, 769 miles, averaging 62.9 mph.

I

EXCELLENCE:

THE ROAD RACING TRADITION

The Grand Prix has been the ultimate test in motor racing for nearly a century. The Formula 1 World Championship, which has been awarded to the driver with the best overall performance in Grand Prix racing each year since 1950, is the ultimate prize in world motor sport by a wide margin. Each race is a spectacle, a clash of high technologies which have evolved behind closed doors, literally from race to race. Each race is a test of supreme driving skill and strong nerves, making Formula 1 the most expensive sport in the world, also by a wide margin. These lasting traditions, of self-conscious excellence, of being the ultimate proving ground of men and machines, were established over a century ago. Although these traditions are the dynamic force behind both evolutionary and revolutionary change in the sport, they are, in turn, based on even more fundamental ideas and themes which have endured in a highly recognizable form since the turn of the last century.

Motor racing began on public roads in France in 1894. There was no regulation: the pioneers drove for days at a time in epic races from Paris to Bordeaux, Paris to Vienna, Paris to Amsterdam, and back, along roads with other traffic, lined with spectators. Speeds increased prodigiously, largely by the expedient of making engines bigger and bigger, and public hostility to the obvious dangers grew. It was banned in France in 1900 but the political influence of the motor lobby was so powerful, not unlike today, that after a brief hiatus, the politicians relented and racing started again. By 1903, engines were around 20 litres and speeds had risen to 80 mph and that year a great race was planned from Paris to Bordeaux and back. There were 275 entrants, starting at intervals, but long before the leaders reached Bordeaux, eight people had been killed, including Marcel Renault, one of the founding brothers of the firm, and many more injured. The race was stopped; racing on open roads was banned in France and this time it stuck.

Motor racing has always been political. To mark the beginning of a new century, in 1900, a series of international races were sponsored by the American publisher James Gordon Bennett. These races were designed to encourage competition between national teams with each race being held in the country of the previous winner. The Automobile Club de France (ACF) was hostile to the Gordon Bennett races because they were only entitled to the same representation as the minor nations in motor car manufacturing; the ACF saw motor racing as a French sport and intended to keep it that way. The 1905 race was held in the Auvergne in France, and a Frenchman, Leon Thery, won whereupon the ACF announced it would neither sanction nor enter another Gordon Bennett Trophy race. Instead it planned what was billed as the greatest motor race ever: the Grand Prix, worth 100,000 francs, to be won by the best driver in the best car. The first Grand Prix was scheduled for two days in June 1906 on what is still, largely, the circuit used today for the Le Mans 24-hour sports car race. The formula was simple: 1000kg weight limit with no regulation on engine size. Entry was limited to manufacturers and there were ten from France, two from Italy, one from Germany and none from Britain.

The first ever Grand Prix was won by François Szisz in a Renault largely because his car was fitted with detachable wheel rims which saved up to 10 minutes at each of the numerous tyre changes. The other competitors had to slash off the old tyres with a knife and lever on the new tyres. Grand Prix racing had been born. In 1907 it was won by an Italian driver in a Fiat and in 1908 by a German in a Mercedes.

Grand Prix racing was as costly then as it is now, and in the world recession of 1908–9 entries fell as the big companies pulled out, forcing change on the sport. There were no Grands Prix for three years, but in response to motor racing's continuing popularity in France, 'voiturette' racing, where the emphasis was on lightness and getting more power out of ever smaller engines, filled the gap. Economic necessity produced a technical revolution in 1911–12, the first double overhead camshaft engines designed to get more power out of each litre, engines which are essentially the basis of those used today.

In Britain and America, motor racing took a different course. Unable to race on the roads, entrepreneurs built banked, oval circuits, the first at Brooklands in Surrey in 1907, the second at Indianapolis in 1909. Circuit racing was completely different from road racing with its variety of corners, inclines and cambers which took far more skill. In circuit racing, drivers could optimise their cars for that circuit alone. Indianapolis attracted crowds, Brooklands less so, but neither challenged the primacy of road racing as the top of the sport.

The recession had eased by 1912 and the ACF reinstituted the Grand Prix on a closed road circuit at Dieppe, with a separate race for voiturettes. French drivers won both races. French engineers had become the masters of the smaller engine, and to capitalize on it, a formula, limiting engine size to 4.5 litres, was introduced for the 1914 Grand Prix at Lyons. Mercedes and Peugeot built cars specially for the race, creating another lasting tradition in Grand Prix racing – the special car, the pure thoroughbred, representing the pinnacle of automotive engineering, built for one race only, adding even more lustre to Grand Prix racing as the ultimate contest. In 1914 the principle ingredients of Grand Prix racing were in place and they remain the same today: the idea of a great contest using cars built specially for the occasion with a lightweight, powerful engine, driven by the best drivers.

Mercedes won in 1914, just weeks before the First World War. When motor racing started again in 1919, Germany was a pariah state, France was shattered and Britain was still limited to racing at Brooklands. The big French manufacturers had been depleted by war so in France a private, specialized company, Ballot, started building

Thoroughbred: Christian Lautenschlager's winning 4.5-litre Mercedes, winner of the 1914 Grand Prix at Lyons.

Grand Prix cars. Fiat and Alfa Romeo picked up the baton for Italy, Sunbeam for Britain and Duesenberg for America. The French Grand Prix was run again in 1921, but it was won by an American, Jimmy Murphy, in a Duesenberg. In the same year, the Italian Automobile Club took up the idea of the national Grand Prix and staged the first race on closed roads at Brescia; Jules Goux of France won in a Ballot.

Ballot expired through lack of funds and Fiat dominated road racing during the early 1920s. Britain's first and only Grand Prix victory until the 1950s came when Henry Segrave won the 1923 French Grand Prix in a Sunbeam. Alfa Romeo then dominated with their 1.5-litre supercharged P2s, winning in 1924 and 1925, including the first Belgian Grand Prix that year, on a road circuit at Spa. The Italian Alfa Corse team was run by a man who had driven for the company until 1924 when a nervous breakdown had forced him to retire from driving. Enzo Anselmo Ferrari was a hugely complex, emotional, unpredictable and autocratic man whose name has been at the forefront of road racing ever since.

Born on 18 February 1898 in Modena, the son of a metal worker, Ferrari failed at college but was supremely ambitious, and after service as a farrier in the Great War, set his sights on being a racing driver. Fiat rejected him so he joined Alfa Romeo. In 1923 Ferrari won the Circuito di Savio Acerbo where he met Count Enrico Barracca, the father of Major Francesco Barracca, Italy's top-scoring fighter pilot in the First World War. The count bestowed upon Ferrari the honour of carrying on his car the emblem which his late son had emblazoned on his Spad fighter – a black prancing horse on a yellow and black shield. In 1924 Ferrari won three major road races carrying the Prancing Horse, including the Coppa Acerbo where he beat the much-fancied Mercedes team; Mussolini awarded him the title *Commendatore*. Ferrari was a fixer and one of his early coups had been to lure Vittorio Jano, a great designer of the day, away

from Fiat to Alfa where he designed the P2. Poaching talent from rivals has been another feature of Grand Prix racing ever since; John Barnard, Ross Brawn and Adrian Newey are the most recent examples, part of the process of putting together the best team or package, as it is called today. Ferrari's great skill was in spotting driving talent, design talent and engine-tuning talent and making deals to get that talent together using cajolery, force of personality and where necessary, money

Racing on open roads was wonderfully romantic but it was also dangerous and uneconomic. France and Italy built artificial circuits at Montlhéry and Monza so that spectators could see the whole race and, like Brooklands, be charged for entry, but they were artificial road circuits rather than banked ovals, reproducing the conditions of road racing, albeit somewhat tamed. As these circuits were being built, recession hit again and in the mid-1920s, the big manufacturers stopped building new, expensive Grand Prix cars each year. National Grands Prix, run to an international formula, were held up to 1928, using existing cars, but they were shadows of the great events of 1921–5. From 1929, the Alliance Internationale des Automobile Clubs Reconnus (AIACR), the sport's governing body, abandoned true Grand Prix racing altogether.

Recession did not blunt the demand for racing and to meet it, small specialist manufacturers flourished. Among the greatest was Ettore Bugatti who sold racing and sports cars to rich, private entrants while racing a small number of his cars with paid professional drivers to enhance the name. Enzo Ferrari did the same for Alfa, and this lean era produced the idea of the 'stable', the *scuderia* in Italy, the *écurie* in France. These small operations honed their skills in race management and financial juggling, and found out by experience and competition what it took to win races when times were hard. The origins of this system are still recognizable in Formula 1 today.

Just as silver McLarens and red Ferraris dominate the late 1990s, so the late 1920s were dominated by red Alfas and blue Bugattis, whose team was run by Ettore Bugatti himself with the help of an ex-driver, Bartolomeo Costantini.

They raced at local circuits which often used the title Grand Prix, but were run under open formulae with little of the sense of a great event. One such was the Monaco Grand Prix, today the most prestigious Grand Prix in the world, which was run for the first time in 1929. The Bugattis, Alfas and Maseratis of this period are some of the most beautiful racing cars ever made, but for economic reasons, they were raced from year to year with only minor technical advances, and the tradition of the thoroughbred Grand Prix car, the best, regardless of cost, went into abeyance.

By meeting a need, the *scuderia* showed what a small dedicated team, rather than a department of a large corporate entity, could do. The single most crucial element in that system was the dedicated individual, working at one remove from the manufacturer or completely independently. They were driven to win in a way that big corporate bodies could not summon up, men with the ability to create the small group dynamics which were vital to winning. Enzo Ferrari was one such individual and wanted his own *scuderia*. He went into partnership with three wealthy businessmen to form Societa Anonima Scuderia Ferrari, putting in 50,000 lire of his own money. The papers were signed on 1 December 1929; the emblem of the new *scuderia* was the black prancing horse against a yellow shield.

Scuderia Ferrari relied on sponsorship in the form of cars and spares from Alfa provided at cost along with other parts such as tyres, fuel, spark plugs and carburettors. He employed the best drivers he could find to drive his works cars and serviced cars for rich no-hopers, the equivalent of the pay drivers of today, to provide income for the operation. The other source of funds was starting money which race organizers paid to the big names

to attract the crowds. The benefit to Alfa Romeo was that if its cars were successful, the spin-off came in sales of their more exclusive sports cars, and it came at a low and easily controllable cost.

The first German Grand Prix was held at AVUS, a specially built test track near Berlin, in 1926, then in 1927 the second was held at the Nurburgring, a 14.7-mile circuit in the Eifel Mountains which had been built as a public enterprise to put unemployed people to work. The first race was won by Rudolf Caracciola in a Mercedes Benz; attendance was measured in hundreds of thousands of patriotic fans. It was the same in Italy where motor racing produced a unique phenomenon, the *tifosi*, literally those who shout, from the wonderfully evocative Italian word *tifare*, to shout. They supported Scuderia Ferrari's Alfas as a national team, as well as an Alfa team. Road racing in Europe was a sport which, though you had to be rich to compete, was also one which involved national pride and people, ordinary working people did go to races for the thrill, for patriotism and for the escape which the spectacle provided from economic depression.

British motor racing operated in a different social *milieu*. Brooklands started up again after the war but it was run as a club for a social elite, further isolating drivers and engineers from the continental tradition. The first British Grand Prix was held in 1926 just as the economic climate was changing, and it was held at Brooklands because there was nowhere else. To simulate the conditions of road racing, a twisting circuit was marked with straw bales and oil drums on the vast concrete apron. A second race was held in 1927 but the club members were not particularly interested and any stirring of interest by a mass audience was quickly damped down by the high entry charges which kept out the hoi polloi. In 1928 the RAC was offered the opportunity to run the rather grandly titled European Grand Prix, but declined.

Road races had been held in America and American drivers had come to Europe to take part

Social impact: Britain's answer to the popularity of road racing in Europe was Brooklands, where social standing was of supreme importance.

RACE CARDS

in Grands Prix, but US manufacturers also pulled out and specialist racing car builders took over. The greatest was Harry Miller who built superbly engineered cars for Indianapolis and supplied cars to American drivers for what became the indigenous form of racing in the US – short oval racing on hastily built, wooden, banked ovals capable of packing in paying spectators, running it as a mass entertainment business.

True Grand Prix racing was revived in 1933, not with money from the motor industry but on the back of the election of Adolf Hitler. Hitler understood the mass appeal of Grand Prix racing and how it could be mixed with national pride to generate a powerful political tool. Within weeks of being elected, he started pouring money into Mercedes Benz and Auto Union, specifically to create racing cars which would dominate the top level of the sport. The effect of the injection of the right kind of money was swift: of the 20 races in 1933, Alfa Romeos won 11, Maseratis won 4 and Bugattis won 5. Of 12 major races in 1934, Alfa won 4, Bugatti 1, Mercedes 4 and Auto Union 5. In 1935, the German teams wiped the floor, winning 13 of the 14 major races. Their most compelling victory was in the French Grand Prix, a crushing blow to French pride. The one anomaly was the German Grand Prix, where Tazio Nuvolari, arguably the greatest racing driver to date, won in a Scuderia Ferrari Alfa P3 in the face of German might, one of the most fabulous drives in the history of Grand Prix racing.

Nuvolari's victory was an exception. Money talks in motor racing and money wins; France effectively withdrew from Grand Prix racing in the face of the German onslaught. The ACF changed its rules for 1936–7, running the French Grand Prix for sports cars instead; Talbot, Delahaye, Delage, Amilcar and Bugatti responded, but it was not Grand Prix racing. The ACF set up a Million Francs race and a Racing Fund Committee to channel funds into French racing car makers, particularly Antonio Lago, who established Talbot

as a sports car company. He built a 4-litre engine which was successful in local Grand Prix, but only when Mercedes and Auto Union were away. With few exceptions, Mercedes and Auto Union won all the true Grands Prix until the outbreak of war in 1939, a period of dominance unparalleled in the history of Grand Prix racing until McLaren's dominance in the late 1980s. It was then, as it is now, based on money.

In Italy, Benito Mussolini copied his German fascist colleague by putting money into Alfa Romeo, the only company to offer real competition, although they could not match the Germans. Enzo Ferrari had been successful, but as Mercedes and Auto Union continued to trounce everything in sight, he and Vittorio Jano were treated as scapegoats. Jano was sacked and Alfa tried to close down Scuderia Ferrari and bring Enzo Ferrari back inside to pursue voiturette racing instead. Ferrari developed the Alfa Tipo 158 with Gioachino Colombo; Maserati followed suit with the 8CLT, largely as a way of racing without facing the Germans, but Mercedes responded with its own voiturette, the W165. The new voiturettes met for the first time at the Tripoli Grand Prix, 28 Italian cars, the star drivers being Dr Giuseppe 'Nino' Farina and Luigi Villoresi for Alfa, against two Mercedes, driven by Rudolf Caracciola and Herman Lang, who came first and second.

Enzo Ferrari was not there to see it. He could not work with Wilfredo Ricart, the new chief engineer at Alfa. Ferrari was a man used to having his own way and in the inevitable power struggle which followed, he left Alfa in 1939. Alfa Romeo created its own in-house racing team again, Alfa Corse, and under the terms of his severance Ferrari was not allowed to be involved in racing as Scuderia Ferrari for four years, years which coincided with the Second World War.

While Germany dominated Grand Prix racing in Europe, it was banned in Britain. The RAC was tied to Brooklands' thinking, creating two barriers to the advancement of road racing in Britain, technical and social, and Brooklands never spawned the superb cars and heroic drivers which emerged on the continent, making it a sport with a mass appeal. Motor cycle racing was the common man's motor sport in Britain. There was popular interest in motor racing in Britain in the 1930s but, bereft of a focus, it centred on building 'specials', usually modified Austin 7 saloon cars raced on any piece of open ground that the enthusiasts could find. One man who built such specials was Charles Cooper, who owned a garage in Surbiton, not far from Brooklands. Charles Cooper's son John had been gripped by racing from the age of eight when his father had built him a kiddy car with a real engine, and from the age of twelve, he and his great friend Eric Brandon, formed a motor cycle racing club with friends, hiring local fields and racing bikes they bought for under £1. John Cooper was typical of many people who raced for fun, graduating from bikes to specials, knowing little about road racing on the continental scale.

In the mid-1930s, the first glimmerings of change appeared in Britain. Two initiatives, one which provided the circuit and another which provided the cars, were started by two very different individuals. The first was a rather gruff Midlands motor trader, Fred Craner, of the Derby and District Motor Club, who wanted a more popular form of motor racing in Britain and set out to provide it, locally. He started by persuading the owner of Donington Hall, one of Derbyshire's great houses, to allow the club to run motor cycle races along the private roads within the grounds in 1931. The response was so positive that he was able to raise £12,000 to widen the course to take cars in 1933. He had created an artificial road racing circuit which was tiny by continental standards, but it attracted huge crowds.

Craner held a local Grand Prix at Donington in 1935. It was not big enough to attract the continental teams but Giuseppe Farina entered his private Maserati and Raymond Sommer his private Alfa Romeo, similar to the one Tazio

Nuvolari had just driven to beat the Germans in their own Grand Prix. It was the first single-seater Grand Prix car to come to Britain. Richard Shuttleworth, a wealthy British playboy entrant, drove another Alfa. British enthusiasts had never seen anything like it: Farina and Sommer made the running until mechanical problems intervened and Shuttleworth won.

In fifth place in that race was Prince Birabongse of Thailand who was studying at Cambridge, driving an ERA. English Racing Automobiles (ERA) was started in 1933 by Humphrey Cook, who had inherited huge wealth at the age of twelve and led a life of leisure which included racing at Brooklands. There he met two other leisured individuals, Raymond Mays and Peter Berthon, an ex-RAF officer who had spent time as a racing mechanic at Brooklands. They wanted to build cars to match Bugatti in France and Alfa in Italy, cars which could be raced and also be sold to wealthy private customers.

Humphrey Cook put up the money, Mays and Berthon provided the technical expertise, and the chassis for the first ERA was built by Brooklands specialists, Thompson & Taylor. It was then shipped to the Mays family home where the stables were converted into an assembly shop to match it with the 1.5-litre supercharged engine. The first was ready for Easter 1934 and made its debut at Brooklands, then Mays took it to Donington for the Nuffield Trophy, the first long-distance road race at Donington, which he won. Private customers started to order ERAs at £2000 each, three times the price of a family house at the time.

Mays took the works car to the continent where the ERA's first real success came when they took four of the first five places in the Eifelrennen at the Nurburgring, applauded by 400,000 people, which was a novel experience for the British road racing pioneers. In 1936 Craner held another Donington Grand Prix attracting five privately entered ERAs which were all eclipsed by Richard Seaman in an Alfa Romeo.

In 1937 Fred Craner's dream of attracting the Mercedes and Auto Union teams to Donington came true. On 2 October, 50,000 British fans were treated to a spectacle they could hardly believe, the true, staggering power and speed of real Grand Prix cars at full throttle, covering their ears against the sound of Mercedes and Auto Unions at 170 mph. Bernd Rosemeyer won for Auto Union with Manfred von Brauchitsch second for Mercedes; Prince 'Bira' was sixth in a Maserati and Earl Howe seventh in a works ERA, many laps behind. This was the day that a true understanding of Grand Prix racing struck home in Britain, the sheer spectacle, sound and competitive surge of the great cars stirring hearts in Britain to wish for something similar.

In 1938, having learned a great deal from voiturette racing at Donington and on the continent, ERA started development on a true Grand Prix car. Then Cook and Mays split, and Berthon went with Mays to start a luxury car company. Cook, who had already put some £75,000 into ERA, could not support the Grand Prix project on his own so he appealed for public subscription and government funding on patriotic grounds. The public response was disappointing and the government declined. Working on a shoestring, ERA produced 'the GP car' as it was called, which was unveiled at Reims on 6 July 1939, though not raced. It was raced once, at Albi later that month: Arthur Dobson, the ERA works driver, lead at the start but not for long because of mechanical problems. That summer, as Britain was on the brink of producing its first Grand Prix car, Europe went to war again.

When hostilities ended in 1945 motor racing had changed forever. The French establishment saw France, the inventor of Grand Prix racing, as the natural home of the sport. Germany and Italy, the other two great road racing nations, were out, having been defeated in the war, so the ACF grasped the opportunity to re-establish its pre-eminent position. The first post-war meeting was held on 9 September 1945 in the Bois de Boulogne near Paris, using pre-war cars. The French government backed a national motor racing project through the Centre d'Etudes Techniques de l'Automobile where the designer Albert Lory laid out a 1.5-litre V8 supercharged engine. It was a patriotic gesture, a national emblem in tune with the times; although the engine produced 260 bhp, the handling was very poor. At Talbot, Antonio Lago set about putting France back on the map again, resurrecting his pre-war 4.5-litre 1939 car while making plans for a new Talbot, the T26C, a 4.5-litre unsupercharged single-seater.

Germany had been beaten in the war, and the Mercedes and Auto Union factories had been flattened. The country was divided between East and West, and the Iron Curtain went straight through Germany's circuit at AVUS. The mastermind of Mercedes' pre-war team, Alfred Neubauer, was still there and had been employed supervising the repair of military vehicles; so was Rudolf Uhlenhaut, the race engineer. Dr Ferdinand Porsche, the designer of the Auto Unions, was in prison in France. Slowly, Germany would be rehabilitated, but in the immediate post-war era, its cars and drivers were not welcome.

Italy on the other hand had been beaten but not flattened. Monza had been used to store military vehicles and had been bombed by the Allies but it was largely intact; work began on restoring it. Most important, the great Italian motor racing fraternity had survived the war, and in 1945 they were eager to get going again. To escape the attention of their allies, the Germans, a number of the Alfa 158 voiturettes had been hidden in a cheese factory and as soon as the war was over the Alfa management decided to get back into racing using these cars in a works team. Maserati, the other great Italian name of the 1930s, planned a works team, Scuderia Ambrosiana, with Count 'Johnny' Lurani as manager, using its Maserati 4CL which also became the car of choice for privateers as they geared up after the war.

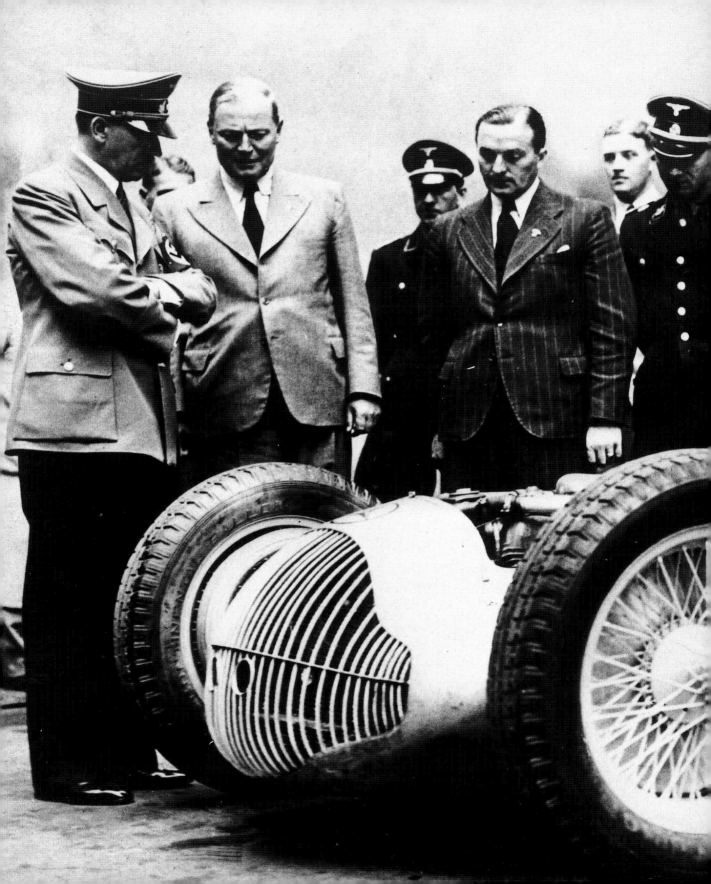

Nazi business: Adolf Hitler admiring the Mercedes W154 in 1938; Grands Prix were state-funded to promote German superiority.

The third strand in the renaissance of Italian motor racing was Enzo Ferrari and his famous *scuderia*. In the war years, he had turned his skills to manufacturing machine tools and done well, expanding his business on government contracts, attracting design and engineering talent. Part of that growth was a new factory on land he owned at Maranello, and once the war was over, he turned that factory over to building a range of luxury sports cars to challenge Alfa and Maserati. To promote the sports car business, Scuderia Ferrari was reborn at Maranello so that Enzo Ferrari could realize another dream, building and racing Grand Prix cars under his own name. He was married and he had a son, Dino, born in 1932, but he also fathered an illegitimate child, Piero with one of his factory employees, Lina Lardi, whom he kept a great secret.

Britain had harnessed the whole country to achieve victory, and by 1945 it was exhausted and impoverished. People and organizations started out by trying to re-establish pre-war attitudes, preserving imperial greatness abroad and industrial greatness at home, but the war had brought about a quiet revolution; people wanted something new. A great deal of the pre-war British motor racing infrastructure had been destroyed by the war. Brooklands had been taken over by Vickers to build Spitfires and been bombed. The members tried in vain to persuade the new Labour Government to give it back, but it was sold to Vickers in the interests of national security and lost forever to racing. Donington had been turned into a vast park for military vehicles and in 1945 was covered in unused trucks and jeeps. The ERA voiturettes had mostly survived, preserved on blocks in garages by enthusiasts waiting for the war's end.

Ironically, what the war had taken away with one hand it replaced with the other: literally hundreds of airfields with long tarmac and concrete runways and perimeter tracks were quickly surplus to requirements. The war had changed attitudes, and the armed forces discharged millions of men into civilian life with new and different aspirations. Most things were rationed – sugar, clothes, petrol – but war surplus materials were plentiful and cheap, and combined with the enthusiasm of the motor cycle world and special builders, racing started up again on disused airfields. The first race was held by the Cambridge University Club in 1946 on a disused airfield at Gransden; it was as near road racing as could be permitted in Britain and when it was repeated the following year it attracted a crowd of 15,000. Following a hill climb at Shelsley Walsh, some of the participants went to another disused airfield in the Midlands and held an impromptu race; the name of the airfield was Silverstone.

The interest which had been sparked in road racing in Britain in the 1930s was rekindled, and it took two forms: the old order based on the pre-war experience, and a new, brasher order which started right down at the grassroots. Colonel Stanley Barnes, the competitions secretary of the Royal Automobile Club (RAC), was part of the old order, but he saw the potential in using disused airfields as a temporary measure and negotiated a lease to hold a Grand Prix at Silverstone in 1948.

The old order, represented by the ex-ERA people, looked to the motor industry. Humphrey Cook started up again after the war, but Mays was in the forefront of Britain's most serious attempt yet to join the front rank of Grand Prix racing. Mays had planned it all during the war, and in 1945 he wrote to every captain of industry asking for support. Mays' plan, which he called the British Racing Motor Research Trust, was heavily reliant on personal connections and a curious combination of private and public endeavour; it was hailed as a breakthrough in a leader in *The Times*. He had secured industrial backing from over 100 British companies with pledges of support including parts and money.

The end of the war also saw a burgeoning of tiny British firms which built racing cars to order for privateers. One was Geoffrey Taylor whose firm, Alta, was based at Tolworth in Surrey. He designed and built a 1-litre engine which he put into sports cars and sold to selected customers in the 1930s, graduating to single-seater voiturettes along ERA lines. After the war he turned to Formula 1, building a 1.5-litre supercharged Grand Prix car. The whole operation was tiny and there was never enough money to do what was wanted, but there was plenty of talent and enthusiasm.

Another was Hersham and Walton Motors. An RAF bomber pilot during the war who later landed agents in France, George Abercassis had been an Alta customer before the war, but in 1945 he joined forces with a gifted engineer, John Heath, to form HWM to supply sports and racing cars to private customers, mainly in the Home Counties. It provided a stable from which Abercassis could race. For engines they turned to Geoffrey Taylor at Alta at nearby Tolworth. Another small operation was Connaught, started by two ex-RAF pilots, Rodney Clarke and Mike Oliver with backing from Kenneth McAlpine, heir to the construction business. Clarke was a perfectionist and as a result progress was slow.

Alta, HWM and Connaught were run by and for the monied classes. Elsewhere in Britain, a completely new level of racing was emerging from the motor trade as opposed to the industry or the artisan bespoke builders. This trade was based on hundreds of garages, second-hand car dealers, small engineering workshops and scrapyards. It was into this world that many recently demobbed soldiers, sailors and airmen chose to make a living in post-war Britain, many of them interested in racing, not as a gentlemanly hobby but as part of their business.

In December 1945, a group of special builders in Bath formed the 500 Club which used 500cc motor cycle engines and a basic chassis built by enthusiastic amateurs for around £150. The secretary was John Siddall and two of the most advanced builders were Clive Lones and Colin Strang. Strang built his special using a Fiat Topolino chassis and a Vincent motor cycle engine behind the driver, driving the rear wheels. The 500cc movement grew and before long it could boast its own magazine, *IOTA*. The first edition in April 1947 had an editorial which defined the 500 Club's primary function – 'to assist the ordinary man in the street to obtain motor racing at something like an economical cost. This is an ideal which we hope will be very shortly attained'. The idea that motor racing was an activity with ideals and that those involved felt themselves to be part of a 'movement', seems quaint today, but it was part of the spirit of the times, the determination of ordinary people not to be excluded as they had been before the war.

While the 500 Club built cars from scratch, special builders adapted cars from the cheaper passenger cars. One group, led by Holland Birkett, formed the 750 Club, dedicated purely to building specials out of Austin 7s. Their main activity was trials, but they also did some circuit racing. To supply the needs of the enthusiasts, a trade developed in second-hand parts run by dealers from their kitchens and from lock-up garages around London.

All this was a long way from motor racing at the international level where Grand Prix racing resumed in 1946. The AIACR, based in Paris, changed its name in 1946 to the Fédération International de l'Automobile (FIA) and created the Commission Sportive Internationale (CSI) to govern international racing. The FIA set the formulae in 1947, largely by the expedient of including the pre-war cars which were available. The formula for Grand Prix racing was called Formula A, for 1.5-litre supercharged cars such as the pre-war Alfa Romeos, Maseratis and ERAs, or 4.5-litre normally aspirated cars like the big Talbots. This was to be Grand Prix racing until the motor industry got back on its feet and new racing cars came along. To cover what had been the voiturette class before the war, the FIA introduced

Formula 2 for 500cc supercharged cars or 2-litre normally aspirated cars. The 500 Club was keen to see its cars covered by an official formula so that it could hold international races, but the FIA decided to wait a while.

The most exciting car in the immediate post-war period was the Alfa Romeo 158. Sixteen had been built between 1937–8 and another six had been started before Italy came into the war in 1940 and were completed to a new specification for the works team. Gioachino Colombo was still retained by Alfa but had been working for Ferrari on its first post-war car, the Tipo 125, a derivative of the Alfa Romeo 158, until Alfa Romeo made it plain that he should come back to Alfa. The Talbot 4.5-litre single-seater was very different from the Alfa which weighed just 700kg and produced 310 bhp compared with the Talbot at 910kg producing 245 bhp. The Alfa was much thirstier than the Talbot which did not have to refuel nearly as often.

In 1948 the Automovil Club Argentino bought two Maserati 4CLTs for Argentinian drivers to drive against visiting Italian drivers. The new president, Juan Domingo Perón, had been a student of Mussolini and he saw motor racing as a wonderful opportunity to fuse patriotism at home with profile abroad. One of the drivers was Juan Manuel Fangio who showed huge promise when he raced against Luigi Villoresi, Achille Varzi and Jean-Pierre Wimille, three of the finest European drivers of the day. Another was a friend of Fangio, Froilan Gonzales, an ex-motor cycle racer.

An essential ingredient in the post-war set-up was the renaissance of the *scuderia*, the *écurie*. Direct sponsorship of motor racing was banned by the FIA in Europe, unlike in America where Indianapolis cars carried the names of their sponsors. In the absence of support from the volume car manufacturers like Fiat, Renault and Peugeot, or the luxury car manufacturers like Mercedes and Auto Union, the *scuderia* bosses turned to accessory manufacturers for tyres, fuel, oil and spark plugs. Enrico Plate formed a team

around his own name to provide a home for Baron de Graffenried and Prince Bira; Ecurie Bleue was founded by Laury and Lucy Schell, a rich expatriate American couple who lived in Paris, for French drivers and their son Harry. Other stables had national overtones: Ecurie France and Ecurie Belge. In Britain it was different; the teams were mostly based on garages like Cooper and HWM, although in Scotland the RRC Walker Racing Team emerged, owned and run by Rob Walker, heir to part of the Johnnie Walker whisky business, which ran its cars in dark blue for Scotland.

Racing started up again most swiftly in France and Italy because both countries still tolerated racing on closed public roads. In 1946 a number of local Grands Prix were run in France, which saw the first appearance of the Alfa Corse team, with Alfa 158s for Giuseppe Farina and Jean-Pierre Wimille and Maseratis driven by Raymond Sommer and Tazio Nuvolari. Both Alfas retired leaving Sommer to win. A month later on 21 July came the restoration of full international Grand Prix racing with the Grand Prix des Nations in Geneva where Alfa Romeo made it a clean sweep – Farina first, Count Carlo Trossi second and Wimille third.

The French motor racing establishment did not invite Alfa to enter the 1947 French Grand Prix. Raymond Sommer drove the new V8 super-charged CTA-Arsenal designed by Albert Lory, even though it was only just out of testing; it broke a drive shaft and Sommer retired. The race was won by Louis Chiron in a 4.5-litre single-seater Talbot, but only because the Alfas were away. As if to highlight the difference, the Alfa Corse 158s came first, second and third in the Swiss, Belgian and Italian Grands Prix that year.

Enzo Ferrari wanted to beat the Alfas, and beat them in his own name. He hired Gioachino Colombo who suggested building a mid-engined car like the Auto Union, but Ferrari responded with a famous remark which was to haunt him in later years. He said no, the horse should be in front

Peace dividend:
Maserati 4CLTs lead
the start of the 1946
Nice Grand Prix, the
first in a series of
international street
Grands Prix.

Rear end solution:
the MK1 Cooper 500,
built from Fiat parts
in 1946 by John
Cooper and his friend
Eric Brandon in
Surbiton, in Surrey.

of the cart, not behind it. Consequently, Ferrari's first Grand Prix car, the Tipo 125, was deeply conservative and bore a strong resemblance to the Alfa 158, the car they had conceived together before the war, now the main opposition.

In 1948 Grand Prix racing expanded from four to six races. Alfa missed the Grand Prix des Nations in Switzerland and the Monaco Grand Prix, both of which were won by Farina in a Maserati, but it did enter the Swiss, French and Italian Grands Prix winning all of them. The Ferrari Tipo 125 made its debut at the Italian Grand Prix with cars for Farina, Sommer and Bira, and although Sommer was up behind the leading Alfas early in the race, the best he could do was third. The Talbot T26C made its debut in 1948 at the French Grand Prix at Reims only to be trounced by Alfas with Jean-Pierre Wimille, Consalvo Sanesi and Alberto Ascari coming first, second and third ahead of the Talbots, a profound shock to the French establishment. The only British car in the race was an Alta driven by John Heath which retired after seven laps.

In Britain the conversion of Silverstone for the first British Grand Prix was completed on 2 October 1948. The supporting race was a 500cc event which attracted 25 starters and was won by Alvin 'Spike' Rhiando in a special he had made himself. Alfa was not there, giving the opposition a chance and Luigi Villoresi won for Maserati.

Alfa Romeo withdrew from Formula 1 in 1949 to concentrate on production of its 1900 saloon car and improve the 158s. It also suffered three tragedies: Achille Varzi had died in an accident in practice for the Swiss Grand Prix at Bremgarten the previous year, then their star driver, Jean-Pierre Wimille, was killed in January 1949 driving Simca-Gordini in Argentina, then in May, Count Carlo Trossi died from an illness. The deaths of its three drivers clearly played a part in the decision, but so too did the possible threat from Ferrari whose Tipo 125 won a minor Formula 1 event at Lake Garda in October in the hands of Dr Giuseppe Farina,

Ferrari's first victory in Formula 1.

The British Grand Prix was awarded full international status for 1949, although even that accolade failed to attract the Ferrari works team. Nevertheless, there was a crowd of around 120,000 to see mainly privateers race in Maseratis, ERAs and Lago-Talbots. There were two Ferraris, one driven by Raymond Mays and owned by Tony Vandervell, one of BRM's sponsors, whose company manufactured Thin Wall ball bearings in Britain. He had bought the Ferrari (naming it the Thin Wall Special) so that the team could gain some experience of racing at the top level. The RAC had bridled at his use of a trade name on the car but Vandervell won the argument.

The works Ferraris of Villoresi and Ascari were at the Belgian Grand Prix but, like the Alfas and Maseratis, they were supercharged, comparatively thirsty and had to make more pit stops than Louis Rosier's 4.5-litre Talbot. Rosier won with Villoresi second and Ascari third. Ferrari then won the Grands Prix in Switzerland, Italy and Czechoslovakia, making it the most successful team that year. Largely as a consequence of the Belgian experience, Enzo Ferrari decided to build a 4.5-litre unsupercharged engine as well. It was designed by Aurelio Lampredi who was instantly able to call on men with decades of racing experience, and were able to design and build the engine in months.

By comparison, progress at BRM was slow: the parts started to come together in 1949 when a complete, but untested, car was unveiled to the members of the Trust. Under pressure from the Trust it was made public for the first time on 15 December 1949 at Fokingham airfield, and although nowhere near ready to race, it was trumpeted in the press as a British success, raising impossible expectations.

Progress elsewhere was better: in 1948 George Abercassis bought the first Formula 1 Alta from Geoffrey Taylor. Abercassis took his racing seriously and started campaigning in Europe to

Unbeaten: the pre-war
Alfa Romeo 158, the
Alfetto, won every race
it entered between
1947 and July 1951,
when it was beaten by
the Ferrari 375.

gain experience, making long trips financed in part by starting money and winnings. He took on as race mechanic an ex-engine fitter called Alf Francis whose real name was Kovaleski, the son of a Polish garage owner who had fought with the 1st Polish Armoured Division and could not return to Poland after the war. Francis knew nothing of racing cars, but proved himself not only competent as a mechanic, using a natural ingenuity when necessary, but somehow completely in tune with the needs of racing.

The grassroots motor racing fraternity widened. John Cooper had seen Colin Strang's 500cc car and was inspired. There was an insurance write-off Fiat Topolino at the Cooper garage which had been shunted in the rear. Cooper sliced it in half, preserving the good end, then went to John Heath down the road and bought a second Topolino, also with a damaged rear. Cooper welded the two front ends back to back and installed a JAP 500cc engine behind the driver. The Cooper Mk 1, as they called it, was ready for the Prescott Hill Climb on 28 July 1946 where, after a series of mechanical failures, Cooper finished well behind Strang and about two seconds down on Lones. Eric Brandon was two seconds slower than Cooper. A second car was built for Brandon and in 1947 the pair entered more hill climbs and speed trials and Brandon was showing that he was the most successful driver.

John Cooper was just one young man recently released from the rigours of war who had a passion for racing. Another, who was serving in the RAF at the time was Colin Chapman, whose passion for motor racing was to last his whole life. Chapman had graduated from University College London that year having learned to fly in the University Air Squadron; although he had been offered a regular commission he decided against it. He had studied civil engineering, but his main interest was making money. Chapman had started a small business in second-hand cars, buying from dealers in Warren Street, the home of the motor trade, then doing them up and selling them at a profit.

Another devotee was Ken Tyrell, the son of a gamekeeper. He left school at 14 hoping to go to technical college but he failed to get in. Instead he joined the RAF to train as a mechanic and graduated to flight engineer on bombers. He flew several missions over Germany during the war and left the RAF with just £30 and a demob suit in 1946 to join his brother in a tree-lopping business in Surrey, from which he derived his nickname 'Chopper' Tyrell. In his spare time he played football and one weekend his club organized a trip to Silverstone to watch 500cc racing. He was hooked immediately and started saving money to buy a racing car.

On the other side of the world was Jack Brabham, born in 1928, the son of an Australian greengrocer. He joined the RAAF in 1944 hoping to become a pilot but had finished up as a mechanic. After the war he set up his own engineering business and swiftly became involved in the Australian equivalent of the 500 Club, midget car racing on rutted oval dirt tracks. He became New South Wales champion in a JAP-powered special which he helped build for another driver who gave up under pressure from his wife.

Bernard Ecclestone was born in St Peter's, Suffolk in 1930, the son of a trawler-man whose family settled in South London before the war. He developed a passion for motor cycles but from the start he had to finance his hobby by dealing in spare parts which he did from his mother's kitchen. One of his customers was another teenage motor cycle rider, John Surtees, who came with his father. The young John raced at Brands Hatch, a well-established grass track circuit in Kent where Ecclestone also raced. Ecclestone is secretive about his early life and career, but variations on the following story have circulated for many years, that he had a job with the Gas Board which involved cleaning filters. He continued to run his motorcycle business from work and at one point failed to check one filter which resulted in a loss of pressure over large parts of south London.

The motor car and cycle industry were both being exhorted to export all they could produce creating a demand for second-hand cars and bikes at home. Most were bought and sold from dingy sheds, but when Ecclestone moved from spares to complete bikes himself, opening a motor cycle shop in Bexleyheath, it was immaculate, light and airy, a delight to be in. He prospered and soon branched out into cars. Long before his twentieth birthday, he was not only a competitive grass track rider but an instinctive and accomplished deal-maker.

Another figure to emerge from the war was Jean-Marie Balestre, a Frenchman born in 1920 who fought in the International Brigade in the Spanish Civil War as a 16-year-old, followed by a stint as a journalist in the left-wing press. His record in the Second World War included service in the Resistance, arrest by the Gestapo, a sentence of death, which he escaped to return to France in 1945 a very sick man. It was some time before he established that he had been in the Resistance, in fact, for which he was later honoured.

The 500 Club in Britain had 16 members with cars in 1947 and it had organized a meeting at Silverstone airfield by arrangement with the landowner, but not the War Department police, which cleared them off. The members repaired to a local pub in Towcester where their plight was relayed to local landowner Lord Hesketh, who promptly invited them to hold their meeting on his land instead. The Duke of Richmond opened Goodwood on what had been Westhampnett Battle of Britain fighter base, which was on his estate in Sussex. The inaugural race was on 18 September 1948, preceded by a 500cc race with a 20 guinea prize from the *Daily Graphic*. There were 9 entrants, 5 of them Coopers, and the race was won by a young man called Stirling Moss in one of them.

Since John Cooper had built his Mk 1, the Cooper garage at Hollyfield Road had become a place of pilgrimage for young men who wanted to race, so much so that at the beginning of 1948,

Charles and John Cooper had a family conference and decided to go into production of 500cc racing cars. They planned to build twelve cars in the first year, most to order, but the orders were hardly from the common man. Among the first were Sir Francis Samuelson, Squadron Leader Ronald 'Curly' Dryden, an ex-speedway motor cycle rider, Alvin 'Spike' Rhiando, and George Abercassis and John Heath of HWM. Stirling Crauford Moss, the 19-year-old son of a dentist and former amateur racing driver, was burning to find a way into competitive racing, saw the Cooper Mk 1 in the showroom and ordered one. His father cancelled the order because Stirling was a minor, but relented. Of 15 events for 500cc in 1948, Moss won 11, showing real talent as a driver and attracting attention to Cooper. Cooper was becoming the core of the 500cc world, not quite what the idealists had planned, but it was growing and attracting attention to Britain which was dominant in the class. The 500cc race supporting the 1949 Grand Prix at Silverstone attracted 40 starters, 19 of which were Coopers. Moss won in a Cooper followed by two other Coopers.

At another 500 Club meeting at Silverstone, there were 11 Coopers out of 17 starters and Peter Collins, the son of a Kidderminster garage owner, won his first race. Coopers won 10 of the 11 races at the meeting, the only one not won by a Cooper was a race for non-production cars, the 500 Club's way of giving amateurs a race which they could win. The stirrings were clear and for the 1950 season the FIA decided that the 500cc movement should have its own formula, Formula 3, based largely on the Cooper specification and the British phenomenon.

The new formula was just one of a number of changes planned by the FIA in 1949 in response to fundamental changes going on in the automobile industry in Europe, changes which were further separating the manufacturers from racing. The artisan-based manufacturing culture, the European model based on coach building traditions in which cars were as much works of art as they were a means of transport, was dying. It was costly and without the solid backing of the manufacturing industry or government support, building Grand Prix cars was an uphill struggle. In France as a way of promoting the mass production of cars, the government introduced a selective employment tax making it very expensive for motor companies to employ anything over a minimum number of employees. French racing car builders struggled, and Lago-Talbot, Amédée Gordini and CTA could not find the combination of people, money or will to do it. The culture and structure of Grand Prix racing was based on too many strands from the past: Italian domination, French paranoia, German exclusion and discreet sources of finance provided by industry or government.

In Britain there had never been either motor industry or government support. British racing had always been self-financed with most of the money coming from the super-rich and most of the expertise coming from small engineering shops and highly motivated individuals. The Brooklands mentality was dying, and as the expertise was redirected into road racing, out of the ashes came a new breed of entrepreneur and a new generation of drivers who saw Grand Prix racing close up as they drove their Cooper 500s in warm-up races for the British Grand Prix. The likes of Stirling Moss, Peter Collins, Tony Brooks and Mike Hawthorn wanted to be part of Grand Prix racing, competing at the top level, in Formula 1, not Formula 3 or 2.

The 500 Club, the 750 Club, the Coopers, HWM, Connaught, Alta, ERA, Raymond Mays and BRM were pursuing the same end by different means, all of them part of a new, rather fragmented road racing fraternity which was gathering in Britain. Whatever their different backgrounds and sources of finance it was a fraternity of necessity based on individual commitment, business acumen and effort; a fraternity of people willing to challenge the big Italian and French manufacturers on limited funds. They took the *scuderia*, the *écurie*, as their model but then created a rougher, tougher version, a motor trade, wheeler-dealer version instead of the manufacturer-based continental tradition with its reliance on industrial, public or private wealth.

These fragile but vigorous developments in Britain came at a time when the FIA was planning for change. By 1950 Grand Prix racing needed to boost its profile in order to encourage new backers to provide finance. By happy coincidence the 1949 Motor Cycle World Championship had been a great success, so the FIA decided that the mid-point of the twentieth century was the time to introduce a World Championship for racing drivers, based on the Grand Prix tradition. Germany was re-admitted to the fold and Mercedes started planning a return. To mark Britain's entry, the first race in the World Championship was to be the 1950 British Grand Prix at Silverstone, a huge boost to those who were determined to make Britain a major player in international road racing,

Magic moment: Jack
Brabham in 1957,
driving to the limit
at Madgwick corner,
Goodwood, in his
grimy Formula 2
Cooper.

2

GENTLEMEN

& PLAYERS

The announcement that the British Grand Prix at Silverstone on 13 May 1950 would be the very first race in the new World Championship captured public imagination in Europe and in Britain. By 1950 the worst post-war privations, rationing and restrictions were disappearing and a fragile economic and cultural renaissance had begun. Britain was looking to prosperity rather than austerity and there were plans for a Festival of Britain in 1951. The country which was emerging from the post-war era was very different from that of the 1930s, and embracing change was a very strong theme of the times. A great deal of that change came from the bottom up, from the generation which had fought the war. They were looking to participate to a greater extent than social and economic norms allowed before the war. This was happening at the same time as the old order was visibly trying to reassert itself from the top down, and the result was a curious mixture of the old and the new.

Both forces were evident in motor racing in Britain as it surged in popularity. The old order was represented by BRM – in the great tradition of Alfa Romeo, Bugatti, Mercedes and Ferrari – a thoroughbred car designed, engineered and built under one roof, each car a classic, aesthetically pleasing as well as fast and functional. The bottom up process was represented by the enthusiasts of the 500 Club and the 750 Club who built cars out of what was available. By 1950, the 500cc movement was becoming more professional and an editorial in *IOTA* magazine in January 1950 warned against allowing Formula 3 to get too big for fear of it losing touch with its roots in the 'racing for the common man' movement. Formula 3 had its own successful racing stables. Eric Brandon and Alan Brown had become professional drivers, working outside the Cooper works team with Ecurie Richmond, a very professional stable set up by Jimmy Richmond, a civil engineering and haulage contractor from Repton, Nottinghamshire whose immaculately turned out trucks, cars,

drivers and mechanics were a feature of all the best Formula 3 events. Charles and John Cooper supplied the top drivers and Cooper's order books were full to bursting. To catch the mood of change and in recognition of its success, it was Cooper rather than BRM that was asked to build a car for display at the Festival of Britain.

British drivers were becoming well known through Formula 3; Stirling Moss, in particular, was looking to move up from Formula 3 to Formula 2 with HWM, but Britain still lacked drivers with the experience to be a serious challenge in the World Championship. To become World Champion a driver had to gain points over seven races including, bizarrely, the Indianapolis 500 in America, partly to include a race outside Europe to give idea of a World Championship credibility, but also to keep the US in the loop. The backbone of the Championship was the six European races: the British, Monaco, Swiss, Belgian, French and Italian Grands Prix. The winner was awarded 8 points, with 6 points for second place, 4 points for third, 3 points for fourth and 2 points for fifth place, with an additional point for the fastest lap; a further incentive to win came from the rule that only the four best results counted.

The Championship also encouraged drivers and teams to compete in all the races, since missing one would put one at a disadvantage, and it was this that attracted the great Alfa Corse team to Silverstone in May 1950. The disused airfield had come a long way since a rather motley bunch of 500cc enthusiasts had descended on it four years earlier, and a crowd of 150,000 was there on race weekend to watch and to soak up the atmosphere.

The RAC clearly hoped that the British Grand Prix would become part of the social season, much like Henley or Ascot, and it was rewarded by royal attendance: King George VI, Princess Elizabeth, Princess Margaret and the Earl and Countess Mountbatten. The atmosphere reflected that of the country – the old order that picnicked from hampers stowed in the boots of their Bentleys, ghosts of Brooklands and its social exclusivity roaming the paddock side by side with people who had arrived by motor bike, coach and train.

In the morning the Half Litre Club, as the 500 Club had been renamed, put on a major event which was well supported by mainly British drivers, among them John Cooper, Stirling Moss, Ronald Dryden, Tommy Aitkens and Peter Collins, in British racing cars with Triumph, Norton and JAP engines. The racing was wheel to wheel, with drivers hanging out of the sides of their cars round the corners, and the crowd loved it. Stirling Moss won his heat and John Cooper won his; Moss led the final almost to the chequered flag until he broke down on the last corner, handing the race to Aitkens in the IOTA-Triumph.

During the lunchtime interval, a completely different sound filled the grandstands as Raymond Mays gave a demonstration in the V16 BRM, the mixture of its high revving and its Rolls-Royce supercharger giving it a sound closer to an air raid siren than a car. It was described by *The Motor* as 'manifestly the most advanced 1.5-litre racing car of this epoch'. It was certainly complicated, and the engine produced huge amounts of power, but it was the butt of a good many jokes for the time taken to get it made. Given the problems of catching up with other countries in just a few years, given the years of post-war austerity, this was unfair, but the sight of Britain's great hope slowly circulating during the lunchbreak did little to inspire confidence.

The Ferrari team was not at Silverstone that afternoon and there were plenty of rumours about why. They had been given a drubbing at the San Remo Grand Prix a month previously when Juan Manuel Fangio, driving a solo Alfa 158, had beaten 6 works Ferraris, 6 works Maseratis and 9 privately entered Maseratis. The Alfa Corse team filled the first four places on the grid at Silverstone but after all the build-up, the race was something of an anti-climax. Farina led the four Alfas away, followed by two Plate Maseratis ahead of the Talbots. The

Alfas got through 70 gallons of fuel before having to refuel, but the pit stops did not change the positions and the four Alfa drivers swapped places, seemingly just to entertain the crowd. Fangio put some pressure on Farina but in doing so, hit a straw bale, damaged an oil pipe and eventually retired. Farina then led Luigi Fagioli, the two Italians a full minute ahead as the race came to a close. Prince Bira retired, as did Baron de Graffenreid, leaving the two Talbots of Giraud Cabantous and Louis Rosier to take the last points in the first race of the World Championship. Bob Gerard was in sixth place in the ERA, just outside the points.

The World Championship changed the mood of Formula 1, introducing a sense of real competition outside the races themselves, and a momentum began to build towards the next race. Monaco was just two weeks after Silverstone, including a Formula 3 supporting event. This time Moss won the 500cc race in his Cooper and in second place was Harry Schell in another. Schell even managed to wangle his way into the Grand Prix in his Cooper JAP, starting right at the back of the grid, the first ever appearance of a Cooper in a Grand Prix. It was also the first appearance of Froilan Gonzales for whom Fangio had arranged a Maserati 4CLT with Scuderia Achille Varzi. Sadly, both Schell and Gonzales were involved in a multiple crash on lap two which eliminated 10 of the 19 starters, including Fagioli and Farina. In his account of the race, Fangio told a very revealing story about the crash and the close-up reality of being a racing driver at the top level. He was well behind on lap two, approaching the crash at full speed when, out of the corner of his eye he noticed that the heads of the spectators, which would normally be turned up the circuit looking to see what cars were coming, were turned down the track looking at the crash which he could not see; he instinctively slowed and managed to thread his way through the debris to win. Alberto Ascari was second for Ferrari and Bob Gerard was once again in sixth place, just outside the points again.

Dr Giuseppe Farina clinched the first World Championship by winning the Italian Grand Prix. The race was a turning point: the Alfas were dominant, but Ferrari had shown that its simpler, less thirsty cars could match the supercharged Alfas. The Alfa engine was at the limit of its development, signalling the end of Alfa's years of supremacy. Having won the first World Championship, Alfa stayed away from the Penya Rhin Grand Prix, leaving Ascari and Serafini to fill the first two places for Ferrari. Both BRMs at Penya Rhin, driven by Reg Parnell and Peter Walker, retired. Raymond Mays and his backers had taken five years and £250,000 to build the BRM V16 to the 1.5-litre supercharged formula, but it had taken so long to build that it was obsolete before it arrived on the scene. Ferrari had come up with the Tipo 375 in a year, demonstrating not only how far behind BRM was, but the value of experience and skill to remain competitive at the top of motor racing. The BRM was a fine piece of technology, but Formula 1 was about winning, which needed a great deal more than elegant engineering. The V16 made its long-awaited racing debut at the International Trophy at Silverstone driven by Raymond Mays and Raymond Sommer. Mays' car was not ready. Sommer lined up for the first heat, but when he let in the clutch, the wheels spun in a cloud of smoke, demonstrating that the power was too much for the rest of the system. Within seconds the transmission failed and the car sat motionless on the grid. Farina won for Alfa Romeo with Fangio second. As it was pushed into the pits the expectant crowd jeered, many of them throwing pennies at it, an ironic comment on its huge cost.

The V16's greatest moment came on 30 September 1950 in the Goodwood Trophy. There were no Italian works teams and one BRM for Reg Parnell in a field of privateers including Stirling Moss in a Formula 2 HWM which had only come off the drawing board the previous year and came to the grid with only a fraction of the financial backing enjoyed by BRM. Parnell managed to ease away without letting the power of the engine destroy some other part of the car, and won.

The real British success story in 1950 was in Formula 3 when Cooper won 13 of the 15 races. The order book at Cooper was so full for 1951 that it started selling its 500cc cars in kit form which also avoided purchase tax. In that order book was an entry for a Mk V with a Norton engine and gearbox finished in polychromatic blue with red upholstery and long-range fuel tanks for a Bexleyheath motor trader, Bernard Ecclestone. The price was £575, evidence of the progress that had been made by Ecclestone and Compton, the motor cycle business in which Ecclestone had bought out his partner.

Business was also growing at Lotus. On 3 June 1950 Colin Chapman had taken his Lotus Mk II to an Eight Club event at Silverstone. Having qualified through a speed trial, he took part in a circuit race and after a great battle with a Bugatti, came second. He decided to build a car to compete in the 750 Club Championship. The Austin 7 was not designed for competition, and two of the drawbacks were the flexibility of the chassis and the design of the engine inlet ports which served two cylinders each. In the first of many innovative moves, Chapman designed a triangulated cage of welded steel tubing to make the whole structure more rigid, and a new inlet manifold which separated the inlet valves, giving more power. He dominated the 750 Championship in 1951, so the Club banned his inlet ports. His reputation, however, spread through the 750 fraternity and he was soon building cars for other people, just like Cooper in Formula 3.

Germany was admitted to the World Championship fold in 1951 with the German Grand Prix at the Nurburgring. Then Spain was admitted, but Monaco pulled out, leaving a total of seven races in Europe. Alfa Corse was back for 1951, having squeezed the last drop of power out of the 158's engine, the same output as the

First among equals: Juan Manuel Fangio (*centre*), Champion in 1951, 1954–7, with Giuseppe Farina (*right*) 1950 and Alberto Ascari, 1952–3.

unsupercharged Ferrari Tipo 375, but the Alfa was slightly faster in a straight line. It was a classic season: normally aspirated Ferraris versus supercharged Alfas, with the driving talent split between the two teams – Farina, Fangio, Fagioli and Sanesi for Alfa Romeo and Ascari, Luigi Villoresi and Piero Taruffi for Ferrari.

The first Championship race was the Swiss Grand Prix, which Fangio won with Taruffi in second place. Farina won in Belgium, with Ascari and Villoresi second and third in Tipo 375s. Then came the French Grand Prix: Ferrari had signed Froilan Gonzales, making it four Ferraris and four Alfas. Ascari fought his way into the lead followed by Fangio but the strain showed on Ascari's Ferrari and Fangio's Alfa and both retired. Villoresi's Ferrari also failed, leaving Gonzales in the lead with Fagioli second, but when Fagioli came in, he was told to hand over his car to Fangio, the faster driver. The Ferrari team responded by calling in Gonzales and putting Ascari in his car. Fangio led, then Ascari, and for six laps it looked as if Ferrari might snatch a famous victory, but Ascari's brakes gave up under pressure and Fangio won with Ascari second. Fagioli was so angry at being dropped for Fangio, he swore never to drive in Grands Prix again.

At the British Grand Prix, Gonzales rewarded Ferrari by setting fastest time in qualifying, breaking the lap record and taking pole position. Reg Parnell and Peter Walker failed to arrive for practice so they started from the back of the grid in their BRMs. The start was a surprise: Felice Bonetto, who had replaced Fagioli, took the lead for Alfa, then Gonzales passed him, the Alfas weighed down with fuel. Fangio then overtook Gonzales, the two Argentinian friends out on their own, battling it out for Ferrari and Alfa in a memorable drive, Fangio ploughing though a line of straw bales, until Gonzales took the lead on lap 39, thrilling the crowd. Gonzales toiled away for forty laps until it slowly dawned on the Alfa team, the Ferrari team and the crowd, that they were witnessing a landmark race, the end of the Alfa Romeo's

Prophetic: BRM's Raymond Mays exchanging information with his much-loved Argentinian driver Froilan Gonzales, who spun off on lap 3.

magnificent period of dominance and the birth of a new era. It was not Alberto Ascari, the Italian hero, who gave Ferrari his first Grand Prix victory, but the great bear Froilan Gonzales, the first time Alfa had been beaten on the race track since 1946. The score between Enzo Ferrari and his erstwhile employers had been partially settled; he sent a cable to an ex-colleague at Alfa Romeo, saying that he felt 'the adolescent tenderness of first love' towards the Alfa 158, although elsewhere he said that 'I killed my mother today'.

To rub salt into the wounds, Ascari won the German Grand Prix with Fangio second, then Fangio managed to give Alfa a swansong by winning the Italian Grand Prix with Gonzalez second. The Championship was finely poised between Fangio and Ascari: both could win it with victory in the Spanish Grand Prix where excitement turned feverish in the crowd of 300,000, policed by armed soldiers. Ascari led from Farina and Fangio at the end of the first lap, then Fangio overtook Farina, but the Ferrari's tyres started disintegrating and the time lost making changes cost Ferrari the race. Fangio had to make more fuel stops, but he made it, giving Alfa its second World Championship and his first. Ascari, a true sportsman if ever there was one, was fulsome in his congratulations, but the Spanish crowd, identifying more with Fangio, a fellow Spanish speaker, went as wild as the soldiers would let them.

Stirling Moss won his first race of the season in a Formula 2 HWM at Goodwood, then set off on the continent with Alf Francis, picking up a string of good places and qualifying for his first World Championship race, the Swiss Grand Prix at Berne, where he came eighth. At Le Mans, he set a new lap record for Jaguar. This brought him to the attention of Enzo Ferrari who offered him a drive in the French and British Grands Prix, a huge opportunity, but Moss was already committed to drive for HWM in a Formula 2 race in Germany on the same day as the French race, and said that he was unavailable but would accept for Silverstone. Ferrari replied that it was both or nothing, so the offer lapsed. Ferrari approached Moss again later in the year, offering him a drive in a new Ferrari, the Tipo 166, in the Bari Grand Prix, then to accompany Ascari and Villoresi to Argentina for the Temporada series in early 1952. Ferrari also enquired whether Moss would sign for Ferrari in Formula 1 for 1952. Moss was intensely patriotic and wanted to drive a British car, so he was tentative about signing for Ferrari, but he did enter the Bari race as a way of trying out the relationship with Ferrari. He found out the hard way that, for Ferrari, deals with drivers were not regarded as binding and when he turned up in Bari to race, Ferrari reneged on the deal and arranged for Piero Taruffi to drive instead, without informing Moss. The approach was intended as revenge for Moss having turned him down earlier. This rudeness set the tone for relations between Moss and Ferrari for a decade.

In November 1951, the FIA announced that from 1 January 1954 Formula 1 would be for 2.5-litre normally aspirated and 750cc supercharged engines. The announcement was the death knell for the BRM V16, a cruel blow to Raymond Mays' dreams and British national aspirations. One man who had been a great supporter of BRM up to that point was Tony Vandervell, who decided to end his association with BRM and go it alone; with his departure, backing for BRM weakened. One man stuck with it, Sir Alfred Owen of Rubery Owen, who took on Mays and Berthon without the complications of the Trust, and started work on a car for the 2.5-litre formula.

Vandervell bought a 4.5-litre Ferrari which he entered as the Thinwall Special through his own team, the Vandervell Racing Team. He improved the Ferrari, starting with the brakes which he changed from drum to disc provided by Goodyear's aircraft division. The experience was invaluable, but it only made him realize that the way forward for the new formula was to build his own all-British racing car. He commissioned a

Racing for all: 500 Club Junior racing at Brands Hatch in 1951. Bernie Ecclestone, No. 9, was black-flagged for cutting across the grass.

modified version of the Ferrari chassis from Charles Cooper and an engine from Norton, the motor cycle manufacturer. He called it the Vanwall.

Alfa announced that it would not take part in Grands Prix for 1952, so with BRM out of the running too, the only competitive cars in Formula 1 were the Tipo 375 Ferraris. Any Grand Prix would be a walkover, so the FIA put the 2.5-litre formula on hold until 1954, giving the teams two years to prepare and in the meantime ran the World Championship under the Formula 2 specification where Ferrari was clearly the best-placed contender with its Tipo 500.

Maserati was working on a new Formula 2 car, the A6GCM, and its strong works team included Fangio, who joined after Alfa pulled out, Froilan Gonzales, who moved from Ferrari, and Felice Bonetto. The new car would not be ready until midway through the season so Fangio and Gonzales drove for BRM and the Thinwall Special in non-Championship races. Gonzales won the Goodwood Trophy in the BRM and the Richmond Trophy in the Thinwall Special. When the A6GCM was ready in June, the works team appeared at the Monza Grand Prix. Fangio had been at Dundrod the day before, driving for BRM, and after driving across France to make it in time, arrived without sleep and at the back of the grid. He fought his way through the pack but crashed badly, was thrown out of the car, broke his neck and spent five days unconscious in hospital; the new World Champion was out of racing for five months convalescing.

With Fangio and Alfa Romeo absent, the 1952 season was a clean sweep for Ferrari: Taruffi won the Swiss Grand Prix; Ascari the Belgian Grand Prix with Farina second. Ferraris filled the first three places in the French Grand Prix at Rouen with Ascari, Farina and Taruffi. Ascari won at Silverstone with Taruffi second. If Ascari could win the German Grand Prix, the first works outing for the Maserati A6GCM, he would be World Champion. He took pole position, fastest lap and won after a brief battle with Farina. Ferraris filled the first four places in the race and in the World Championship.

It was Ferrari's finest season and its first World Championship: Ascari with 36 points, Farina with 24 points, then Taruffi with 22 points, all for Ferrari. The change to Formula 2, while hugely benefitting Ferrari, gave the British teams and drivers just the opportunity they were looking for. It was noticed widely, not least by Ferrari, that in equal fourth place in the Championship was Mike Hawthorn, the best result by a British driver in the World Championship to date. The 1952 season saw significant advances by the British teams, at the back of the grid admittedly, but compared with only a few years previously it was very heartening. At the British Grand Prix there had been 8 red Ferraris, 4 blue Gordinis and 16 cars in British Racing Green and at the Italian Grand Prix there were 4 Cooper-Bristols, 3 Connaughts and 2 HWM-Altas.

The Cooper factory produced one new Formula 3 car a week in 1951, but when the World Championship switched to Formula 2, Cooper responded with the T20, using a Bristol engine some 35–40 bhp more powerful than the Alta. Cooper dispensed with the mid-engined layout for the Cooper-Bristol Mk 1, putting the engine in the front. To run the team, he turned to a superbly run Formula 3 stable, Ecurie Richmond with its drivers Eric Brandon and Alan Brown. Brown came fifth in the Swiss Grand Prix, the first World Championship points ever gained in a Cooper car, and sixth in Belgium. Evidence of British progress was clear: Cooper T20s came first, second and third at Goodwood in the hands of Mike Hawthorn, Alan Brown and Eric Brandon, and Hawthorn, who raced a T20 owned by Bob Chase and prepared by his father Leslie Hawthorn whose main contribution was adding nitro-methane to the fuel, came fourth in the Belgian, third in the British and fourth in the Dutch Grand Prix. Connaught produced just four cars for 1952, the

complete antithesis of the Coopers; Connaughts were made to last while Coopers were made to win, and Connaughts driven by Dennis Poore and Eric Thompson came fourth and fifth in the British Grand Prix, behind Hawthorn. At HWM-Alta John Heath took on Peter Collins who made his debut in the Swiss Grand Prix and finished sixth in the French Grand Prix. Alf Francis had fallen out with John Heath. There was never enough money to make the team work and it was bedevilled by breakdowns, and by the end of 1951, they were losing out to the Cooper-Bristols.

Stirling Moss realized that HWM was declining, but kept his options open, staying with the team on an informal basis while joining forces with a leading light in the Half Litre Club, Ken Gregory. Moss took him on as personal manager, with Alf Francis to build a Formula 2 car based on a Cooper chassis. While it was being built, Moss drove an HWM in the Swiss Grand Prix and was lying third before he had to have a plug change and was later withdrawn. He then went to ERA which was overcomplicated in the tradition of its BRM cousin, and it broke down on the first lap in the Belgian Grand Prix, then again at Silverstone and Zandvoort in Holland. Moss switched to Connaught for the Italian Grand Prix and put it ninth on the grid ahead of Hawthorn in eleventh place, but retired with a broken push rod. Moss was an outstanding driver, but he scored no points in 1952 because his choice of cars made winning difficult.

Meanwhile Hawthorn was having more success in the Cooper-Bristol. The *Daily Mail* Trophy at Boreham airfield in August included Formula Libre and Formula 2 cars, two of the big Tipo 375 4.5-litre Ferraris driven by Luigi Villoresi and Francisco Landi racing at the same time as Hawthorn in his Cooper-Bristol and Moss in an ERA. Hawthorn put on a magnificent display, leading the two Ferraris on the track at one point, and winning the Formula 2 race a lap ahead of the rest of the field; Moss was third. Enzo Ferrari

Rite of passage:
Bernie Ecclestone,
aged 21, came second
in his heat and in the
final of the Open
Challenge race at
Brands Hatch in 1951.

Master class 1955: a serene Fangio in the Mercedes W196, displaying the skills which made him a legend in the World Championship.

decided that he wanted Hawthorn and Hawthorn had no qualms about driving an Italian car if it would get him to the top of Formula 1. He signed up immediately, the first British driver to get a works drive for one of the top continental teams.

Lotus was budding, if not exactly flowering. Chapman rented a stable block behind the Railway Hotel in Tottenham Lane from his father, and on 1 January 1952 Lotus Engineering Ltd opened for business with one employee, Michael Allen, who had bought Lotus Mk II, and Colin's girlfriend Hazel Williams, who ran the office. The production process was crude but effective, the jig for the chassis an old bedstead, welded up to give it rigidity. The stables became a magnet for enthusiasts and from these premises, Chapman built 80 Mk VI Lotuses with Ford Ten engines, gathering people around him who worked for the excitement of being there; men like Mike Costin, a draughtsman from the de Havilland aircraft factory at Hatfield and an accountant called Fred Bushell from Peat Marwick Mitchell, whose arrival was to stop Lotus from being something of a club built around a love of cars and started it on the road to being a business.

The 1953 season was run under the same formula as 1952. During 1952 Gioachino Colombo had left Ferrari to join Maserati to make the A6GCM as good as the Tipo 500; they were quicker in a straight line but the Ferrari had better braking. Fangio was fully recovered and signed up for Maserati with Froilan Gonzales and Felice Bonetto. The Championship started in Argentina, the first time it had moved outside Europe, leaving aside the anomaly of Indianapolis. There were only four teams: Maserati, Ferrari, Cooper and Gordini from France. The race was held in a specially built autodrome in Buenos Aires and was attended by President Perón whose wife Eva had recently died. The circuit would have been full to bursting with 100,000 spectators but an estimated 500,000 turned up and simply ripped up the barriers so that when the race was due to start, the circuit was lined with people on either side, some of them on the track itself. Ascari led from start to finish, with Villoresi second, Froilan Gonzalez third, then Hawthorn. Fangio retired. Farina was the only Ferrari driver not in the points because on lap 30 a spectator walked in front of his car and in trying to avoid him, Farina lost control and went into the crowd. The official death toll was one, with six injured, but unofficial estimates were higher.

Ascari won in Holland and Belgium with Ferraris second in all three, then came the French Grand Prix at Reims which turned into *the* classic battle between Maserati and Ferrari. Maserati was determined to displace Ferrari, just as Ferrari had displaced Alfa Romeo. Onofre Marimon, another Argentinian, had joined the Maserati team, making it four from each factory, and the eight red cars filled the first three rows of the grid. When they growled away together, Gonzales, who had opted to start with half tanks, went into the lead for Maserati. At the end of the first lap, Gonzales was ahead with three Ferraris on his tail, ahead of the other three Maseratis, with Farina eighth. They circulated as a bunch, blasting through the countryside, the three Ferraris changing places until Gonzales had to come into the pits. He was not far enough ahead and rejoined just behind the leading pack. The leaders were in two groups: Hawthorn and Fangio out front with Gonzales, then Farina and Ascari a few seconds behind. Towards the end of the race, the lead changed several times, and as it did so, Hawthorn and Fangio turned towards each other, laughing and exchanging words at 160 mph. Neither could get an advantage until the final moments when Hawthorn just managed to get a better line on the final corner at Thillois and went on to win by a second, with barely eight seconds covering the first five cars after $2\frac{3}{4}$ hours of racing.

It was a triumph for Ferrari, it was a triumph for Hawthorn, and though it was an Italian car, it was a triumph for Britain. In four years, Hawthorn had gone from nowhere, through 500cc Coopers in

Formula 3 and Cooper-Bristols in Formula 2, to Formula 1 Ferraris, and won his first Grand Prix in only his fourth race against three former World Champions – Farina, Fangio and Ascari.

Ferrari remained ascendent: Ascari won at Silverstone from Fangio, and Farina won at the Nurburgring, also from Fangio. If Ascari could win the Swiss Grand Prix at Bremgarten, then he would take the title. Fangio led from the start but retired and it was Farina, Marimon, Hawthorn and Ascari towards the end, then Hawthorn got past Marimon whose transmission failed, leaving the Ferraris first, second and third. A pit signal was held out telling the three drivers not to race each other and risk a calamity, but Ascari charged, taking Hawthorn and Farina to win. Ascari claimed that the setting sun in his eyes had prevented him from seeing the board, but Farina was furious and berated Ascari in the pits. It was too late – Ascari had become the first man to win consecutive World Championships. At Monza, in front of the home Italian crowd, Fangio broke Maserati's World Championship duck by winning in brilliant style from Farina, Villoresi and Hawthorn, the first time the Ferraris had been beaten in a Championship event for two years, marking the end of Ferrari's supremacy.

The 1953 season had been an Italian season, dominated by Ferrari and Maserati, confirming Italian dominance even without Alfa Romeo. Italy claimed four World Championships out of four, three of them to Italian drivers. British hopes and aspirations still looked rather paltry by comparison, but Grand Prix racing was about to change forever. Italian, French and British teams were preparing for the new 2.5-litre formula, and the hottest news was that Mercedes Benz was to re-enter Grand Prix racing. Most could remember the pre-war *blitzkrieg* by Mercedes and Auto Union fifteen years earlier, and although Mercedes was no longer supported by the German government, it was a symbol of German excellence in engineering. That was the point, to promote the Mercedes name

rather than the country, through immediate and assured success.

At Maserati, Gioachino Colombo had started work on a completely new car, the 250F. Maserati had become a wide-ranging engineering company which did a great deal of business in machine tools and agricultural machinery in Argentina, and Argentinian drivers were always welcome at their factory in Modena – Fangio, Gonzales and Onofre Marimon all made it their first port of call. The Argentinian dictator, Juan Perón, like Hitler and Mussolini, wanted to use motor racing as a national symbol of success and by giving Argentinian drivers a place at the top, Maserati fostered an ever stronger relationship with the country.

Mercedes and Maserati were the largest operations in Formula 1, with huge internal resources, but the new formula had stirred other great names from the past: Lancia was in the hands of Gianni Lancia, the son of the man who started the company before the First World War. He hired Vittorio Jano to design a new sports car, but what he really wanted was a racing department like Maserati. Jano designed a new Formula 1 car, the D50 with its V-8 engine used as a structural member to maximize lightness.

Even in comparison with Lancia, Ferrari was a small operation, run as the personal fiefdom of Enzo Ferrari, a man with limited engineering and management skills who drove the business by the sheer force of his personality. This personality was flawed by delusions of grandeur and a desire to see his cars triumph, a flaw which periodically threatened to tear the company apart. He believed it was the car rather than the driver that mattered and he believed he had the best cars. As a result he did not have any big plans for the new formula, believing that he could uprate the Formula 2 Tipo 625 to the Tipo 553 Squalo or Shark, which was not a good car; it had very poor handling and the drivers preferred the old 625. Ascari and Villoresi, who were inseparable friends, were worried about the Mercedes threat, and lacking confidence in the

Hope and glory: Mike
Hawthorn in 1956, on
the way to becoming
the first British World
Champion in 1958,
giving British motor
racing a great boost.

Squalo went to Lancia. Hawthorn stayed at Ferrari where he was joined by Froilan Gonzales.

The new formula encouraged the British constructors to find what they needed most, a more competitive engine. They approached Coventry-Climax which made engines for generators, fire pumps and fork-lift trucks. During the Korean War, Climax had produced 1000cc fire pump engines to a featherweight specification (FW) using an aluminium block. Wally Hassan, an engineer who started out in motor racing in the 1920s and worked on the ERA, had joined the company in 1950 with another former racing engineer, Harry Mundy, who had worked at ERA and BRM. They were natural targets for Cooper, HWM and Connaught, and under their pressure, Hassan and Mundy persuaded the managing director of Climax to look at a V-8 design named Godiva which produced 246 bhp in tests. However, as the season approached they decided not to release the engine to be pitched against the might of German and Italian racing manufacturers. Cooper and Connaught in particular had their plans set back by this decision. What Climax did do, under pressure from Cooper and Chapman, was to develop the existing fire pump engine for their sports cars under the designation FWA. Sports car racing was beginning to replace Formula 3 as a local spectacle and the years in which Formula 2 had been the World Championship formula had left a vacuum. Cooper produced a sports car around the FWA which kept its traditional mid-engined layout; it sold for £1350.

Moss was keen to drive a serious Formula 1 car and the best on the horizon was obviously Mercedes. Ken Gregory went to Stuttgart and was granted an interview with Alfred Neubauer, the legendary team manager, who said no, but he had clearly been watching Moss and left the door open if Moss got some real Formula 1 experience. Neubauer suggested that Moss look at the new Maserati 250F to gain that experience and although Moss was disappointed, he took the advice. It was good advice. Gregory went to Modena to buy a car while Moss's father underwrote the £5500 necassary. To run it, they formed Equipe Moss, a tiny dedicated stable around Moss with Alf Francis as mechanic. Dunlop supplied tyres and BP 200 gallons of fuel.

Mercedes was not ready for the opening races of 1954, so it was business as usual with Ferrari versus Maserati. Neubauer wanted Fangio to drive for Mercedes, and to back up Fangio there were three Germans, Herman Lang, Karl Kling and Hans Herrmann. While he was waiting for Mercedes, Fangio drove the new Maserati 250F; the first race of the season was on his home turf in Argentina, and he won. Mercedes chose the French Grand Prix on 4 July for its debut, the time and the place being no coincidence, there being more than a hint of nationalism in unveiling a new German Grand Prix car in France as happened in 1914 and 1934.

The gleaming Mercedes 196 Streamliner looked more like a sports car than an Formula 1 car. No expense had been spared: it was a technical marvel with fuel injection, desmodromic valve drive and a straight eight engine lying on its side to get the weight low. There were three Streamliners, for Fangio, Kling and Herrmann; Fangio took pole with Kling next to him, then Ascari driving a Maserati 250F because the Lancia was not ready. There were only six finishers: Fangio who won, with Karl Kling second, both in Mercedes, then four Maseratis led by Robert Manzon a full lap behind, a humiliation for everybody except the Germans.

At the British Grand Prix there were two Mercedes 196s for Fangio and Kling, three Ferraris for Hawthorn, Gonzales and Maurice Trintignant, all in 625s, a works Maserati team of Ascari, Villoresi and Marimon, and Moss in his private Maserati. Moss had been third at Spa and as a result Maserati gave him works support, undertaking to rebuild the engines if he blew them under pressure. Fangio took pole followed by Gonzales, Hawthorn and Moss. Gonzales led Moss from the start but Hawthorn and Fangio managed to get past Moss, then Fangio moved into second place and had a 25-lap fight with Gonzales. Moss and Hawthorn were having just as good a struggle until Moss managed to get past Hawthorn as Fangio started to fall back, his car leaking oil, putting Moss second, until his transmission failed. Fangio managed to keep his car going but Marimon got past, so the final placing was Gonzales, Hawthorn, Marimon and Fangio.

Onofre Marimon was under considerable pressure in practice for the German Grand Prix. He was the No.1 Maserati driver but Moss was faster and the works support made him more competitive. Marimon was a proud and competitive man but he qualified only eighth on the grid with Moss third, and in trying to improve his place, he left the circuit at a lonely spot, was thrown out of his car and killed. Omer Orsi, the Maserati boss, was in Argentina at the time and when he heard, he ordered the official Maserati team to withdraw out of respect. The Owen Organization, which was using a 250F to gain experience for BRM also withdrew, but the privateers, including Moss, raced. So did Fangio and Gonzales, Marimon's great friends, although Gonzales was visibly shaken. Fangio won for the home crowd with Gonzales second, a sad and sombre tribute to their friend.

The sad mood continued at the Swiss Grand Prix which Fangio led serenely from start to finish. Second place went to Froilan Gonzales for Ferrari, an Argentine 1-2 win and a second World Championship for Fangio who insisted on sharing his laurel wreath with Gonzales, their two faces still etched with sorrow for their friend and countryman, Onofre Marimon.

Moss had been right to go for Maserati. Cooper, Vanwall and Connaught were still not up to Formula 1, and he temporarily gave up the unequal struggle to find a British car. On 4 December 1954 he had a test drive for Mercedes and was invited to join. Maserati had considered offering Moss a works drive for 1955 but they prevaricated and by the time they did decide, Mercedes had signed him up to partner Fangio. Moss and Fangio were professionals who knew their value and they were not prepared to accept that team managers could exploit their enthusiasm and desire to get into the sport by offering split winnings and starting money. Mercedes adopted a professional approach too, and Ken Gregory was able to accept Mercedes' first offer of £28,000 for the 1955 season, five times the salary of a cabinet minister at the time and fifty times the industrial wage.

A new face arrived in Britain and gravitated towards the Cooper works at Hollyfield Road. Jack Brabham wanted to move on from midget racing in his native New South Wales. He had driven a Cooper-Bristol in Australia, attracting sponsorship from ReDex whose name he put on the side of the Cooper; the Australian authorities were no less stuffy than the British, and Brabham had to take it off before racing. Another new face appeared around the same time at Lotus. Graham Hill, the son of a stockbroker, had been apprenticed as an engineer before doing his National Service in the navy, and found his way to Tottenham Lane where he was taken on as a mechanic at £1 a week. Another old face returned – Mike Hawthorn was not happy living at Maranello nor did he like the Ferrari atmosphere any more than other drivers had and he signed for Vanwall for 1955.

Ten Grands Prix were planned for 1955, but Mercedes was not only planning an onslaught on the World Championship, it was also entering the World Sports Car Championship with the 300 SLR. Fangio won his home Grand Prix at Buenos Aires eclipsing the Ferraris, then he and Moss drove 300 SLRs in the Mille Miglia sports car race in Italy. Fangio drove alone, but Moss took Denis Jenkinson as navigator. Jenkinson and Moss had been over the 1000-mile course before and made detailed pace notes for every corner, straight and gradient on a continuous roll of paper which he read out to Moss. They won in record time, beating the old record by 32 minutes with Fangio taking second place; Moss's talent had found a worthy home at last.

There was a sense of awe and triumph building up around the Mercedes team; they seemed unstoppable, but this was checked at Monaco when both Mercedes developed valve problems. Fangio dropped out and Moss fell right back leaving Alberto Ascari in the lead in one of the new Lancia D50s. Then Ascari made a serious error and spun off into the harbour and was out, handing the race to his team-mate Maurice Trintignant. Four days later Ascari was at Monza testing a Ferrari sports car for Le Mans when he crashed and was killed; the reason for the crash was never discovered. Ascari's death sent Italy into shock, the Italian fans going into mourning for the loss of a double World Champion at a time when Italian dominance was under attack from Mercedes. Ascari's great mentor Villoresi, who was with Ascari when he died, announced his immediate retirement.

Gianni Lancia was distraught; he was not used to violent death and although he was on the brink of success, the company was not in good financial shape because the D50s had cost vastly more than expected. Ferrari was shocked by Ascari's death but he was hardened to death in motor racing and he saw an opportunity. His own cars were simply not competitive, so he started negotiations with Lancia while Gianni Lancia was at his most vulnerable. He persuaded the Agnelli family, owners of Fiat, to finance a plan which involved $100,000 a year for a five-year period to take the Lancias into his *scuderia*, just as he had done with the Alfa P3s before the war, complete with spares and Vittorio Jano as consultant. He sold it as a plan to provide for the renaissance of Italian motor racing and Lancia accepted, handing over everything to Ferrari, the master businessman. The whole deal was concluded in a matter of weeks.

Mercedes challenged Ferrari and Jaguar for the jewel in the crown of sports car racing, the Le Mans 24-hour race. The favourites were Fangio and Moss, driving together for once. Three hours into the race Fangio was contesting the lead with Hawthorn's Jaguar, when Pierre Levegh's Mercedes hit Lance Macklin's Austin Healey and spun off into the crowd where it caught fire. Levegh and 81 spectators were killed and another 100 injured. In what seemed an insensitive decision by the organizers, the race went on as the dead and injured were carried away. At two in the morning the Fangio-Moss car was two laps ahead of Hawthorn when orders came from Mercedes head office in Stuttgart to withdraw; Hawthorn won.

It was, and remains, motor racing's worst ever accident. The fallout was immediate – religious and political figures denounced motor racing in general, and editorials in newspapers sought to ban it. The French, German, Swiss and Spanish Grands Prix were cancelled, reducing the World Championship to six races. The British Grand Prix went ahead. Stirling Moss took pole position with Fangio just behind, followed by a works Maserati driven by Jean Behra, then two other Mercedes. The other three works Maseratis were split by Harry Schell in one of two Vanwalls and Robert Manzon in one of three Gordinis, then came the three Ferraris of Eugenio Castellotti, Trintignant and Hawthorn who had left Vanwall after disagreements with Tony Vandervell. In last place on the grid was Jack Brabham driving an awkward-looking, mid-engined Cooper-Bristol T40 with a sports car body. It was another triumph for Mercedes: Moss won by a tenth of a second from Fangio. The best British car was Schell's Vanwall in ninth place. Brabham retired. There was speculation that Fangio had let Moss win his home Grand Prix, but if he did he made sure nobody could see how he had done so, and as ever, was first to congratulate his team mate. It was a personal triumph for Stirling Moss, his first Grand Prix win; he moved up the ladder as a driver, joining Hawthorn as one of the British drivers who could genuinely win the World Championship.

Fangio took the World Championship for

Mercedes at Monza but it was a short-lived celebration because Mercedes pulled out of racing at the end the year. The arrival and departure of Mercedes on the Grand Prix circuit was swift and impressive, and although it had little impact on the design of racing cars, it did have an impact on the expectations of the racing public, reinforcing the idea that it was the most powerful cars competing at the topmost level that was the biggest attraction.

The departure of Mercedes left the Championship much more open. Amédée Gordini was perennially short of money. Bugatti, which had come back into the fray with a car designed by Gioachino Colombo who had moved from Maserati, still had a long way to go to make it competitive. Vanwall, Connaught, Cooper and Lotus were making progress but still lacked a really competitive engine, and few observers of the time saw them as serious contenders for the title. The two Italian marques, Maserati and Ferrari, were clearly the most competitive, especially Ferrari with the Lancia D50s. Enzo Ferrari, who had been master of all he surveyed at the end of 1953, had been humiliated by Mercedes' success, and by the end of 1955 his *scuderia* was seen as second in Italy, behind Maserati.

In the great swirling of nationalism and patriotism which followed the Mercedes victories and the death of Ascari, the *tifosi* wanted a star Italian driver to win races in an Italian car. But it was the car that mattered to Ferrari, and if the driver was Italian so much the better. Mercedes' decision to withdraw had left Fangio and Moss, the two top drivers of the period, without a job but neither was Italian. However Ferrari needed to win and either Fangio or Moss could do it for him. Ferrari claimed to be 'an agitator of men', getting them to do what he wanted by a crude mixture of flattery, manipulation and brinkmanship, motivating people by setting them against each other. Moss and Fangio were both professionals. Moss was out. Not only did he want to drive a British car, he still harboured memories of the way Ferrari had treated him in 1951, so he signed up with Maserati for 1956 alongside Froilan Gonzales. However, in his search for a British car, Moss's contract allowed him to drive for Vanwall when Maserati did not require his services. Fangio was 46 years old. He was the best driver in the Championship and the team which had Fangio had the huge advantage of his skill and the psychological advantage of having the man to beat. Enzo Ferrari was used to dealing with drivers direct, bludgeoning them into driving for him for a pittance, using the mystique which he had created around the name Ferrari. Fangio knew all about Ferrari, and like Moss, he had a personal negotiator Marcello Giambertone, whom he took with him to Maranello. Ferrari was outraged, but Fangio was not phased by his tantrums. Fangio had won three World Championships, knew his own value, and in the final analysis, both men knew it. Reluctantly Ferrari conceded 12 million lire for the year. Having secured Fangio, Ferrari then sacked Farina, Trintignant and Schell; Hawthorn left of his own accord. Ferrari then signed the rising British driver Peter Collins, a Spanish amateur, the Marquis de Portago and two Italian aristocrats, Eugenio Castellotti and Luigi Musso, grooming them as Italian stars of the future.

Hawthorn had never been happy living in Italy, but there were now pressing reasons to return to Britain. His father had died and he had inherited the family business, the Tourist Trophy Garage in Surrey. Tony Vandervell offered him a contract to drive for Vanwall but the experience of the previous year was still fresh and he went to BRM instead to drive a new car, the P25. He signed the contract in a flamboyant patriotic gesture, live on the BBC's *Sportsnight* programme, the great all-British hope for Grand Prix victory and even a World Championship. Hawthorn's partner at BRM was another rising British driver, Tony Brooks, a dental student who was still only 23.

It had not been a good year at Vanwall and the problem was diagnosed as the Cooper chassis.

Respect: Juan Manuel Fangio and Stirling Moss after the 1957 Italian Grand Prix. Moss won for Vanwall with Fangio second for Maserati.

Derek Wooton, who drove the Vanwall transporter, had served with Colin Chapman in the RAF and he suggested to Tony Vandervell that Chapman, a trained engineer, be asked to design a chassis rather than relying on the Coopers' empirical methods. Chapman started from scratch, designing a space frame chassis to take a shapely, aerodynamically clean body designed by ex-aircraft designer Frank Costin, with a ducting system to keep the driver cool and all excrescences such as exhaust pipes faired in. The result looked like a tear drop and the car became known as the Tear Drop Vanwall.

Jack Brabham had settled in as a full member of the fraternity at Cooper, working variously as fitter, welder, design assistant, truck driver and racing driver where he also built his own mid-engined Formula 1 car using a Cooper chassis and a 2-litre Bristol engine. Brabham entered his creation in the ReDex Trophy at Snetterton in August 1955, as did Moss in his private Maserati 250F. Moss took pole ahead of Harry Schell and Ken Wharton in works Vanwalls. The two Vanwalls left the rest of the field behind, including the Maseratis, hard evidence of the improvement in the new Vanwall. Behind them Brabham was giving Moss a real fight for third place in the awkward-looking Cooper-Bristol. The two passed and repassed each other until Brabham spun, leaving Moss to take third place. It was a great day for British cars, especially the Vanwalls, but Brabham had shown what his little car, half a litre down on the others, could do.

The Argentinian Grand Prix was a straight fight between Ferrari and Maserati which Fangio won, giving the Lancia-Ferrari D50 its first World Championship points. Moss took pole in the British Grand Prix with Fangio second and Hawthorn third. Moss led until his rear axle failed, then Fangio took over and won. Fangio won the German Grand Prix from Moss, making the Italian Grand Prix the showdown race for the title. Moss could not win it. Fangio had 30 points and needed to finish second or higher to take the title, but Collins was second with 22 points, so if he won,

took fastest lap, and if Fangio failed to finish, then Collins would be Champion by 31 points to 30. It was the first time a British driver was in contention for the World Championship. Fangio, Collins and Luigi Musso filled the front of the grid and Fangio led until Schell and Moss overtook him by slipstreaming each other, Schell led on lap 11, the first time a Vanwall had led a World Championship race for a whole lap. Moss took the lead back, then Fangio's car developed an alarming tendency to pull to the right under braking, so he had to go into the pits. Musso, in the meantime, was lying third when the Ferrari pits signalled to him to come in and hand over to Fangio, but Musso drove on and refused to hand over when he came in for tyres. Fangio was completely dignified as he waited for his car to be repaired, then Collins came in lying third. Castellotti had already wrecked a second D50, and if Moss dropped out and Collins won and took fastest lap, then he would be Champion. But when asked to hand over to Fangio, Collins never hesitated and jumped out. Fangio embraced Collins briefly for the respect he had shown to his team leader, then Fangio jumped in. Schell retired, then Moss coasted into the pits leaving Musso in the lead. Moss's car had sprung a leak and he had run out of fuel but was soon back in the race in second place behind Musso, whereupon Musso's car suffered a broken steering arm. Moss won, while Fangio in Collins' car, the last serviceable Ferrari, settled for second place and the World Championship. Fangio never forgot Collins' great sporting gesture. If the cards had fallen differently, Collins could have been Britain's first World Champion, but the twists of fate gave Fangio his fourth title and Ferrari its third, albeit with a Lancia car.

By the end of 1956, the cloud that had descended on Ferrari appeared to be lifting. Castellotti's victory for Ferrari in the Mille Miglia brought renewed hope to the *tifosi*, and Fangio winning the *scuderia*'s third World Championship really did seem to signal a renaissance, albeit at the hands of Argentinian genius. But the gains soon withered. Juan Manuel Fangio and Enzo Ferrari were completely different characters – Fangio was precise, cool, self-confident and straightforward, while Ferrari was moody, manipulative, unreliable and a control freak. At the end of the last race of the season Fangio left Ferrari as swiftly as possible. He was fed up with the man at the top, the way that Ferrari saw his cars as the most important element and the drivers as not much more than a commodity to be bought, hired and fired, all for the greater glory of the name Ferrari. For a highly intelligent, civilized and talented man like Fangio, Ferrari's childish mind-games and divisive tactics – setting drivers against each other, denying them drives he knew they wanted – was something he was not prepared to tolerate for a second year. It had been a good year for Ferrari in racing, but he was in turmoil personally: on 30 June 1956 his legitimate heir, Dino Ferrari, had died, pitching him into grief and guilt.

Fangio went home to Maserati and his place was taken by Mike Hawthorn. Peter Collins stayed at Ferrari, but he got married which upset Enzo Ferrari who saw it as a distraction from his job of winning races; Collins began to fall from grace while the more flamboyant Hawthorn's star began to rise. Maserati, especially with Fangio, would clearly be a challenge for Ferrari in 1957. BRM and Connaught were still disappointing, but Vanwall was making progress against the Italians, and in his search for a British car, Moss signed for Vanwall alongside Tony Brooks.

Cooper reverted to a mid-engined layout for its Formula 1 T43, a beefed-up version of the Formula 2 T41. It was a joint effort between the *ad hoc* team of Charles and John Cooper, North London car dealer Roy Salvadori, racing driver Jack Brabham and Rob Walker. Walker ran his RRC Walker team from his garage business in Dorking with Alf Francis as chief mechanic; Francis had left Equipe Moss when Moss went to Maserati. There had been virtually no Formula 2

racing between 1952 and 1956 but from 1 January 1957 the FIA announced there would be a new Formula 2: 1.5 litres. Charles Cooper saw a new market for private entrants and persuaded Climax to produce a lightweight version of the FWA engine, the FWB, which he matched with a modified Bobtail chassis as a single seater. The first order for the T41 came from Rob Walker.

The Lotus factory at Hornsey in London, like Cooper at Hollyfield Road, continued to attract young men who wanted a taste of the vibrant atmosphere created by the mixture of motor racing and the charisma of Colin Chapman. The Cooper and Lotus efforts were not a movement, in the way that the 500 Club had been; they were businesses out to make a profit, but in both places there was a sense of being part of a wider family, and help was extended across company boundaries out of mutual respect and a common desire to make money. Chapman developed a design concept based on good handling and lightness of construction in order to maximize the use of available engine power rather than simply increasing engine output as the key to victory, as at Ferrari.

In 1957 Ken Gregory and Alfred Moss, Stirling's father, set up a racing team they called the British Racing Partnership. Clearly the idea was that Stirling Moss would one day drive for BRP, an all-British team. They bought a Cooper T45 and arranged that Stuart Lewis-Evans, a rising star at Vanwall, would drive for them when he could. His father ran a garage in Bexleyheath, and he was a friend of Bernie Ecclestone.

The 1957 World Championship was a tumultuous struggle. The Argentinian Grand Prix was an all-Italian race between six Lancia-Ferrari D50s, six Maserati 250Fs and a single Ferrari 500. Moss and Fangio were together again at Maserati with Jean Behra and Carlos Menditeguy; Ferrari sent a works team consisting of Hawthorn, Collins, Castellotti, Musso, Froilan Gonzales and Cesare Perdisa. Fangio fought off the Ferraris, and Collins,

Brothers-in-arms: Stirling Moss and Tony
Vandervell after trouncing the Italians at Monza
in 1957, writing Britain into racing history.

Musso, Hawthorn and Castellotti all retired under the pressure, leaving 250Fs in the first four places.

Ferrari's stable of hopeful drivers – Alfonso de Portago from Spain, Phil Hill from America, Olivier Genderbein from Belgium and Count Wolfgang 'Taffy' von Trips from Germany – provided him with the opportunity to use the black art of setting men against each other to get into the Formula 1 team. In March, news reached Enzo Ferrari that the much improved Maserati 250F was threatening to break the lap record at Monza which was held by a Ferrari. Ferrari called Castellotti back from holiday to raise the record in the new Tipo 801; he crashed and was killed in a futile attempt to add lustre to the Ferrari name. Then came the Mille Miglia in May, an obsolete race which nevertheless gripped the Italian nation every year. For Ferrari, with his ever backward-looking stance, winning the Mille Miglia was the ultimate badge of honour. Ferraris came first, second and third, but the fourth entry, driven by de Portago crashed and killed him, his co-driver, 10 spectators including 5 children and injured 20 more. There was outrage, and Italy was forced to join the other nations which had long ago banned flat out racing on unprotected roads. It was the end of an era, but there had to be a scapegoat; Enzo Ferrari was charged with manslaughter although he was eventually cleared.

The British Grand Prix at Aintree was a landmark in the battle between the Italian and British teams. Ferrari and Maserati had 4 cars each, Vanwall fielded 3, BRM 2, and there were 2 Cooper T43s – Roy Salvadori in a works car and Jack Brabham in the Rob Walker car. There were no Connaughts; the team had give up the unequal struggle with the cost of getting to the top of Formula 1 and had put the entire team up for sale by auction. Bernie Ecclestone bought the lot. Moss took pole position at Aintree, Jean Behra took the lead but Moss overtook him on the first lap and held the lead for 20 laps until his Vanwall started misfiring and he came into the pits. Brooks, who

was lying ninth, got out and Moss got in and started a charge, setting lap records as he went and working his way up to fourth behind Lewis-Evans, Hawthorn and Behra, who was still leading. On lap 65, Behra's clutch disintegrated and Hawthorn ran over the remains getting a puncture for his pains. Suddenly the two Vanwalls were leading the British Grand Prix without a red car in sight. Then Lewis-Evans' throttle broke and Moss was in the lead with Musso a distant second. Moss won and the British crowd went uncharacteristically wild. Musso, Hawthorn and Collins filled the next three places and in fifth place was Salvadori in the works Cooper who had passed Trintignant's Ferrari to give the Cooper works team its first World Championship points. Ferrari had yet to win a Championship race in 1957.

The showdown in the World Championship came at the Nurburgring, a classic race, possibly *the* classic of all time. It was certainly Fangio's finest hour. Seven drivers – Fangio, Hawthorn, Behra, Collins, Brooks, Schell and Moss – broke the lap record of 9 minutes 41.6 seconds. Hawthorn took the lead followed by Collins, but Fangio was in control after three laps, pulling away because he had started on half tanks. He went into the pits on lap 12, 28 seconds ahead of Hawthorn but the pit stop went wrong when Fangio's pit crew fumbled the wheel change and instead of getting out in the lead, he rejoined 45 seconds behind Hawthorn. He appeared not to be pushing, so the Ferrari pits signalled to Hawthorn and Collins to slacken off the pace, but the Maserati team had set a trap and Ferrari gobbled up the bait: on a signal from his pits Fangio attacked, taking 7 seconds out of the Ferrari lead on lap 15 and a further 9 seconds on lap 16. Fangio was now in some kind of altered state, taking corners where he would normally have slackened off at full power and taking others a whole gear higher. On lap 18 he had brought the lap record down to 9 minutes 25.3 and the Ferraris were only 25 seconds ahead with four laps to go. The protagonists could not see each other, and although the Ferrari pits signalled frantically to their two drivers to speed up, Fangio's sublime drive continued and by lap 19 he had the gap down to 13.5 seconds. With two laps to go, Fangio saw a red car in the distance, and by lap 20 he was just 100 yards behind Collins; he had the lap record down to 9 minutes 17.4 seconds. Fangio passed Collins by taking the outside line, going on to the grass and showering Collins with pebbles, one of which broke his goggles. With one lap to go Fangio went inside Hawthorn on a sharp left hander and into the lead. There were wild scenes in the grandstand as Fangio started the last lap with Hawthorn doing everything he could but making no impression. When they came round again Fangio was 3.6 seconds ahead and took the chequered flag, giving him his fifth World title. Fangio admitted after the race that he had done things he should never have done, but that is what set him apart as a driver beyond mere talent.

There was little sense of it at the time, but with Fangio's fifth title, Grand Prix racing was about to change forever. Cooper was poised to make a leap ahead, persuading Climax to build a new engine, the FPF, the Fire Pump Featherweight, for Formula 2, the first racing engine to go into production in Britain, giving 141 bhp from 1.5 litres. Roy Salvadori had the idea of a Formula 1 car based on the new engine in discussion with the Coopers, Jack Brabham and Rob Walker in the Hollyfield tradition. A 2.5-litre purpose-built engine was the best idea, but in the meantime, they toyed with the idea of boring out the Formula 2 engine to 2 litres, and because the car was so much lighter than the Ferraris, Maseratis and Vanwalls, it could be competitive as it would rely on fewer fuel stops.

Wally Hassan at Climax was sceptical and Cooper would not finance the experiment, so Rob Walker decided that he would. He ordered a Formula 1 Cooper with an engine which Alf Francis would prepare at the Cooper works. The idea was to have it ready for the 1957 Monaco Grand Prix on 19 May. Alf Francis gave the engine

its first bench test on 10 May, then put it into a modified Formula 2 chassis and took it to the 1957 Monaco Grand Prix where the brakes locked in practice and Brabham crashed into the wall at the Hotel de Paris corner. Francis and his team took the engine out and put it into a spare Formula 2 chassis brought for just such an eventuality. Brabham put it on the fourth row of the grid. It was a race of attrition but Brabham hung in and was lying third at one point before the fuel pump broke loose; he coasted to a stop and pushed it over the line for a sixth place, another step forward in the progress of the mid-engined car builders.

BRM was still looking for that elusive success and to achieve it, Tony Rudd was recruited from Rolls Royce in 1957. He had a long association with BRM while still at Rolls Royce, since he had been assigned to install the superchargers in the ill-fated V16. One of his first moves on arriving at BRM was to consult Colin Chapman over the P25/48, as Vanwall had done, and the result of the collaboration was a much improved car.

Bernie Ecclestone had given up driving in races, but he had bought the Connaught cars to start his own dedicated team built around Stuart Lewis-Evans, in much the same way that Ken Gregory was seeking to do with Stirling Moss at BRP. Ecclestone loved the racing world, but at heart he was a dealer, a businessman whose motivation was profit. He was already successful with a string of profitable motor cycle shops and dealerships. In January 1958, he took two Connaughts to New Zealand, hiring Lewis-Evans and Salvadori to drive them in a non-Championship race, after which he hoped to sell them. Jack Brabham won the race in a 2-litre Cooper-Climax, demonstrating the apparent obsolescence of the finely engineered, front-engined Connaughts and Ecclestone had to bring them back to Britain unsold.

The elegant front-engined Maserati 250F, by any measure the finest car of the the front-engined era, was the end of the Maserati line. President Perón had been overthrown by the army in 1955 and the Argentinian economy descended into a shambles which damaged Maserati's business in Argentina. At the end of 1957, its most successful year, Maserati pulled out of racing.

The formula was supposed to change in 1959, but only minor adjustments were made. Fuel had never been specified, teams used whatever they wanted, including nitro-methane which was favoured by Vanwall. The petrol companies saw no real advantage in this arrangement and lobbied for pump fuel to be used. However pump fuel varied enormously in specification and was not suitable for high-performance engines, so it was decided to use 130-octane aviation fuel which was made to an international standard. Races were shortened from 500km (310 miles) to 300km (186 miles); the practice of changing drivers during a race was banned; and from 1958 a Constructors' Championship was introduced. Cooper and Lotus were delighted with the changes – the standard fuel led to better fuel consumption which, combined with the shorter races, meant that they could carry less fuel, which in turn meant that cars could be lighter.

The changes looked small but they had a profound effect. On 15 January, Stirling Moss put Rob Walker's Cooper T43 with the new FPF engine seventh on the grid at Buenos Aires for the first Championship race of the season, the Argentinian Grand Prix. Neither Vanwall nor BRM were there; they were still trying to adapt to the changes in the fuel formula and Maserati was only there because of its commitment to Fangio who was going to drive in his national Grand Prix for the last time. The strongest team was Ferrari – the venerable D50s had been pensioned off and Musso, Castellotti, Hawthorn and Collins were all driving the new Ferrari Dino, a development of the Formula 2 Ferrari with a new 2.5-litre engine. Moss's Cooper was giving away around 80 horsepower to the Ferraris and it had four studs holding on the wheels as opposed to Ferrari's quick-release hubs. But the car was much lighter, it

was very quick, it was nimble, it was less thirsty and it was driven by a master who could make the best use of those strengths.

In another classic race, on which the history of Formula 1 sometimes hinges, Moss started seventh out of ten, with the Maseratis of Fangio, Behra and Carlos Menditeguy, and the Ferraris of Hawthorn, Collins and Musso ahead of him. The little car caused amusement more than anything; it looked awkward and lacked the classic lines of the 250F and the Dino. Hawthorn took the lead, then Fangio overtook him on lap 10 as Moss moved up to fourth behind Behra, causing a great deal of concern in the Ferrari pits. Fangio, Hawthorn and Behra then made pit stops on lap 34, leaving Moss in the lead at the halfway mark. Romolo Tavoni, the Ferrari team manager, was not unduly worried as they expected Moss to come in for fuel and tyres. On lap 47, Behra dropped back and Musso took over the job of catching Moss, but he did not try too hard because he thought that Moss was going to have to come in. In the Cooper pit, Alf Francis did nothing to prevent the Ferrari people from thinking that, putting fresh wheels and tyres out as if getting ready for a pit stop. It never came – Moss, a superb driver with a really light touch, had husbanded his tyres all the way through the race and with fuel enough for the whole race, it suddenly became clear to Ferrari that he was not coming in. Moss was driving on tyres worn right through to the canvas, but he chose his path carefully in order to stay on oily and rubberized patches of the track. Although Musso caught him up, Moss had judged it perfectly and crossed the line 2.7 seconds ahead of the Ferrari to win his second all-British race in Formula 1.

The victory was widely reported and for many it was just another Moss win. However, to the small band of people behind it, then gradually to a wider audience, it was a win of enormous significance, a victory for a small, mid-engined car over much larger front-engined cars, built by a small *ad hoc* team rather than a big manufacturer, two features which would greatly alter the whole basis of road racing. The architects of that victory were Charles and John Cooper, Jack Brabham, Roy Salvadori, Alf Francis, Stirling Moss and Rob Walker.

British cars filled the first six places on the grid at Monaco in a sea of green: Brooks' Vanwall, Behra's BRM, Brabham's Cooper, then Salvadori in a works Cooper and Trintignant in Rob Walker's blue Cooper which Moss had driven in Argentina. Then there was a flash of red from Hawthorn's Ferrari, followed by more green from the Vanwalls of Lewis-Evans and Moss, ahead of the Ferraris of Collins, Musso and von Trips, then the two Lotuses of Cliff Allison and Graham Hill. Behra led from Brooks but Hawthorn forced his way through the sea of green into third place by lap eight, second on lap twenty, then into the lead on lap twenty-eight when Behra retired with brake problems. Moss challenged Hawthorn but his engine failed, then Hawthorn's fuel pump failed, handing first place to Trintignant who managed to hold off Musso and Collins to notch up two wins in a row for Rob Walker's Cooper, with Brabham fourth in the works Cooper.

Enzo Ferrari was furious. Vanwalls had won the last two races of 1957 and now the upstart Coopers, privately entered at that, had beaten the cream of his drivers and cars. Even his best two drivers, who were also British, could not do anything about it. It got worse. Moss won the Dutch Grand Prix for Vanwall, with the BRMs of Schell and Behra second and third, and Salvadori's works Cooper fourth, ahead of Hawthorn, and in sixth place was Cliff Allison in yet another British car, a Lotus. The Belgian Grand Prix was only marginally better for Ferrari – Tony Brooks won for Vanwall with Hawthorn second, Lewis-Evans third for Vanwall then Allison for Lotus and Schell for BRM.

Ferrari put Hawthorn and Collins together for Le Mans. Hawthorn burned the clutch but managed to stay in the race. When he handed over to Collins it started giving problems again and they

retired. They then left the circuit without telling Ramolo Tavoni who became furious and phoned Enzo Ferrari who blamed Collins. Ferrari's next step was to instruct Tavoni to withhold a Formula 1 drive from Collins in the next race, the French Grand Prix, and give him a Formula 2 car instead. Collins did not find out about the arrangement until he arrived at the circuit with Hawthorn. Collins and Hawthorn were great friends and their friendship irked Ferrari because it made it difficult to set them against each other. They stuck together and with Ken Gregory, who was also managing Collins, spent an uncomfortable time with Tavoni in Collins' hotel room, arguing about Le Mans and demanding a Formula 1 car for Collins. It finished with Tavoni calling Ferrari in Maranello and persuading him to reinstate Collins which he reluctantly did.

Ferrari was a deeply conservative and manipulative man. He believed that racing cars should be as he had known them all his life, big, beautiful and above all powerful, all made under one roof, including the engine which should be in the front. He believed that raw power and drivers manipulated to go to the edge were the key factors in victory, and he saw drivers who stood up to him and the unworthy little British mid-engined Coopers as a challenge to his exalted position. He did not like the direction he saw them taking the sport and resisted it instinctively, ignoring the siren messages from Carlo Chiti, his chief designer, who could see that the British teams were on to something, and that to stay ahead Ferrari would have to follow them.

The raw power of the Ferraris showed at Reims, where the circuit had been modified in 1953 using a long stretch of new road to bypass the village of Gueux, creating a tricky bend which only the best drivers could take flat out. Hawthorn took pole position with Musso second. On the third row of the grid, behind Brooks, Moss, Trintignant, Schell and Musso was Fangio in his own Maserati 250F. Enzo Ferrari put great pressure on Musso, the great Italian hope for the race. Musso had run up debts and before the race he had received an anonymous telegram which warned that winning would be a good idea for Musso if he wanted to clear those debts.

The Ferrari's straight line speed was an advantage at Reims and Hawthorn led with Musso second after two laps. As they passed the pits at the end of lap 10, Musso was beginning to close up on Hawthorn. As they entered the new right hander at Gueux, Musso was slightly off the racing line as he went into the corner flat out. Musso did not have the skill to take the bend flat out; he lost control, spinning off into a ditch which threw the car into the air and him out of the cockpit. He was killed on impact. Hawthorn continued to lead and as the race neared its sombre conclusion he came up on Fangio. Whatever the consequences with Ferrari, this was between drivers at the top of the sport who respected each other according to their own rules. It was Fangio's last Grand Prix and Hawthorn, who could easily have lapped him, held off out of respect for motor racing's greatest legend. Hawthorn won by 25 seconds from Moss with Wolfgang von Trips third for Ferrari and Fangio, unlapped, was fourth. Ferrari had something to celebrate, its first victory since Fangio had won the German Grand Prix in 1956, but Luigi Musso was dead. Enzo Ferrari's rather obvious comment on the result was 'the price of victory is too high'.

Victory for Ferrari came again at the British Grand Prix where Collins and Hawthorn managed a 1-2 win. Hawthorn took pole at the Nurburgring but Moss put in a blistering first lap, breaking Fangio's lap record of the previous year. Then his Vanwall failed under the strain, leaving Hawthorn and Collins in the lead with Brooks fourth and closing. He continued to put pressure on the two Ferrari drivers, then Collins spun off and crashed. Hawthorn had seen the crash in his mirror and instinctively knew the worst; he retired at the end of the next lap, reporting clutch failure. Brooks won for Vanwall, followed by Salvadori and Trintignant in the works and Rob Walker's Coopers respectively, then von Trips in a Ferrari with Bruce McLaren, a newcomer from New Zealand, fifth in a Formula 2 Cooper. The British contingent was subdued; Collins had sustained severe head injuries from which he died later in hospital. It was a massive personal blow for Hawthorn. With two of his top drivers dead in a month Enzo Ferrari came under enormous criticism at home, especially from the Vatican which called for all motor racing to be banned. Phil Hill was promoted from Formula 2 to Formula 1 to fill the gap.

The World Championship went down to the last Grand Prix of 1958 in Monaco. Whatever happened, there was going to be a British World Champion. Moss, who had been second in 1955, 1956 and 1957 had 32 points and Hawthorn had 41 points, so Moss could win the title if he won the race, took fastest lap and Hawthorn was lower than second. On the other hand all Hawthorn had to do was come second to clinch the Championship. Hawthorn had already decided privately, that whatever the result, he would retire after the race. He was fed up with the political culture at Ferrari and trust was at such an all-time low that he insisted that the Jaguar racing manager, Lofty England, who had masterminded Jaguar's successes against Ferrari at Le Mans, be brought in to manage his pit team.

Hawthorn took pole position but Moss led from the start and put up the fastest lap, seven seconds ahead of the rest. His problems lay behind him where Phil Hill, Tony Brooks and Mike Hawthorn were battling for second place. Brooks held Hawthorn off until lap 30 when the Vanwall's engine failed and Hawthorn moved up to third. The inevitable signal from the Ferrari pits told Hill to let Hawthorn through. Hill obliged and all Hawthorn had to do, with Hill guarding his tail, was keep going and finish second. Two laps later, Stuart Lewis-Evans' engine failed and as he coasted off the track, the Vanwall caught fire.

Evans jumped out with his overalls ablaze; he ran away and suffered massive burns. Moss won by 38 seconds and once again there was a tragic conflict of emotions in the British contingent: great goodwill towards Hawthorn, sympathy for Moss and Tony Vandervell who had come within a hair's breadth of taking both titles, all under the shadow of grave concern for Stuart Lewis-Evans who was clinging to life by a thread.

Vanwall had won the Constructors' Championship and Hawthorn was World Champion, the first British driver to make it; Moss was second again, despite having won four Grands Prix out of Vanwall's six, to Hawthorn's one of Ferrari's two victories. Despite Ferrari's win, the points table showed that there was a real threat to Italian supremacy from Britain. The first five drivers in the Championship were British: Hawthorn, Moss, Brooks, Salvadori and Collins, then came Harry Schell driving for BRM and Maurice Trintignant driving a Cooper for Rob Walker, on the same points as Musso, the first Italian driver who had won no races and was dead. Vanwall had beaten Ferrari in the majority of the races and Cooper, with what Ferrari still regarded as a ridiculous little car, had come third in the Constructors' Championship with BRM fourth.

Stuart Lewis-Evans finished ninth in the World Championship, one point behind Musso. He had been strapped across three seats in a chartered Viscount and flown back to Britain where he was put in the care of Sir Archibald McIndoe at the famous wartime burns unit at Roehampton Hospital where he died two days later. Lewis-Evans' death had a huge effect on Tony Vandervell. Like Gianni Lancia, Vandervell had never had the experience of a driver dying in one of his cars, and he never really got over the death. On 12 January 1959 he retired on medical grounds and without him, the Vanwall team just withered away.

It was a landmark year in the Championship, a year of progress and of fatal accidents which affected both the top teams. Vanwall had lost one of its top drivers and missed a sensational double for Britain while Ferrari had lost two top drivers and won a title with a British driver who announced he was retiring as soon as the race was over. Ferrari made strenuous efforts to get Hawthorn to sign up for 1959 but Hawthorn was not tempted; he had seen too much death and he wanted to concentrate on the Tourist Trophy Garage, using his new fame to boost business. Ferrari signed Cliff Allison from Lotus instead.

There were two sad postscripts to the British side of the story of 1958. Britain's two World Champions, Hawthorn and Vandervell, were not included in the New Year's Honours while Stirling Moss was awarded the OBE. Soon after the Honours List announcement, on 22 January 1959, Mike Hawthorn was driving his Jaguar on the Guildford bypass where he overtook Rob Walker in his Mercedes at high speed, then crashed into a tree and was killed. The news spread quickly through his friends in the vicinity, then to London and finally to the press. Britain's first World Champion was dead at 29.

The team of young drivers that had gathered at Maranello just two years previously had been decimated. Castellotti, de Portago and his co-driver Nelson, Musso, Collins and now Hawthorn were all dead. Wolfgang von Trips left to test for Porsche which was contemplating getting into Formula 1, and Ferrari responded by signing up Jean Behra from BRM and Tony Brooks from Vanwall to partner Phil Hill and Olivier Genderbein.

Vanwall was replaced in the vanguard of the British revolution by Cooper. Coventry-Climax produced a full 2.5-litre Formula 1 engine which gave the new Cooper T51 around 240 bhp. The Cooper works drivers were Jack Brabham, Bruce McLaren and Masten Gregory. Rob Walker bought T51s for Stirling Moss and Maurice Trintignant. But just as the British acquired a new tailor-made engine at the end of 1958, a new formula was announced which was to take effect

Lotus blossom: Innes
Ireland raced his own
Lotus XI until he got
a works drive in 1959.
He gave Lotus its first
Grand Prix victory in
1961, then was fired.

from the beginning of 1961 – 1.5-litre unsupercharged and no less than 1.3 litres with a minimum weight of 450kg. There was no supercharged option, an attempt at least in part to reduce speeds in the wake of the death toll. The FIA also looked at the anomalous position of the Indianapolis 500 as part of the World Championship. No Formula 1 driver had ever won points at Indianapolis so it was dropped, and plans were made to replace it with a US Grand Prix. Ironically, within a few years British teams would be attracted to Indianapolis, not for Championship points, but for money.

Lotus made it into Formula 1 when Graham Hill gave the front-engined Lotus 16 its debut in the French Grand Prix. The Lotus 16 had more than a hint of the look of the Vanwalls, but since the bodywork had been designed by Frank Costin this was not surprising. Even though they were several laps behind the leaders, Hill and Allison managed to finish tenth and sixteenth in the Italian Grand Prix that year, and it was on the strength of that performance that Allison was offered a contract by Ferrari. Stirling Moss's quest for a British car led to a test for BRM. Afterwards he agreed to drive one in the International Trophy race under an arrangement like that with Maserati in 1954 – BRM maintained the car while Moss drove it for BRP.

The look and feel of the World Championship wwas very different in 1959. With Fangio in retirement, Maserati out and Perón in exile in Spain, there was no Argentinian Grand Prix. Most of the big cars – the Maseratis, Vanwalls and Connaughts – had disappeared either completely, or been banished to the back of the grid. Ferrari, BRM and Lotus still had front-engined cars but they were all much smaller. The greater part of any entry list for Grands Prix was made up of mid-engined Coopers. Moss put the Walker team's Cooper in pole position at Monaco but Brabham won against determined opposition from Brooks for Ferrari, to take his first Grand Prix victory. Behind him, Coopers powered by Climax FPF

engines took four out of the next five places.

The British invasion at the top continued in the Dutch Grand Prix when Jo Bonnier took his and BRM's first victory, a tribute to the work of Tony Rudd and Colin Chapman. Brabham was second, giving him the lead in the World Championship after two races. Brooks won the French Grand Prix with Phil Hill second and Brabham third. This left Brabham in the lead in the World Championship which he held down to the last race, the first US Grand Prix at Sebring in Florida. The position was tantalizingly similar to the previous year in Casablanca. To take the Championship, Moss needed to win and take a point for fastest lap with Brabham no higher than second. Moss sailed away from Brabham, gaining on every one of the first three laps until transmission problems put him out of the race and the Championship. Brabham led until near the end with McLaren in second place and Trintignant in third, all in Coopers, with Brooks a distant fourth. Then it happened – about half a mile from the chequered flag Brabham ran out of fuel. He was coasting along towards the line when McLaren came through and slowed briefly, seeing that his team-mate in trouble. Brabham urged him on; he needed McLaren to finish first in case Brooks made fastest lap and won, which would give Brooks the Championship. McLaren went on to win by a fraction of a second from Trintignant just as Brabham came to a halt. He jumped out, took off his helmet and goggles and started to push up the gradient to the finishing straight. Brooks shot by as the crowd went wild to see a man pushing his car to the line for the World Championship. He made it in fourth place and took the title.

It was the final triumph for the mid-engined revolutionaries and it came not from a scion of the old order – a Vanwall, a BRM or a Connaught – but from the heart of the revolutionary new order, from the back of Charles and John Cooper's Surrey garage. Here a Scottish toff with a passion for racing, Rob Walker, an ex-soldier from Poland,

Alf Francis and an ex-RAAF mechanic, Jack Brabham, designed cars by a rule of thumb. They made a clean sweep for Cooper – Driver's Championship and Constructors' title, the first time anybody had won the double.

The change of formula was heralded as a good thing on the continent but was widely condemned in Britain where it was felt that just as Cooper, BRM and Lotus were getting under way, the cards were restacked in favour of Ferrari and Porsche which was planning to enter Formula 1. It is difficult to see why the British were so hostile since the lighter British cars were already doing extremely well against Ferrari and Porsche in Formula 2. The problem was engines – the British teams relied on Climax which, after a costly development process, had produced the 2.5-litre version that would now have only two seasons before being rendered obsolete with nothing else on the horizon.

If engines were troubling the British teams, it was the success of their mid-engined layout, a change outside the scope of the formula, which concerned Enzo Ferrari. However, even he could now see that change was imperative if Ferrari was to be competitive, and work started on a mid-engined Ferrari for 1961 using a development of the Formula 2 engine. BRM started work on a smaller mid-engined car, and like Ferrari, built its own engine. The Lotus team followed, using a Climax engine.

One of the constant problems facing the British teams was money. The first signs of what would eventually become a fundamental change in the economics of the World Championship came when credit companies sponsored a team in return for publicity. Ken Gregory had a business that rebuilt and repaired cars for insurance companies which were then sold on through the motor trade. This brought him into contact with Yeoman Credit, a subsidiary of the Bowmaker Group, run by the brothers Paul and Fabian Samengo-Turner. The other main credit company supplying the needs of

the domestic car market was United Dominion Trust. UDT had backed Formula 2 drivers and teams, and Yeoman Credit wanted to go one better by getting into Formula 1. It chose BRP, pledging £60,000, a far greater and more stable source of funding than that of Cooper and Lotus which relied on selling racing cars to private entrants to provide revenue.

Gregory would have loved to have Moss as a permanent driver, building the team around him. Although Moss had driven two races for BRP in 1959, he stuck with Rob Walker. BRP had its share of tragedy in 1959. In July, Ivor Bueb was driving a BRP Cooper-Borgward in the Trophée d'Auvergne at Clermont-Ferrand when he lost control, spun off, was thrown out of the car and killed. He was replaced by the ebullient and charming Harry Schell, who spun in the wet in practice for the International Trophy at Silverstone and was also killed. Undaunted, Gregory took on Tony Brooks for 1960.

Ferrari signed up Phil Hill and Ritchie Ginther, another American driver, who had been a USAF mechanic and had raced Ferrari sports cars in America. He also had Cliff Allison and Wolfgang von Trips, who had returned from Porsche. Graham Hill walked out on Lotus after a poor year, to join Jo Bonnier and Dan Gurney at BRM to drive the mid-engined P48. Colin Chapman's first mid-engined car, the Lotus 18, was very light and fast, worrying the Cooper camp. Innes Ireland stayed with Lotus. Cooper used the previous year's car with two works cars for Brabham and McLaren as drivers.

The last year of the 2.5-litre formula, 1960, was a triumph for the revolutionaries. The demise of Vanwall and Connaught, with their copies of the big continental cars, was matched by the rise of Cooper and Lotus. There was only one of the new generation of cars on the grid at Buenos Aires, a Lotus 18 driven by Innes Ireland. Moss was on pole in a Rob Walker Cooper T51, but Ireland, who had been two seconds down on Moss in qualifying,

Cooper climax: John Cooper and Jack Brabham on the podium in 1961. The Championships of 1959–60 were the high tide for Cooper.

shot into the lead and was several seconds ahead of the pack on the first lap, only to spin on the second lap and start again in sixth place. Jo Bonnier led for most of the race and Ireland fought his way back to second place. Then Bonnier's BRM developed engine problems and he slipped back, giving Ireland the lead again until Ireland's gear linkage jammed and he slipped back as well, leaving the lead to McLaren who won for Cooper. It was McLaren and Cooper's second victory in a row, but the race showed that Cooper's dominant position was under pressure from Lotus. Ireland finished sixth showing that, except for the gear linkage problem, the race might have seen an upset on the scale of Moss's victory in the Cooper in 1958. The point had not been lost on the Cooper team, which increased the pace of work on the T53 as soon as they were back in Britain.

The completely rebuilt T53, nicknamed the 'Lowline' because it was so close to the ground made its debut just four months later at Monaco. It was here that Ferrari brought out its mid-engined 246P, in reality a 246 with the engine behind the driver rather than a new design. Rob Walker bought a Lotus 18 for Moss who duly took pole, ahead of Brabham and Ireland. Brabham showed the new Cooper's potential, leading from start to finish, winning by 25 seconds from Ireland.

The Belgian Grand Prix two weeks later was one of the most sobering races of the era. Stirling Moss was driving Rob Walker's Lotus 18 in practice when a rear stub axle broke and the wheel came off. He crashed and was thrown clear but broke both his legs. Then the steering wheel on Mike Taylor's works Lotus 18 broke and he crashed into a tree, breaking ribs and his neck. He never raced again and successfully sued Chapman for damages. In the race, Jack Brabham led ahead of a terrific battle for fifth place between Chris Bristow in the BRP Lotus with Willy Mairesse, a Belgian driver, in a Ferrari. On lap 17 Mairesse passed Bristow who then tried to take his place back. He tried too hard, spinning off to be decapitated by a low branch on a tree by the circuit. Then Alan Stacey hit a pheasant which sent him careering off the track where he crashed and was killed. Two deaths and two serious injuries in Lotuses at one meeting cast a grave shadow over their progress which many put down to the lightness of the construction used by Lotus, a theme which was to recur.

Brabham won the next three races – the French, British and Portuguese Grands Prix – which settled the Championship. In the French, Coopers and Lotuses filled all five places in the points, and in the British and Portuguese Grands Prix there was just one Ferrari placed in each. Brabham had won five races in a row, and with the Italian Grand Prix to come he could equal Ascari's run of six in 1952, and even beat it if he could win in the US. The comparison with Ferrari in 1952 and 1953 was there for all to see; the new overturning the old, except that this time the old was Ferrari and the new was Cooper. The Italian Automobile Club suddenly announced that parts of the Monza circuit not used in recent Grands Prix would be included, favouring the Ferraris over the much lower, lighter Coopers and Lotuses. The season ended on a sour note: Cooper and Lotus boycotted the race and it was a Ferrari procession won by Phil Hill. Lotus was back on top in America, with victory for Moss.

The 1960 Championship was a clean sweep for Cooper again; Jack Brabham took his second Driver's title with Bruce McLaren second, well ahead of Stirling Moss in third place. Coopers won six of the nine Grands Prix, Moss and Lotus won two and Ferrari only one, when there was no competition. Coopers filled the first three places in the Belgian Grand Prix, the first four in the French with Brabham, Genderbein, McLaren and Taylor, and following them were two more Climax-engined cars, one driven by newcomer to Lotus, Jim Clark. A decade on from the first World Championship race at Silverstone, Formula 1 had been transformed into a British province.

The same was true in the lower formulae. For the first half of the decade Formula 3 had prospered, but from 1956 it started to decline as support races were increasingly run for sports cars. The problem was that Formula 3 cars did not change much, and while there was still plenty of good racing, many local motor races were opened up to Formula 2. Cooper's order book showed 19 cars for 1957, 6 for 1958 and only 4 in 1959. The cars which had given Britain its great leap forward and the movement which had been built around them was passing from the scene. The debt was a big one: the British drivers who had learned their trade in Formula 3 Coopers – Moss, Hawthorn, Collins, Brooks and Lewis-Evans – had gone on to the commanding heights of the World Championship. Certainly Vanwall, BRM and Lotus had all benefitted from the interest which Formula 3 had generated as an outlet for both excitement and patriotism.

The first Coopers made to the replacement formula rolled off the production line in 1960 – Cooper-Austins for Formula Junior. The new formula was the brainchild of Count 'Johnny' Lurani, once of Maserati. In 1956 he suggested a formula based on Fiat production engines as a way of encouraging new driver talent in Italy in the same way that Formula 3 had produced the current crop of British drivers. It was adopted as an international formula in 1959 with cars of up to 1100cc using pump fuel, and it flourished in Italy. British interest was sparse at first, but Charles Cooper saw the potential and started building Formula Junior cars in 1959, using a specially tuned version of the Austin A35 engine. Ken Tyrell was an early customer.

The first Formula Junior race in Britain was on Boxing Day 1959. Four Cooper-Austins took part, the best coming fourth, behind two Elvas and a Lola, but in the same race were a Gemini and a Lotus, both powered by Ford 105E production engines. Neither made much impression: the Gemini engine was damaged in practice and the Lotus was fitted with an untuned version because the tuners had only managed to get the Gemini engines ready in time. The name of the tuning company was Cosworth, a combination of the names of two men who had met working at the Lotus factory: Mike Costin and Keith Duckworth. They set up Cosworth in 1958 and Duckworth left Lotus while Costin stayed. In 1959 the company was almost insolvent, then Chapman chose the 105E engine for the Formula Junior Lotus 18.

Chapman also signed up 23-year-old Scottish driver Jim Clark, the only son of a prosperous farming family from Dundee in Fife, Scotland. Clark's first contact with motor racing had been at Charterhall, a disused airfield in Berwickshire, in October 1952 when he saw Farina and Moss. After visiting Brands Hatch several times, he started racing a Sunbeam in club events at Crimond, another disused airfield in Scotland during 1956. Clark drove a Lotus Elite against Colin Chapman at Brands Hatch on Boxing Day 1958. Chapman beat him, but he was aware that Clark had rare talent and invited him to drive the Formula Junior Lotus 18, and signed him up early in 1960. The next race was on 19 March at Goodwood. There were two Cosworth-tuned Ford 105E engines in two Lotus 18s driven by Jim Clark and Trevor Taylor. Ken Tyrell's Cooper was driven by John Surtees, the World Motor Cycle Racing Champion who was making his debut in racing cars having met Tyrell at Hollyfield Road. Surtees took pole position ahead of the two Lotus Cosworths and Bruce McLaren in a works Cooper. Clark won, the first race won by a Cosworth-tuned engine, with Surtees second, Taylor third then another works Cooper driven by Henry Taylor in fourth.

The race established the Lotus 18 as the best Formula Junior car. Orders poured in to Lotus which meant a huge increase in business for both Lotus and Cosworth which never really looked back. Lotus produced over 120 Formula Junior cars in the first year and in the process helped to establish Cosworth as a business. British teams had hijacked Formula Junior just as the proving ground for drivers capable of challenging for a drive in Formula 1 was passing from Formula 3. That Formula Junior race on 19 March 1960 was a long way from the World Championship, but it saw the coming together of a number of key names in the story of the British revolution – Lotus, Cooper, Cosworth, Tyrell, Surtees, McLaren and Clark – names which would echo through the next decade of the World Championship and beyond.

The change in the formula marked the passing of an era. There was only one World Champion still racing in 1961: Jack Brabham. The first, Nino Farina, had retired in 1955 and tried his hand at other forms of racing including Indianapolis, but he had a great many accidents and eventually gave up, only to be killed in a road accident in 1966. Fangio, five times Champion, a record which still stands, retired in 1958 to concentrate on his business in Argentina, the Mercedes Benz concession. He regularly attended Grands Prix over the next three decades and was held in universal respect not only for his ability at the wheel and his courage, but for his integrity; he died in 1995 at the age of 84. The other two World Champions, Alberto Ascari and Mike Hawthorn, were dead.

Of the serious challengers in the 1950s, Luigi Fagioli was dead, killed in the sports car race which replaced the Monaco Grand Prix in 1952, as was Louis Rosier, who was killed racing in 1956. Froilan Gonzales, who had captured the affection of British fans for his sheer guts, effectively retired in 1955 although he appeared in Argentinian Grands Prix up to 1960. He concentrated on building up his motor business in Argentina. Piero Taruffi retired in 1957 to set up a racing drivers' school in Italy; Prince Birabongse, Louis Chiron, Baron de Graffenried and Bob Gerard all retired before the decade's end; Luigi Villoresi, who had never really got over the death of Ascari, also retired. Jean Behra, Peter Collins, Stuart Lewis-Evans, Eugenio Castellotti, Onofre Marimon and Harry Schell were all dead.

Power Play: the Cosworth DFV engine, the kit
car teams' saviour from 1968 to 1982, giving
12 drivers and 10 constructors their titles.

3

KIT CAR KIDS

The introduction of the World Championship ushered in a decade of technical advance, financial innovation and international growth which changed the face of road racing entirely. The romantic idea that unfettered racing on open roads was the only way to remain true to the past had been sullied by the moral impact of so many deaths. It was time for change, and the power and influence of the old order began to erode under the twin pressures of commercialism and the need for greater safety. The new order was a small, tightly knit community of largely British enthusiasts who had found their way in by taking on the motor racing grandees and winning, wrenching the initiative away from the big manufacturers and making Formula 1 the province of small entrepreneurs. The kit car teams, a term originally applied patronizingly and derisively, had been turned into a badge of honour by 1960. These teams had carried out a very quiet revolution with victories in two Driver's and two Constructors' World Championships. The symbols of the revolution were the dark blue mid-engined Cooper T51, Stirling Moss and his victory for Rob Walker in Argentina in 1958.

Moss had continued to drive for Rob Walker whose cars were still tended by Alf Francis. He was at the height of his powers in 1961, and though he had been the perpetual runner-up in the World Championship, his name was synonymous with the best in motor racing. He would have stood a better chance at the World Championship if he had signed for Ferrari, but Moss was his own man; he wanted to beat those red cars, not join them.

Jack Brabham was the great success story of the kit car revolution. He stayed at Hollyfield Road while nurturing ambitions to build Formula 1 cars himself and run his own team. He had established a garage business in Chessington as a way of capitalizing on his success, and in 1959 he invited Ron Tauranac, his partner from his midget car racing days in Australia, to join him in a new business, Motor Racing Developments. They

started out building a Formula Junior car for Australian driver Gavin Youl, in a shed in Esher. Clearly MRD was going to be a direct competitor to Cooper and not only for the lower formulas since Brabham and Tauranac were planning to go into Formula 1.

A new generation of drivers was coming into Formula 1. Brabham's team-mate at Cooper was his friend and protégé Bruce McLaren; still only 24, he had made a huge impression since he first raced in Formula 1 in 1958. In the off-season McLaren raced in the Tasman Series in his native New Zealand, and from 1960 he became a regular driver in American sports car races. McLaren was a year younger than Jim Clark, who had moved from Formula Junior to Formula 1 at Lotus, winning his first non-Championship race at Pau in 1960. Clark's arrival at Lotus put him alongside John Surtees who had graduated to Formula 1 by way of Ken Tyrell's Formula Junior team and Reg Parnell's Formula 2 team in a single season. Graham Hill had left Lotus in 1959 to go to BRM after experiencing a series of failures in the front-engined Lotus 16 and, in his own words, being 'brassed off' with Lotus. The parting was not amicable; Chapman sued him for breach of contract and lost. A year later Hill's wife Bette produced their eldest son, Damon, the first of a future generation of racing drivers.

Roy Salvadori, who had also played a great part in the revolution, was driving a Cooper for BRP under its new title Yeoman Credit Racing. The Yeoman Credit and UDT-Laystall teams owed their existence to direct sponsorship, a new idea in motor racing. At the end of 1960, Ken Gregory discovered that the manager of his car repair business had been indulging in some creative accountancy. Worse, the financial irregularities involved large sums of money owed to Yeoman Credit, the sponsor of Gregory's racing team. Among the other creditors was Bernie Ecclestone who, as a large motor trader, had been a customer of the business. Yeoman switched its allegiance to

Driving lesson: the superior handling of Moss's
obsolete Lotus 18 gave him victory over Ritchie
Ginther's new Ferrari 156 at Monaco in 1961.

Reg Parnell who was also starting out in Formula 1. Undaunted, Gregory promptly went to UDT, a competitor of Yeoman, which put in around £80,000. A publicity tussle between credit companies was a small beginning, but as the first direct sponsorship it was a landmark in the development of Formula 1.

The new 1.5-litre formula was really the old Formula 2. This should have been good for the kit car teams which had triumphed over Ferrari and Porsche in the lower formula. The difference was that the Italian and German companies developed their Formula 2 cars for Formula 1, while the British-based teams had resisted the change and were left behind. Porsche's Formula 1 car was late for the new season so its drivers, the Swede Jo Bonnier and the American Dan Gurney, drove an uprated Formula 2 car instead. At Ferrari, Carlo Chiti had been joined by a new designer, Mauro Foghieri, a 26-year-old engineering graduate of Bologna University whose father already worked at Ferrari. The drivers were Wolfgang von Trips, Phil Hill and Ritchie Ginther, and the car was the first mid-engined Ferrari; the Tipo 156 with a new six-cylinder V engine came in 120° and 65° versions. The Tipo 156 made its debut in Formula 2 form at the Syracuse Grand Prix on 19 March 1960 in the hands of von Trips who won. Ritchie Ginther then drove it in the 1960 Monaco Grand Prix and came sixth. By late 1960 the Tipo 156 was ready in full Formula 1 specification and the first true Formula 1 car made its debut at Syracuse, on 25 April 1961, driven by Giancarlo Baghetti, a young Italian driver who had distinguished himself in Formula Junior. Baghetti won from Dan Gurney for Porsche, Bonnier and Brabham, setting the stage for a clash between the kit car teams and the manufacturers.

Coventry-Climax and BRM were both working on new V8 1.5-litre engines but they were not ready for the start of the season. To bridge the gap the British teams had to make do with an uprated Climax Formula 2 engine, the FPF Mk II. Climax

produced 8: 2 for Cooper, 2 for Lotus and 1 each for BRM, Rob Walker, the UDT-Laystall and Yeoman Credit teams.

The first of eight Grands Prix in 1961 was held in Monaco and it was another historic race. Of the 21 entrants, 12 were powered by Climax engines. Moss was in pole position, then came Ritchie Ginther for Ferrari. Ginther led from the start, opening up a five-second lead over Moss and Jo Bonnier. On lap 12, Moss and Bonnier managed to pass Ginther, then Moss started to inch away from the Porsche as the Ferraris closed in. Phil Hill passed Ginther, then Bonnier, to attack Moss, managing to reel him in steadily. By lap 60, Moss was five seconds ahead of Hill who had Ginther on his gearbox and was clearly faster. Ginther managed to pass Hill on lap 75, then set out after Moss, but Moss was driving superbly and though Ginther nibbled away at the lead, down to 4 seconds on lap 81, Moss remained in command. Both men managed to put in a fastest lap in the struggle but Moss won a great victory over Ferrari by 3.6 seconds in a car with a 40 bhp disadvantage.

Having lost the first race of the season, Ferrari asserted its superiority over the next four races. Von Trips won the Dutch Grand Prix, with Hill second; Hill won in Belgium with von Trips second and Ginther third; and Baghetti, in his first Grand Prix, won in France. Von Trips won the British Grand Prix with Hill second.

The prospect of a Ferrari revival with a German driver leading the team, attracted a crowd of 500,000 to the Nurburgring for the German Grand Pix. It was a day of great expectations, but for the well-informed, interest centred on the debut of Wally Hassan's Climax V8 engine in Jack Brabham's Cooper T58. It was the only example of the engine, and it had only just been put into Brabham's car a few days earlier. It was the first British car made for the new formula, and both Brabham and McLaren realized in testing at Silverstone that it was in the same league as Ferrari. Brabham put the V8 Cooper in second place on the grid, made a great start but spun off in a pool of water and stalled. Even this brief encounter with the power and acceleration of the V8, convinced him that with it the kit car teams could get back on top.

Moss scored another famous victory at the Nurburgring, all the sweeter for knowing that his friend Fangio was watching. Both men remembered the 1958 race on the same circuit when Fangio won over a clutch of Ferraris, achieved by sheer skill over technical superiority. A triumph of driving skill over engine power set Moss apart with great drivers Fangio and Nuvolari.

The showdown for the Championship came at Monza with the banking included as in the 1960 race. At the end of the first lap, Phil Hill was in the lead from Ginther, Rodriguez, Clark and von Trips. Von Trips moved to pass Clark on lap 2 as they approached the Parabolica corner. Clark pulled out from von Trips's Ferrari slipstream to overtake just as von Trips moved over, his rear wheel brushing the front of Clark's car. Both cars spun off on to the grass. Clark crashed but was unhurt; von Trips hit the barrier, rolled over several times and bounced back on to the track where he was thrown out and killed. So were 14 spectators.

The race continued under a pall of gloom. Phil Hill came round on lap three and saw the mangled Ferrari and Lotus but did not know what had happened to his team-mate. He diced with Ginther for the lead until Ginther's engine failed, then won the race and the World Championship, the first American to win. It was a bittersweet victory since he had no idea von Trips was dead until he saw Carlo Chiti's face at the end of the race.

With both Championships settled and its star driver dead, Ferrari did not attend the US Grand Prix at Watkins Glen. Brabham and Moss battled it out for the first part of the race until Brabham retired when the V8 Climax overheated; then Moss led until a main bearing failed. Innes Ireland took over the lead and nursed his Lotus, which had fuel pressure problems, to the end to win his, and

Lotus's, first Grand Prix. Lotus had arrived, but there was a sad ending to the story – Chapman fired Ireland in favour of his protégé Jim Clark. Ireland and Clark had never got on very well, the former a *bon viveur*, drinker and swashbuckler off the track whereas Clark was shy and abstemious. Ireland was understandably bitter. He moved to the UDT-Laystall for 1962 but took a long time to forgive Chapman.

The end of the 1961 season brought two bitter partings at Ferrari. Enzo Ferrari had invited Ritchie Ginther to stay for the 1962 season, but on terms which left Ginther underpaid and without any real status. When Ginther refused to sign, Ferrari did not negotiate and Ginther left the building immediately, having first handed in the keys to his company Ferrari. He went to BRM. Carlo Chiti, Romolo Tavoni and a number of other Ferrari employees who saw only complacency at Maranello and had finally fallen out with Ferrari, also left at the end of 1961. They formed an Italian kit car team, ATS, in a factory in Bologna with backing from a consortium of industrialists much as Ferrari had done in 1929. Chiti was replaced as technical director at Ferrari by Mauro Foghieri.

Cooper, the prototype kit car team which had won two Driver's and Constructors' titles, failed to win a Grand Prix in 1961. The garage at Hollyfield Road was prospering and a new drawing office adorned the roof of the showroom where Stirling Moss had seen his first racing car in 1947. By 1962 it was full of Austin Mini-Coopers, racy versions of the fashionable production car which were tuned and prepared under the Cooper name. Cooper's lack of success in Formula 1 led to another parting of the ways. Jack Brabham decided that his six-year relationship with Cooper had run its course and in 1962 he started building his own Climax-engined car, the BT3. Brabham had already started to race under his own name, entering the 1961 Indianapolis 500 in a Cooper T54 with a 2.7-litre Climax engine. He came ninth, but he came

Sharknose: the sleek Tipo 156 of Phil Hill, the first US World Champion, who gave Ferrari its fifth Driver's and first Constructors' title in 1961.

World Champion
1962 and 1968:
Graham Hill
with his wife Bette
and their son Damon
aged six at the 1967
British Grand Prix.

home with a fistful of dollars, stirring interest among the kit car teams who were always looking for new ways to earn cash.

With Brabham gone, Bruce McLaren became Number 1 driver at Cooper. McLaren was inspired and hard-working, with good mechanical knowledge, and like Brabham, very much part of the Cooper community. He participated in the development of the cars from drawing board through to test driving. He contributed a great deal to the new Cooper T60, a lighter, narrower car built around the Climax V8, essentially a development of the traditional Cooper.

Cooper's pioneering status had been taken over by Lotus which had grown prodigiously as a business under Colin Chapman's dynamic, if rather esoteric management. He was still producing the Lotus 7 in kit form but had started to produce a range of sports cars too – the Elite in 1958, then the Elan, with fibre-glass bodies. By June 1959 Lotus had outgrown Hornsey Mews and moved to a factory at Delamare Road in Cheshunt, Hertforshire. Chapman blossomed with the challenges which his successful business created; he thrived on new ideas, forging ahead of Ferrari, which actively resisted new ideas.

In 1961 Chapman devised the first and arguably the most influential piece of innovation in racing car design to come from his fertile brain – the monocoque. By using the stressed skin as a structural member of the car, it was possible to do away with all the aluminium tubing associated with space frame construction while providing greater stiffness and far lighter construction. The Lotus 25 was a classic with low, smooth, clean lines giving it a very distinctive appearance. Monocoques had been tried before and had failed, so while Chapman experimented, he also developed a new space frame car with the V8 engine, the Lotus 24, as an insurance policy.

Reg Parnell signed up John Surtees and Roy Salvadori for his Bowmaker Racing Team for 1962. He needed cars, but instead of going to Cooper or Lotus he commissioned a new Formula 1 car from Eric Broadley's company, Lola. It had produced a front-engined Formula Junior car, which sold in small numbers before being eclipsed by Lotus.

BRM was in a parlous state: in thirteen years it had won only one World Championship race – Jo Bonnier's victory in Holland in 1959. In 1961, Hill finished with just three points and Brooks six, and behind closed doors, Sir Alfred Owen gave the team an ultimatum – if they did not win at least two Grands Prix in 1962, he would shut up shop. Raymond Mays remained as a figurehead, but without any power, and Peter Berthon was made a consultant to Rubery Owen, a polite but firm way of sidelining him. Tony Rudd was promoted to finish the P56 engine which Berthon had started and to focus on the short-term objective of winning. The P56 was finished during the summer of 1961 and made its debut in practice for the Italian Grand Prix.

Ferrari was in poor shape again. Enzo Ferrari had lost his senior engineers and top drivers, so two weeks before the start of the 1962 season he invited Stirling Moss to Modena for the first time in a decade. They did a deal: Moss would drive a Ferrari, supplied, owned and maintained by the factory but prepared for the races by Alf Francis and the Rob Walker team in whose colours the car would be painted. This was Moss's title bid, but it was not to be. Moss entered the Glover Trophy at Goodwood in a UDT-Laystall Lotus 18. He was unhappy with the car and stopped in the pits for attention to the gearbox, rejoining nearly two laps down on Graham Hill in the BRM. Moss managed to claw back a whole lap, coming up on Hill at St Mary's corner. He was preparing to unlap himself by overtaking on the outside when he was forced to go wide on to the grass where his wheel got stuck in a gully. He could not control it and crashed heavily into an earth bank. It took 40 minutes to cut him out of the wreckage and he was taken to hospital where he remained unconscious for 38

New face: Max Mosley and his brother Alex in
1958; he considered politics before motor racing,
working his way from driver to president of FIA.

days. He woke up a different man without the same swift, instinctive reactions, and although he gave it time, testing his skills after a period of convalescence, he found them sadly wanting. He retired after a career of 494 races. Stirling Moss is one of the all-time greats, to this day the best driver never to win the World Championship.

The first race of 1962 was the Dutch Grand Prix at Zandvoort where a number of new cars were on display. Jim Clark drove the Lotus 25, which caused much discussion and some irritation to Jack Brabham and Ken Gregory who had both bought Lotus 24s. Bruce McLaren was in the Cooper-Climax T60, John Surtees in the Bowmaker Lola-Climax, Graham Hill in the P57 BRM, and Jo Bonnier and Dan Gurney in a brace of new straight-eight, air-cooled Porsche 804s. Clark made the best start followed by Graham Hill, Gurney and Surtees, and by lap 3 Clark had opened up a 3-second lead. On lap 12 Graham Hill managed to pass Clark who then brought the Lotus 25 into the pits with a slipping clutch, rejoining nine laps down. Graham Hill won, a famous victory for BRM, with Taylor second for Lotus and Phil Hill third for Ferrari.

After a joyless 1961 at Cooper, Bruce McLaren put the T60 back on the map by winning at Monaco. Clark did the same for Lotus at Spa, then came the French Grand Prix at Rouen. Ferrari had entered three cars but none of them appeared; Porsche arrived with Dan Gurney and Jo Bonnier. Clark took pole position, but Hill took the lead with Surtees second. Clark and Hill retired and Gurney held the lead to the end to take Porsche's first and only Grand Prix victory.

The decider was South Africa – whoever won the race took the title. It was Hill, only the second British driver to be World Champion, which made it difficult for Sir Alfred Owen to do anything other than reprieve BRM, which he did amid great celebration.

The nine Grands Prix produced 54 places which earned points in the World Championship,

and out of those, 26 were filled by cars using Climax engines, including four first places. Graham Hill won a further four races and was placed in eight of the nine Grands Prix, giving a total of eight out of the nine races to the British teams. The Climax and BRM V8 engines had put the British kit car teams firmly back on top.

The ninth victory had gone to Dan Gurney. Porsche's experiment had been based on the idea of building a family of racing cars, evolving to a peak in Formula 1. It had been expensive, and just one season had shown the management that such an approach would not be competitive in the face of the kit car teams who went back to the drawing board each year in true Grand Prix tradition. Porsche did not take part in the South African Grand Prix and pulled out of Formula 1 to concentrate on sports car racing to publicize its name, in direct competition with Ferrari.

Ferrari did not win any races in 1962. Enzo Ferrari placed the blame entirely on his drivers rather than his cars, deciding that Phil Hill had lost the will to win. He was not fired but made to feel very uncomfortable, and at the end of the season, fed up with all the intrigue, he left Ferrari to join the other dissidents at ATS. Ferrari signed John Surtees who was popular in Italy from his days riding for MV-Augusta in the World Motor Cycle Championship; he already had an Italian nickname, *Il Grande John*.

Italy was beset by industrial unrest and economic uncertainty and Enzo Ferrari was so depressed in the winter of 1962–3 that he seriously contemplated selling the *scuderia*. Ford was looking for ways to promote its name worldwide, particularly with young people. Ford, however, had agreed with other US motor manufacturers not to participate in motor racing in order to avoid getting involved in what all had seen as a costly distraction. But Ford had identified motor racing as a way of attracting young people to its cars and in a strategic move, began to invest heavily in promoting itself with the slogan 'Total

Performance'. Buying Ferrari would contribute heavily to that image, acquiring prestige, particularly through Le Mans where Ferrari was dominant. Negotiations started at around $19 million, provoking impassioned editorials in the Italian press. Ultimately negotiations foundered, not over money but over control of the racing which Ferrari would not relinquish. Henry Ford was not amused and immediately decided to build a car, the GT40, to beat Ferrari on the race track under the Ford name instead.

The British teams which had upset the balance in Formula 1, the root cause of Ferrari's depression, were part of another social and economic revolution which swept through Britain in the 1960s. It produced entrepreneurs in areas from retailing and pop music to fashion and photography. Motor racing became part of the colourful, exciting and rewarding world which attracted talented people as drivers, mechanics and engineers. Some came and disappeared quickly, others made a passing impact, but a few went on to build teams which would produce multiple World Champions and ultimately dominate the sport.

Frank Williams was one such person. He was born in 1942 in Jarrow while his father was a bomber pilot in the RAF. His parents divorced, but his mother was determined that he would have a good education and despite the shortage of family money, he went to a boarding school in Dumfries. Motoring was his boyhood passion; when he left school in 1960, he took a job as a management trainee with a Nottingham motor distributor. He bought his first car in 1961, an Austin A35 from Graham Hill's company, Speedwell Conversions. At weekends he raced it in club events where he met Jonathan Williams and Piers Courage, both wealthy young men trying to get into racing. They became firm friends and he became mechanic to Jonathan Williams.

Max Mosley was born in 1940, the son of Sir Oswald Mosley, leader of the British League of Fascists, and divorcee Diana Guiness, one of the Mitford sisters. Shortly after he was born, his mother was interned at Holloway prison; his father had already been imprisoned. After the war, he was brought up and educated in France and Germany, ending up at Oxford in the early 1960s where he studied law and physics and became secretary of the Union. In 1962 he visited Silverstone where his life completely changed direction; he caught the bug and was soon racing in club events while making his way as a barrister. When he moved up to Formula 2, his first car was a Brabham which was prepared by Frank Williams.

Robin Herd was born in 1940 and went to Oxford at the same time as Mosley. He took a double first in physics and engineering and went on to become an apprentice at the Royal Aircraft Establishment at Farnborough where he worked on Concorde. He had a long-standing interest in motor racing and during work experience had worked at Lotus with race mechanic Bob Dance, where he had caught the bug too.

Lotus was the leading kit car team of the day and its success attracted many people to the sport, including Alan Rees who had been at school with Robin Herd, who drove for the works Formula Junior team in 1962. Chapman was forging ahead in Formula Junior based on the relationship with Cosworth, launching the Lotus 22 with the Ford-Cosworth Mk IV engine at the Racing Car Show in January 1962. The new factory at Cheshunt gave new space and impetus to Colin Chapman's ideas and 1963 would see the height of his achievements to date. The Lotus 25 was clearly ahead of its competitors in Formula 1 and although a series of failures left Lotus in second place in the 1962 World Championship, it was the best all-round car.

The Lotus sports car division was supposed to be the profitable side of the business but the Lotus Elite was losing money. The problem was the engine, and for the Elite's successor, the Elan, Chapman was looking at a standard 1500cc Ford production engine. Chapman contacted Walter

Hayes, for whom he had written a column in the *Sunday Despatch* when Hayes had been editor. Hayes had moved to Ford to run the Total Performance campaign, and he suggested that Chapman not only use the Ford engine for the Elan, but that the same engine should be put into a new saloon car, the Ford Cortina, together with other modifications including a green stripe down the side and Lotus badges front and rear. Chapman agreed and the Lotus Cortina was announced in January 1963, echoing Cooper's association with the Mini-Cooper. The Lotus Elan and the Lotus Cortina were both great successes financially, putting Lotus on a far firmer footing.

Not content with all his activities in Britain in road cars, sports car racing, Formula Junior and Formula 1, Colin Chapman also set out to win the Indianapolis 500 in 1963. It was a huge, rich race but it relied on cars that had changed little over the years, all powered by the same Offenhauser engine, designed and set up for the Indianapolis circuit, with its four similar corners. In July 1962, Chapman went to see Ford at Dearborn where the management wanted to get into Indianapolis as well. They agreed to modify a Fairlane engine if Chapman would design a car to take it. Following the 1962 US Grand Prix, Chapman took Jim Clark and the Lotus 25 to Indianapolis and tried it out there in front of a crowd of Indy officials and drivers. He then went on to build an Indianapolis car, the Lotus 29 which was ready for the 1963 500 at the end of May. Clark caused a sensation by challenging the might of the Indianapolis establishment. With just 25 laps out of 200 to go, he was lying second behind Parnelli Jones in an 'Offy' roadster, and was closing on the leader when he had an oil leak. The track became increasingly slippery but the officials wavered long enough for the leak to stop because the oil level had dropped low enough. The orange lights were put on which meant that everyone had to hold his place until the end. Jones won and Clark was second; if there was great disappointment at the apparent lack of

sportsmanship, it was mitigated to an extent by the $100,000 prize for second place which Lotus and Clark took back to Cheshunt.

There were ten races in the World Championship in 1963, the addition being Mexico. BRM started out well with Hill winning at Monaco and Ginther second. Jim Clark then took the Championship by the scruff of the neck as only a truly great driver can. He won in Belgium with McLaren second for Cooper, in Holland with Gurney second for Brabham, in France with one of the finest drives of his life and at Silverstone, his fourth win in a row. He was second in the German Grand Prix, behind Surtees' Ferrari, after a faulty engine slowed him.

The 1963 Championship was decided at Monza between Jim Clark and Graham Hill. Clark could win the title which Hill could not, but if Hill won the race, he could keep his challenge alive with three races to go. Clark won in front of the *tifosi*, a stylish way to take his and Lotus's first World Championship. To celebrate, he picked up Colin Chapman from the pits and drove a lap of honour with Chapman sitting astride the car. It was a great moment and when they came round to the grandstand again, the crowd had burst through the barriers into the pits area. Jim Clark won seven out of ten races and came second at Indianapolis, putting Lotus on top of the world.

The motor racing fraternity in Britain was flourishing. Cooper, Lotus, Brabham and Lola all built cars for customers and made a profit from their expertise. They dominated Formula 1 and they were beginning to move into America. Ford looked to Britain for racing expertise and high performance technology, not to Germany, France or Italy. It was a highly fluid industry in which success was paramount and the ability to wheel and deal essential. New teams came, flourished and died, quietly and spectacularly, depending on the skills of the key people. There were failures as well as successes. Kit car philosophy depended on having an extraordinary figure at the heart of the

Four wheel driver: John Surtees with Enzo Ferrari.
He signed with Ferrari in 1963 and took the
Championship in 1964.

team with the independence of mind and drive to pull the money, engineering and drivers together. The ATS experiment turned sour when one of their industrial backers pulled out, leaving Chiti and Tavoni without the finance to continue. They lacked the entrepreneurial flair which the British kit car team bosses relied on to survive and at the first sign of problems, it folded.

In 1963 John Cooper had a serious accident on the Kingston bypass in an experimental Mini-Cooper. He was hospitalized and Charles Cooper who was now 70, asked Ken Tyrell who was running his own Formula Junior team, to step in and run the Cooper Formula 2 and Formula Junior teams. Cooper was conspicuous for its lack of success and this posed the question: was Bruce

McLaren the cause of the problem or was the lack of success the effect of a wider decline at Cooper. Charles Cooper was conservative by nature, elderly, and he had a heart condition. McLaren was frustrated by Cooper's conservatism, and sensing that Cooper was in decline, was already thinking about starting his own team, like Brabham. Things came to a head when McLaren tried to persuade Charles Cooper to build two special lightweight cars for the Tasman Series of six races in New Zealand and Australia. When Charles Cooper decided against building any new cars, McLaren decided to go it alone.

McLaren built two cars, one for himself and one for Tim Mayer, an American lawyer turned road racing driver, managed by his brother, who had been spotted by Ken Tyrell. He brought along Americans Tyler Alexander and Peter Revson, another driver, who had been at Cornell University with the Mayers. The Mayers, Revson and Alexander were part of a small but determined invasion of Americans to European road racing, most of whom had started out in sports car racing in the US. They were attracted by the gentlemanly tradition of road racing compared with the highly commercial, but generally more blue collar, oval racing tradition in the US. They were also attracted by the burgeoning, flexible, small-team culture and structure of the sport in the Britain of the 1960s. Tim Mayer showed exceptional promise and Ken Tyrell signed him up for his own Formula Junior team; he was soon being spoken about as future Formula 1 material.

McLaren's two Tasman cars were based on the Cooper T66 with an improved short stroke, 2.5-litre FPF engine. To finance, own and enter the cars, McLaren created Bruce McLaren Racing Ltd with Teddy Mayer as a director to raise the capital, manage the business and keep the team going, while McLaren provided the charisma and the leadership around which it revolved. McLaren had the rare ability to make a team work at all levels and the most important ingredient was his own enthusiasm and the way he inspired others.

Jack Brabham had also built two cars for the Tasman Series, using the same short-stroke FPF engines. He took on New Zealander Denny Hulme, who had started in Formula 2 in 1960, to drive the second car. The ability to conceive, design, finance and build a brace of new racing cars, then ship them half way round the world, race them and win, all in a matter of months, then back to Europe to get to grips with another car and another formula, was the youthful, entrepreneurial spirit of the times. McLaren and Brabham became the seeds from which two of the most competitive teams grew and blossomed. This competitiveness was evident in the first Tasman race, the New Zealand Grand Prix in Auckland. Mayer took the

lead, then Brabham passed him before crashing to leave McLaren to win. He repeated his success, beating Brabham in two fierce battles in New Zealand, the Wigram Trophy and at Teretonga. In Australia, Hulme won at Warwick Farm with McLaren second and at Lakeside with McLaren third. The final race was at Longford in Tasmania. In practice, Tim Mayer's car hit a bump at speed, became airborne and hit a tree, killing him. A very subdued Bruce McLaren drove hard in the race to give him second place behind Graham Hill's Brabham and the Tasman Championship.

Tim Mayer's death affected the whole McLaren team, but Bruce McLaren had demonstrated not only his ability to drive and win, but that he could build competitive cars and run a successful team. Tragedy and triumph were common bedfellows in motor racing in the 1960s, and personal loss, however strongly felt, had to be swiftly overcome. McLaren was saddened but never thought of giving up: the excitement came not only from driving, but driving cars with his own name on them. Nor did the loss of his brother deter Teddy Mayer who stayed on at McLaren which turned to building sports cars for racing in the US. McLaren was sensible enough not to make any ill-judged leaps before he was ready, and until he was ready, he continued to drive for Cooper, but the goal, the Holy Grail, was Formula 1.

Tim Mayer's death left a big hole in Ken Tyrell's Formula Junior team. In his search for a new star he heard from Robin McKay, the manager at Goodwood, of a 24-year-old Scottish driver who was having great success for Ecurie Ecosse at Goodwood. His name was Jackie Stewart. Tyrell put him in a Formula 3 car at Goodwood, his first drive in a single-seater, then pitted him against the times set by Bruce McLaren who was testing in a similar car. Within a few laps, Stewart was bettering McLaren, who went out again and set a faster time which Stewart promptly bettered again. Tyrell signed him on the spot, starting one of the most successful partnerships in Formula 1.

The season opened at Monaco, and apart from two Ferraris for Surtees and Lorenzo Bandini and a single private Belgian entry, all the cars were British. Clark led but Hill won, his second consecutive Monaco Grand Prix, with Ginther second, for a BRM 1–2. Clark made up for it by taking the lead from the start of the Dutch Grand Prix, then leading to finish first from Graham Hill who had fuel vaporization problems, then John Surtees. Race order at the start of the last lap was Hill, McLaren, his engine spluttering from a flat battery, then Gurney, also spluttering because he was low on fuel, then Clark. Gurney ran out of fuel and seconds later the same thing happened to Hill, leaving McLaren heading for the finishing line in a very sick Cooper. He was in sight of victory when, fifty yards from the flag, Clark shot past and won.

Clark then led the French Grand Prix from pole until his engine failed, leaving Dan Gurney to win, the first Championship victory for Brabham after two years. Clark's run continued with victory in the British Grand Prix, putting him on 30 points to Hill's 26, with the rest far behind.

As the season developed so did the cars, and things started to change at the German Grand Prix. Jim Clark was driving the Lotus 33, a lighter version of the Lotus 25 with a stiffer monocoque and wider tyres; Ferrari had two V8-engined cars for Surtees and Bandini. Making its debut at the back of the grid was the Honda V12 RA271 of Ronnie Bucknam. Japan's renowned motor cycle manufacturer had decided to enter Formula 1 by setting up a European base with a small team in Holland. Surtees won, a much needed and applauded victory for Ferrari, with Hill second and Bandini third.

Lorenzo Bandini won the Austrian Grand Prix, Ferrari's second Grand Prix in a row when the Championship leaders all retired with mechanical problems. The race saw the Formula 1 debut of a local driver, Jochen Rindt, driving a Rob Walker Brabham-BRM. Rindt was a wealthy young man who had inherited his family's business in 1961. He bought a Formula Junior Cooper and went motor racing, selling the family business to finance a Formula 2 Brabham, then racing at his own expense while looking for a way into Formula 1.

The Ferrari team arrived at Monza to great acclaim from the *tifosi* and Surtees rewarded them with pole position and a near-perfect result – Surtees, McLaren, Bandini. Clark retired with a broken piston and Surtees was the only one of the top three in the Championship to gain points, putting him on 28 points, 2 behind Clark and 4 behind Hill. Clark's run of bad luck continued at Watkins Glen where he retired with fuel injection problems. Hill won with Surtees second, so with only the Mexican Grand Prix to go, Hill, Surtees and Clark could all win the title. Clark went serenely into the lead ahead of Gurney, Hill, Bandini and Surtees. Bandini tried to take Hill but their wheels touched and Hill spun off into the barrier, crushing his exhaust pipes so he could not use full power and he went into the pits. Surtees made full use of the incident to move up to third place, then Bandini recovered and passed Surtees. Clark's oil pipe then failed, putting him out of the running and putting Surtees third, making Graham Hill Champion unless Surtees could pass Bandini. As they started on the last lap, the Ferrari pits signalled furiously to Bandini to let Surtees through. Whether Bandini let him or whether Surtees out-drove him is not clear, but Surtees crossed the line first, adding the Formula 1 World Championship to his list of motor cycle titles. Ferrari also took the Constructors' title, a very timely victory against the tide of British success; the *tifosi* could breathe again.

Ferrari's relationship with the British teams was complex. They wanted to beat each other on the track but at an organizational level they wanted to make more money from race promoters, and it was difficult to negotiate from strength if they were divided. During 1963, the French motor racing federation proposed a series of Formula 2 races in France and wanted an agreement with the British teams, suggesting a Formula 2 Association to negotiate terms. Andrew Ferguson, the Lotus team manager, was appointed to represent the British teams and a deal was struck covering the prize fund, starting money and how the revenues would be split between the teams according to a sliding scale based on performance. Cooper, Lotus and Brabham were also involved in Formula 1, and having seen the benefits of collective action, got together with BRM to create the Formula 1 Constructors' Association, F1CA, not only to negotiate deals but to reduce costs by organizing collective transport of all members' cars to overseas races. Ferguson was appointed secretary of F1CA, a prototype Bernie Ecclestone, on a fee of £15 per annum.

The teams were becoming real businesses with fixed overheads whose only income came from racing, while Honda and before them Porsche and Mercedes, went racing to promote their names and bore the costs of racing internally. Ferrari saw himself as closer to the big manufacturers than the British teams, whom he dismissively called *garagistas* or *assemblatore*. He did not join F1CA, preferring to stay above what he saw as the petty concerns of the lesser teams, but he was a master of Formula 1 politics and he kept in touch with F1CA to see and hear what was going on.

The F1CA teams' emphasis on their distinction as constructors, rather than simply racing teams, was one they were keen to maintain between themselves and the private entrants, small *scuderia* and *écuries* who were, ironically, the main customers for the racing cars they built. The F1CA teams were determined that the fruits of greater commercialization, particularly the prospect of major, direct product sponsorship, would flow to them directly, and not be creamed off by small operators. Ken Gregory, who had pioneered direct sponsorship with the credit companies by using the name of the sponsor as the team name, badly wanted to qualify as a constructor, but he was exactly the kind of small operation which F1CA

members saw as a threat and they decided resolutely against admitting him. He decided not to fight and closed BRP at the end of 1964, leaving racing to develop businesses in air transport and financial investment.

At the end of 1963, the FIA announced a new formula from 1 January 1966: 3-litre or 1.5-litre supercharged, signalling a return to engine power. Fixing the formula generated a great deal of debate, as it had in 1961, provoking contrary proposals from Ferrari who wanted unlimited engine size, and from the British teams who wanted a limit of 2 litres, enabling them to develop existing engines. The new formula suited Ferrari best since he had a well-developed 3-litre engine from sports car racing. Good as it was, the Climax 1.5-litre engine could not be developed to match it, leaving the kit car teams looking to a future with uncomfortable similarities to the previous formula change when waiting for a new engine held them back for a whole season. This position was confirmed in February 1965 when Climax decided it was not going to build a new off-the-shelf engine. Neither Cooper, Brabham nor even Lotus could afford the development costs of a new 3-litre engine, so they all went down different routes for the 1966 season.

The blow fell heaviest on Cooper which was already suffering from a far greater loss. Charles Cooper, whose beautiful little Cooper 500s had transformed British motor racing, died on 14 October 1964. His son John took over the reins and he realized that to arrest the company's decline, he needed more than a new engine supplier; he needed proper financial backing. He found both when Roy Salvadori put him in touch with the Chipstead Group, one of Britain's major motor traders, which had bought all Salvadori's car trading businesses some years earlier. Chipstead saw commercial opportunities in the rights to the Mini-Coopers, which had won the Monte Carlo Rally the previous year in a blaze of publicity. It could promote the company name on the back of

Testing time: Surtees and his wife Pat with Mauro Foghieri at the start of the 1966 season. Surtees left mid-season after a row with Enzo Ferrari.

Cooper's sales of racing cars. In April 1965 Cooper and Chipstead announced they had merged, but the reality was that Chipstead had paid around £220,000 for the company and John Cooper stayed on to run the racing team with Salvadori. For 1965 they signed Jochen Rindt.

Chipstead also provided Cooper with a new engine. One of its directors was Mario Tozzi-Condivi, an Italian living in Britain who was closely connected to Maserati. Tozzi-Condivi was a consummate deal-maker and through his efforts Maserati agreed to build a new flat 12 engine based on its 1957 2.5-litre design. The Formula 1 Cooper-Maserati would be sold to customers as a complete car, including the engine, while the works cars' engines remained the property of Maserati and would be rebuilt by them. It was a deal with a certain irony; Cooper, the pioneer of the new order, providing a route back into Formula 1 for one of the greatest names of the old order. The takeover was the end of the old atmosphere at Hollyfield Road and a number of the old hands left to join McLaren. As part of the deal Cooper moved its premises to Taylor & Thompson where generations of Brooklands cars had been tuned and the ERA chassis built before the war. One of the apprentice engineers at T & T was the 18-year-old Ron Dennis who was working on a yard full of imported Russian Moskvitch cars and was immediately attracted to the idea of a racing team. He quickly engineered himself a position as Jochen Rindt's mechanic.

BRM, which had always produced its own engines, started work on a very complicated H16 layout for 1966. Sir Alfred Owen signed Jackie Stewart to partner Graham Hill. Stewart had won his first Formula 3 race for Ken Tyrell in 1964, then won eight more events, completely dominating his first year in Formula 3. Cooper and Lotus tried to lure him away from Tyrell for their lower formula teams. Although he drove a Lotus in the non-Championship Formula 1 Rand Grand Prix in South Africa, he was very loyal to Ken Tyrell and when he signed for BRM he remained free to drive for Ken Tyrell in Formula 2.

Jack Brabham turned to Australia for an engine. He had a strong relationship with Repco, Australia's largest distributor of automotive parts, and together they provided Repco-Brabhams powered by Climax engines for the Tasman Series. Brabham had realized for some time that if Climax did pull out, he would need a solution to the Tasman races as well as Formula 1 so he persuaded Repco to build a racing engine. Repco's chief engineer, Frank Hallam, suggested using a very light, linerless aluminium block developed for a new General Motors compact car, which GM then abandoned. Repco bought up the discarded blocks and designed a new overhead camshaft, initially for Tasman, but at Jack Brabham's urging, Repco then moved on to develop a 3-litre version for Formula 1. The first Formula 1 engine, the Type 620, was bench-tested on 25 March 1965 in Australia, then brought to Britain for testing in a BT19 chassis. It weighed 340lb and produced around 350 bhp. Brabham was set for the new formula in 1966.

In *his* search for a new engine, Colin Chapman turned initially to Keith Duckworth at Cosworth. It had moved to new premises at Northampton where it was busy building engines for lower formulae. Duckworth had no plans for Formula 1 but he had started on a design for a new 1.6-litre engine for Formula 2 based on the Ford 105E engine which would also be suitable for the Lotus Cortina. Chapman asked Duckworth if he could build a Formula 1 version which would produce 400 bhp and if so, how much it would cost. Duckworth, never one to go about financial matters with the same detail and perfectionism he applied to his engines, put the figure at £100,000 on the development and said he would do it if Chapman could find the money. While Chapman enthused Walter Hayes, Duckworth started work on his new 4-valve, 1.6-litre Formula 2 engine in July 1965. His plan was to see if that worked and if it did, he would double it up to V8 to provide a 3-litre version. Negotiations continued through the summer, including a presentation to Henry Ford III in America. In October, Ford announced it would finance development of an engine, to be designed and built by Cosworth, and that Lotus would have exclusive use of it for one season – 1967. Colin Chapman would have liked a longer period of exclusivity but he had to agree. It became known as the Cosworth Double Four Valve, DFV, and ultimately it would change the face not only of Formula 1, but Indianapolis as well.

Another development which was to have an even more profound long-term effect came when the British Health Ministry announced on 8 February 1965 that cigarette advertising would be banned on British television. Colin Chapman was ahead of his competitors in seeing the huge commercial possibilities that this represented for the kit car teams if the rules on direct sponsorship ever changed.

The first Grand Prix of 1965 was on New Year's Day at East London. Clark took pole position in the Lotus 33, a full second ahead of Surtees in the V8 Ferrari and Jack Brabham in the BT11. Clark led from start to finish; Surtees was second and Graham Hill was third. Jackie Stewart, who was sixth, picked up his first World Championship point in his first Grand Prix.

Jim Clark was not at Monaco because he was driving in the Indianapolis 500 held on the same day. He won a sensational victory and $166,621 in the world's richest motor race. It was the first time since 1946 that a car not powered by an Offenhauser engine had won the race. Lotus and the mid-engined revolution had hit Indianapolis swiftly and surely, and in 1965 mid-engined cars and Ford Cosworth engines dominated the race. Parnelli Jones was second in a Lotus-based car and Mario Andretti, in his first Indianapolis, was third in a Cosworth-engined Brawner.

Clark was back for the Belgian Grand Prix which turned out to be something of a landmark in the demise of the private entrant. The promoters invited ten to attend, then said that only four would receive starting money, so the private entrants refused to take part. A compromise was worked out and most were eventually paid, but it was an example of the pressure which the F1CA teams and Ferrari were putting on the system for more of the starting money to go to them, making all but the richest private entrant an increasingly endangered species. The constructors did not want them squeezed out altogether, but cash was king, and deals that F1CA did make gave its members the lion's share of the purse which became increasingly important to their ability to finance their racing, as did the prospect of direct sponsorship.

It was shaping up into a Lotus versus BRM season: Clark won at Spa with Stewart second and McLaren third. Ginther was sixth for Honda, winning its first Championship points. Stewart, having driven in only three Grands Prix and earned points in each of them, was now third in the World Championship with 11 points to his team-mate Hill's 15 and Clark's 18. Clark was on a roll, winning the next three races: the French, British and Dutch Grands Prix, a total of five wins from five races, putting him on 45 points to Hill's 26 and Stewart's 25.

The Nurburgring had been partly resurfaced for the German Grand Prix. Honda withdrew but Clark was on top form, breaking the lap record, putting it over 100 mph for the first time, 3 seconds ahead of Stewart, Hill and Surtees. Clark won from Hill with an average speed of 99.79 mph, faster than Surtees' lap record of the previous year, in one of the finest drives of his career, worthy of delivering him a second World Championship.

Stewart had retired on lap 2 with suspension problems but came back with a vengeance for the Italian Grand Prix, which produced some magnificent racing. The lead swapped back and forth between Clark, Stewart and Hill. Clark's fuel pump then failed and the two BRM drivers battled it out to the end, swapping the lead four times

Decline and fall: John Cooper briefing Phil Hill and Bruce McLaren at the 1964 British Grand Prix. Hill was 6th and McLaren's gearbox failed.

before victory went to Stewart, his first Grand Prix victory in his eighth race.

Hill won the US Grand Prix, then the circus moved to Mexico for an historic occasion, the last race of the 1.5-litre formula. There was something of an end-of-term feeling, but Honda had been working hard on making the RA 272 competitive in the thin air at 7000 feet altitude. Ritchie Ginther provided a shock result, putting all the European teams in the shade by leading from start to finish for Honda's first Formula 1 victory, sparking off wild enthusiasm in Japan.

The laurels for the 1961–5 formula have to go to Lotus, Jim Clark and Colin Chapman. In five years, Lotus had won 20 of the 46 Grands Prix it entered. It ended on a high note with a second victory in the Driver's Championship on maximum points with a string of lap records, fastest laps and pole positions, a second victory in the Constructors' Championship and victory in the Indianapolis 500. From this high point, Lotus became the biggest sufferer when the new formula came into force in 1966. The Cosworth engine would not be ready until 1967, so Colin Chapman had to make do with a mixture of uprated 2-litre Climaxes and BRM H16s.

The new formula stimulated other kit car teams into existence. American interest continued – Dan Gurney left Brabham at the end of 1965 to form Anglo-American Racing, sponsored by Mobil, and named the cars Eagle for patriotic reasons. The plan was to create an Indy Car and adapt it for Formula 1, reversing the process followed by Lotus. Gurney took on Len Terry who had designed Clark's Indianapolis Lotus 38, setting up the European end of the operation in the Sussex workshops of Aubrey Woods, an ex-BRM engineer who set up on his own as an engine builder under the name Weslake. Len Terry was replaced by an ex-De Havilland aircraft worker and Austin 7 special builder, Maurice Philippe.

Bruce McLaren decided that the new formula was the right time to move up to Formula 1, and in

a radical move, he took on Robin Herd from Farnborough to design the car. Herd had never designed a racing car before, but set about producing drawings for the M2A using an ex-Indianapolis 4-litre Ford V8 engine linered down to 3 litres. The M2A was unveiled to the press in December 1965. Moving to Formula 1 meant leaving Cooper after eight years and the loss of McLaren was another serious blow to Cooper. Jochen Rindt stayed on, joined by Ritchie Ginther on loan from Honda until their 3-litre car was ready. As second driver McLaren signed fellow New Zealander Chris Amon.

John Surtees stayed at Ferrari with Lorenzo Bandini, but the big man's relationship with Ferrari was endlessly dogged by the politicking of Eugenio Dragoni, the team manager, who tried to get Bandini the best cars to drive at the expense of Surtees. Enzo Ferrari also felt that Surtees had lost his edge following an accident in a sports car race in the US. With Surtees driving the new car, the Tipo 312, Ferrari should have been, and was, the best placed of all the teams to benefit from the new formula. The Tipo 312 with its new V12 fuel-injected engine producing 360 bhp, was still fitted into a traditional space frame chassis. Ferrari's emphasis on power rather than handling still hampered the kind of progress which should have been possible with the financial support from Fiat. His treatment of drivers was another problem.

John Surtees was to partner Mike Parkes in the Le Mans 24-hour sports car race. Enzo Ferrari, operating true to form, rather than reassure Surtees, chose to emphasize his concern that Surtees had lost his edge. Parkes and Surtees were not soul-mates. Parkes was a rather aloof, upper-class man with a certain disdain for Surtees' working-class origins and his engineering skills. He was also after Surtees' No.1 seat in the Ferrari Formula 1 team. Ferrari not only put them together, but signed up a third driver, Lodovicio Scarfiotti, as reserve for the entry, a fact which Surtees only discovered when he arrived at the

Driver-constructor:
Bruce McLaren
enjoyed success in
sports car racing in
North America which
eluded him in the
World Championship.

circuit. Surtees refused to drive on that basis and immediately challenged the decision with Dragoni and Enzo Ferrari by telephone. Ferrari was unmoved, so *Il Grande John* returned to England, ending his relationship with Ferrari on a sour note after three seasons. Back in England Surtees went to see Cooper who signed him up for the rest of the season, his arrival displacing Ritchie Ginther who went back to Honda. Surtees was replaced at Ferrari by Mike Parkes.

Ferrari was crushed at Le Mans for his pains: Bruce McLaren was driving the Ford GT40, partnered by Chris Amon. They won with GT40s in second and third place, an ignominious end to the long run of Ferrari victories and sweet revenge for Henry Ford, who was there to see it.

The new era started on 22 May 1966 at Monaco. Clark just managed to take pole position in an underpowered version of the 1965 Lotus. McLaren was tenth, on exactly the same qualifying time as his friend and rival, the only other man to drive a car bearing his own name, Jack Brabham. Surtees led for the first 14 laps, then retired with a broken axle. More retirements followed and only four finishers were classified: Stewart who won, Bandini, Hill and a private entrant, Bob Bondurant, in a BRM.

Ferrari fared no better at the French Grand Prix. Clark brought the Lotus-BRM for its debut but was hit in the face by a bird in practice and did not start. Bandini led for 31 laps until his throttle cable broke and the repair cost him far too much time to have a chance of winning. Brabham was lying a close second at the time and took the lead which he held to the end, the first victory for Brabham-Repco and the first by a constructor driving a car bearing his own name in the World Championship. Ferrari did not attend the British Grand Prix due to a strike at the factory. Brabham won with Hulme second, a Brabham 1-2, followed by Hill, Clark, Rindt and McLaren, his first points in a car carrying his own name.

Only Surtees could stop Brabham taking his third World Championship, by winning the Italian Grand Prix, but no sooner had Brabham retired with an oil leak than Surtees' Cooper-Maserati developed a fuel leak, so Brabham won both the Driver's and Constructors' titles under his own name, a unique achievement which stands to this day.

The race was won by Lodovicio Scarfiotti with Parkes second, much to the delight of the *tifosi*, the first victory by an Italian driver in an Italian car in the Italian Grand Prix since Alberto Ascari in 1952. There was dancing in the streets in Italy following Scarfiotti's victory, but it was a victory gained largely because of mechanical failures among the opposition and many at Ferrari knew it. They also knew that Ferrari did not have the drivers to really put on a convincing show but they were afraid to say so to the patriarch. Enzo Ferrari had been soundly beaten by a small, garage-based operation which had only been in business three years, operating on a shoestring budget, using a reject General Motors production car engine, driven by Brabham, who not only built the cars and owned the team but won the races.

It had not been a good year in Formula 1 for Bruce McLaren, the other constructor driver, who finished in sixteenth place with three points. It was clear that the M2B was not competitive with the Ford engine and McLaren had tried a sports car engine designed by Alf Francis, the Serenissima V6, which fared no better. For 1967 he decided to change to the BRM H16. Largely because of the engine problem, Chris Amon had not had a happy season with McLaren and after his victory at Le Mans had brought him to the attention of Enzo Ferrari, he was on his way to Maranello.

The producer of the film *Grand Prix*, John Frankenheimer, took a lot of advice from Graham Hill, Jackie Stewart and other drivers, but for the central story of the film he went for the passion of Ferrari and the mystique of the red cars rather than the practicality of the British teams, especially after Enzo Ferrari threw the whole weight of the

World Champion 1963 and 1965: Jim Clark in the Lotus 25 at the 1963 Dutch Grand Prix. In 1965 he won the Indianapolis 500 as well.

company behind making it. Passion and emotion are what films and television are about, not technique and business, but while Ferrari captured the headlines, the British drivers and teams who provided the practical advice made money for their teams by staging the racing sequences. One thing it did was to show how motor racing could look on TV – lots of trackside and on-board coverage, lots more behind-the-scenes rather than just racing and commentary. It was not well received by the critics but it was at the box office and it won three Oscars.

The success of the movie was an indication that Formula 1 was increasingly part of popular culture, making it more commercial. That fact increased the pressure to free up the economics of the sport. Costs were rising and the fuel and oil companies were starting to balk at footing the bill.

The trigger for change was Esso's announcement that it was going to withdraw from sponsoring motor racing. Faced with the prospect of such a huge loss of revenue, the CSI cleared the way for direct sponsorship, allowing products to be advertised on the side of racing cars. The first man to take advantage of the new rules was Colin Chapman. During 1967 he agreed a deal with Geoffrey Kent, the chairman of John Player, to change the name of Team Lotus to Gold Leaf Team Lotus for 1968 with the cars painted in the gold and red colours of the Gold Leaf cigarette packet. The energetic and ever-impatient Chapman was still determined to expand his business, and in anticipation of the changes which the Cosworth engine and sponsorship would bring, plus growth in the sports car business, he bought a

Uphill struggle:
after winning the
World Championship
in 1962, Graham
Hill came second in
1963–5 and fifth in
1966 for BRM.

disused airfield at Hethel, just outside Norwich. Here he built a completely new factory and moved the whole Lotus operation, its second move of the decade.

The Cosworth Formula 2 engine, the Four Valve A, was tested in February 1966. It produced 220 bhp, 10 percent higher than expected and was delivered to Formula 2 customers in March 1967, eclipsing Ferrari and Porsche. Its immediate success gave Keith Duckworth confidence that the Formula 1 engine based on it, the DFV, would be as successful, and work started soon afterwards. It was destined for the Lotus 49, a very simple, lightweight monocoque design to which the engine was bolted as a full structural member in the manner pioneered by Chapman with the Lotus 25. It had a ZF gearbox which many thought was unsuitable for the power of the engine, but Chapman insisted on it over the more flexible Hewland box. To drive the Lotus 49, Walter Hayes proposed having a new top-line driver so that Lotus would have greater chances of victory with two No.1 drivers rather than one. That driver was Graham Hill; to start with Chapman resisted, but he gave in and Hill moved back to Lotus after seven years at BRM.

There were eleven races in the 1967 season, starting in South Africa where there was an all-Brabham front row, Brabham just taking pole from Denny Hulme. Hulme then showed great confidence by taking an early lead which he held while his boss and team-mate, Brabham, fought off Surtees, Rodriguez, Clark and a local private entrant, John Love in a Cooper-Climax. The attrition rate among the stars was high and included Hulme, and at the flag it was Rodriguez in the Cooper-Maserati followed by Love, much to the delight of the home crowd, then Surtees.

It was a great day for Cooper, but Ferrari had not been there, the Cosworth engine was still not ready, and Clark and Hill were still in Lotus 33s, so the true opening of the Championship came at Monaco. Mauro Foghieri had improved brakes

and suspension and provided a new, 36-valve cylinder head for the Tipo 312s. There were three at Monaco for Chris Amon, Lorenzo Bandini, under pressure not only from Ferrari but the whole Italian nation, as was Lodovicio Scarfiotti. Brabham was on pole with Bandini second and Bandini took the lead. Hulme and Stewart then overtook him, then Gurney, and Stewart led from Hulme until the BRM's transmission failed. Hulme opened up a lead of around 8 seconds which he never lost. Bandini had overtaken Surtees and was lying second for most of the race until he just clipped the barrier on lap 81, overturned and burst into flames. Bandini was dragged free with a fractured skull and severe burns; he died in hospital three days later. Italy was once again plunged into mourning for a national hero and thousands turned out on the streets of Milan for his funeral.

Bandini's death was a huge blow to Ferrari but another, technical blow was just a month away. On the back of a £100,000 investment, Ford had given Lotus the V8 DFV Formula 1 engine with a performance which exceeded expectations. It made its debut at the Dutch Grand Prix. Hill took pole position, with Clark well down the grid, and he led until lap 11 when his DFV's camshaft drive stripped its teeth and Brabham came round in the lead. Clark then made his challenge, passing Rindt and Brabham then opening up a lead. It was a defining moment in the sport: the British teams had never had a really superior engine, their progress achieved largely by making cars that handled better. But thanks to Ford, Lotus now had an engine which, combined with good handling and a great driver, looked unbeatable. The Dutch Grand Prix of 1967 represented the dawn of a new era and as Jim Clark unrolled the laps from the front, there was a sense of awe; another Championship for Clark and Lotus looked certain. When he came into the pits after taking the chequered flag, he was mobbed.

Clark retired from the Belgian Grand Prix,

and this left Denny Hulme leading the drivers' table after four races, going into the French Grand Prix with 16 points to Amon and Rodriguez on 11 and Clark on 10. Hill led at the start, Brabham overtook him, then Clark came from behind and passed the Brabham-Repco, then Hill did the same and the two Lotuses started to pull away. The dream seemed about to happen when both Lotuses suffered the same problem, the teeth stripped from the final drive, all within ten laps. Brabham took over, Hulme moved into second place in the other Brabham-Repco. It finished with a magnificent Brabham 1-2, putting Hulme on 22 points, Amon and Rodriguez on 11 with Brabham, Stewart and Clark on 10, making it anybody's Championship.

Clark won the British Grand Prix and was on pole at Monza, followed by Brabham and McLaren, Amon in the sole Ferrari, then Gurney, Hulme, Stewart, Hill and Surtees in the new Honda. It was a much more competitive car with far better handling, improvements Surtees had helped initiate at the Slough factory with the help of Eric Broadley of Lola. The start was a shambles because the starter dithered. Gurney led lap one from Brabham, Hill, Clark and McLaren. Clark asserted the superiority of the Lotus-Cosworth combination, moving into the lead on lap 3, then Hill came through too and the Lotus dream looked as if it was about to become a reality again. The dreamers had reckoned without the dogged Denny Hulme, who was in sight of the Championship. He passed Hill, then Clark who had a slow puncture. By the time that had been fixed Clark rejoined in fifteenth place and had been lapped by the leaders. In a sublime piece of driving, he first unlapped himself, giving Hill a slipstream tow into a commanding lead over Hulme and Brabham, then surged off to try and catch up a whole lap. Hulme dropped out with an engine problem, then Brabham's car started to slip back after he over-revved under the pressure. Hill seemed set to win when his engine failed, leaving Brabham in the lead over Surtees. Behind them, having just overtaken Rindt, was Jim Clark, who had driven beyond the limit to make up a whole lap, then overtook Surtees and Brabham to lead, writing himself into history as one of the truly great drivers of all time. Just as the dream was about to come true, it all started to fall apart on the final lap when the Lotus developed a fuel problem and first Surtees, then Brabham passed him. Coming out of the corner into the finishing straight Brabham was slipstreaming Surtees. He pulled out and passed the Honda, but Surtees had crossed the line ahead by a whisker and the Italian crowd, which still loved Big John, roared their approval.

Clark won the US Grand Prix with Hill second, then Hulme third, putting him on 47 points and Brabham on 40. Brabham needed to win the Mexican Grand Prix, with Hulme coming no higher than fifth, to take the title. Tension between the two Brabham drivers was high, not only because of the title position, but because Hulme had already told Brabham that he was going to go to McLaren for 1968 to form an all-New Zealand team. Clark won from Brabham with Hulme third, enough for the burly New Zealander to take the Championship from his boss.

Clark and Lotus failed to win the Championship while they had exclusive use of the Cosworth engine. Clark had won four races, which gave him 36 points, plus one sixth place and a third, but the car failed to finish in so many others that he rarely accumulated other points. This was due to the general unreliability of the engine and the car.

The availability of the Cosworth engine brought new names into Formula 1: Ken Tyrell signed up Jackie Stewart in a one-car team backed by the oil giant Elf, which also sponsored the French team run by the defence conglomorate, Matra. There were many in France who hankered after a French challenge to the British and Italian teams which led to Matra being given a grant of 6 million francs (£800,000) by the French government to develop a new racing engine. Tyrell

Road racing tradition: Jim Clark leads in the wet on the road circuit at Spa, Belgium, one of the most demanding drives in the Championship.

Kit car man: Jack Brabham, the only winner of
both Driver and Constructor titles in his own
name, at Monza in the 1966 Repco-Brabham.

wanted to use the Cosworth which had spurred him into Formula 1 in the first place and he put together a deal to use a Matra chassis which he adapted to take the DFV, the car to be entered by a new team, Matra International.

Bruce McLaren also signed up for the Cosworth engine for 1968 with the new World Champion Denny Hulme and sponsorship from Yardley Cosmetics. His team had dominated the CanAm sports car series in the US, but he had failed to finish in all but two Grands Prix in 1967. The M5A was clearly an improvement, as the Canadian Grand Prix had shown, and McLaren looked increasingly like a real Formula 1 player, but the blow came when Robin Herd left to join Cosworth. Gordon Coppuck, his assistant, rose to the position of designer.

Herd's move to Cosworth was at the invitation of Keith Duckworth who was planning to build a complete Cosworth Formula 1 car – chassis, engine and transmission – and to apply more of the DFV's power to the road, Duckworth planned to use four-wheel-drive. He chose Herd for his technical qualifications, success at McLaren and enthusiasm, all of which meant he would fit in at Cosworth.

The Cooper-Maserati had proved heavy and lacked engine power, and the arrival of the Cosworth suddenly made it look uncompetitive. Cooper could not use the DFV, the one thing which might have arrested its decline, because the association with BMC through the Mini-Cooper barred them from using and promoting an engine made by BMC's main competitor, Ford. Cooper turned to BRM instead, whose engine looked uncompetitive against the DFV. As a family business with strong characters at the heart of it, Cooper was a force to be reckoned with; without that heart it was just a name, with no glue to hold it together. The downward spiral continued when Jochen Rindt left to go to Brabham to fill the spare seat left by Hulme's move to McLaren, taking his personal mechanic, Ron Dennis, with him. Dennis was still only 20, but he made it a condition of his

employment at Brabham that he would not work on the production side of the business, only in the racing department. Dennis had found Rindt rather arrogant and preferred the gentle giant and when Brabham suggested he become Brabham's own mechanic, Dennis agreed.

Lotus was booming. On the back of the sponsorship deal with John Player, Colin Chapman had much needed cash but that was not all; from the new premises in Norwich, Lotus had sold over 3000 cars and made profits of £731,000. Chapman was on a roll, he was highly successful and there was a real chance of winning the Championship again with Jim Clark. Once again he was working at the frontiers of design, looking for a new advantage now that everybody had the DFV. The newest frontier was aerodynamics. The first use of aerodynamics to improve performance was in American sports car racing in 1967 on the Chaparral 2E. It had a large wing attached which could be moved by the driver. The idea was simple; by using an inverted aircraft wing shape, a downforce was created which pushed the car more firmly against the track surface, creating greater adhesion and faster cornering. Chapman experimented with a wing attached to the car high above the rear wheels, but also added little winglets to the nose of the car to work on the front wheels as well as a scallop-shaped scoop in the bodywork at the back of the Lotus 49B.

Jim Clark and Graham Hill appeared in South Africa with their Lotus-Fords painted in British Racing Green for the last time. It was a triumph; Clark won with Hill second, Clark's twenty-fifth Grand Prix victory, beating Fangio's record. Once again, Clark, Chapman and Lotus looked set for the Championship, but just as the Lotus package looked dominant, tragedy struck. On 7 April 1968 Jim Clark and Graham Hill were driving in a Formula 2 race at Hockenheim in Germany, their cars painted in the new red and gold livery of Gold Leaf. Neither qualified well – Clark in seventh place with fuel metering problems and Hill even further back with handling problems. Chapman was away, having a skiing holiday with his family. The weather was poor and Jean-Pierre Beltoise for Matra took the lead and Clark fell back to eighth place. On the fifth lap Clark was coming to the end of a long straight which ended in a tightening right hander. As he entered the corner, the rear of his car twitched out; Clark corrected, and it twitched right as he struggled to control it. He failed and it slid off the circuit sideways, snapping off some small trees at 140 mph, then hitting a big tree broadside, the car almost wrapping itself round the tree under the impact. He was killed instantly.

Chapman was devastated by the tragic end of a decade of friendship, and of a partnership and personal collaboration which had produced one of the fairy-tale stories of motor racing. He arranged for an independent investigation which concluded that a tyre had been cut by something and deflated on the straight. Clark had been unaware of it until he put a side load on the tyres which then set the rear breaking away. Chapman had all the hard skills necessary to be successful in Formula 1, working always with the full knowledge that deaths could, and did, occur. Even through his genuine grief he was able to look to the future, and immediately offered the vacant seat to Jack Oliver.

Shortly before the Grand Prix season got under way again, tragedy struck once more. Jim Clark should have been testing a new Lotus for the Indianapolis 500 but with his death, Mike Spence went instead and was killed in a test accident. Chapman sank briefly under the weight of the two tragedies and his immediate reaction was to give up racing, but he changed his mind when the initial gloom had lifted. Inside the team the greatest burden fell on Graham Hill, a man of exceptional good humour but underneath as steely as it takes to be a World Champion. He gave the Lotus team the hope that it could win again after the loss of two such respected drivers.

The first Spanish Grand Prix since 1954, at Jarama, was a testing time for Graham Hill and Lotus. The Lotus 49Bs appeared without their complete wings and were well down the grid. Chris Amon led for much of the race until his fuel pump failed, then Hill led under pressure from Hulme until the McLaren's gearbox failed. Hill took the chequered flag to huge applause from the grandstand and from his fellow drivers. At Monaco, the Lotus 49B appeared with its complete set of wings, causing quite a stir. Jack Oliver made his debut for Lotus but Ferrari did not appear, Enzo Ferrari expressing concern over the safety of the circuit. Hill won another highly popular victory, his fourth Monaco Grand Prix, putting him first in the Championship at 24 points to Denny Hulme on 10.

The use of aerodynamic devices was even more in evidence at Spa where Brabham and Ferrari both turned up with wings; Ferrari's were moveable from the cockpit. Amon was fastest in qualifying, Jackie Stewart, back in his Matra-Cosworth was second, then Ickx. The early part of the race was a battle between Amon, Ickx, Stewart and Hulme until the pressure started to show. Hill retired with a broken half shaft, Rindt, Brabham, Amon, Surtees and Hulme all dropped out with mechanical problems, leaving Stewart the leader on lap 16 which he held until he ran out of fuel two laps before the end. Bruce McLaren won in a McLaren, the second driver to win a Grand Prix in a car bearing his own name.

The French Grand Prix at Rouen saw Lotus take the aerodynamic experiment even further by mounting its high rear wing directly on to the suspension uprights rather than the chassis, making them more directly effective on the wheels while putting greater loads on the slender parts of the car. John Surtees was not happy with the new RA302 Honda and preferred the RA301, but great pressure was put on for it to appear in the race. A second driver was engaged. Jo Schlesser was an experienced racing driver in sports cars and Formula 2, but had only competed in two Formula 1 races. It was wet, and although Stewart led from the start, Jacky Ickx, a Belgian driver recently signed by Ferrari, was soon in front. Schlesser's Honda had been misfiring, and on the second lap, he lost control when the engine cut out. He crashed into a bank, the car turned over and burst into flames. The magnesium alloy skin of the Honda burned fiercely and the situation was made worse by the firemen using water which only made it burn more fiercely. Some fifteen minutes went by before the car could be approached, by which time Schlesser was dead. Ickx took his first Grand Prix victory which caused some tension in the Ferrari team. Amon, who had striven hard for the *scuderia* during some very difficult times, was still looking for a win and did most of the testing, while Jacky Ickx seemed to have the luck and the glory.

There were three Lotus 49s in the British Grand Prix at Brands Hatch, for Graham Hill, Jackie Oliver and Jo Siffert whose car was entered by Rob Walker, the last of the great private entrants. Oliver led, then Hill passed him and it looked as if the two works Lotuses were having it all their own way. Hill then retired with another drive shaft breakage which may have been due to the effect of the downforce exerted on the car by the wing. Oliver then led, but his transmission failed, leaving Siffert, who had been battling for third place with Amon, in the lead. Siffert drove an inspired race, the privateer against the biggest team, and won, the first Rob Walker victory since the great days with Stirling Moss.

The Cosworth engine was a great boon to the kit car teams, but it was also a great leveller. To look for an edge, more designers turned to the use of wings which proliferated in size, shape and application, high-mounted, low-mounted, some of them fixed, others moveable. There were no regulations regarding their use and Matra even installed tiny electric motors normally used in guided missiles to move them during the race.

The World Championship went down to the last race in Mexico. Hill was leading on 39 points from Stewart on 36 and Hulme on 33; all of them could win it. Hill and Stewart both raced with problems. The Lotus system for moving the wing broke during the race, giving Hill handling problems, and after a titanic battle Stewart's fuel system started playing up ten laps from the end. The Mexican crowd had hacked their way through the barriers and were standing on the verges, cheering on their local hero, Pedro Rodriguez, who had worked his way up as high as third. Hill won the race and his second World Championship. It was a very emotional scene: Chapman was waiting with a bottle of champagne, then Hill and Chapman joined hands and embraced warmly at what was a great moment for both of them, but one tinged with sadness for the absence of Jim Clark.

Just prior to the Mexican Grand Prix, in October 1968, 48 percent of the Lotus sports car company, not the racing team, had been floated on the Stock Market as a way of providing finance for growth. Colin Chapman, who owned most of the shares and who kept 52 percent, was made a multi-millionaire. Chapman's great partner in the kit car revolution, Cooper, was on its last legs. Shorn of its pioneering leadership, John Cooper finally realized that the game was up. There were plans to use the Ford engine and there was talk of a sponsorship deal with Wilkinson Sword, but the heart had gone out of the whole team and when no Coopers turned up at Kylami for the South African Grand Prix, the signs were clear.

It was also the end for Anglo-American Racing's Eagle-Weslake project. Mobil had withdrawn its sponsorship and Gurney closed down the Formula 1 end of the business to concentrate on US racing. Honda also pulled out at the end of the year. John Surtees moved to BRM for 1969 but he also set up a factory at Edenbridge in Kent to build F5000 cars, his sights eventually set on Formula 1.

Jochen Rindt was the fastest driver around and Brabham was keen to retain him for 1969. Rindt was a close friend of Bernie Ecclestone who was managing Rindt's Formula 2 team. Ecclestone had remained on the fringes of motor racing during the

Personal relationship:
Colin Chapman and
Jim Clark had a
special bond; a feature
common to many
winning partnerships
in the kit car world.

1960s, but he had concentrated his entrepreneurial skills on making money through a string of highly successful motor cycle dealerships, the second-hand car business, which included setting up Weekend Car Auctions and property.

By 1969 Ecclestone was very wealthy and looking for a way back into Formula 1; his close relationship with Rindt provided the catalyst. Ecclestone and Rindt were actively planning to go into business in Formula 1, as Ecclestone had planned to do in 1958 with his friend Stuart Lewis-Evans. Rindt did not have a good year with Brabham in 1968 and the obvious place to go was Lotus. Ecclestone could see that, and the money which came from the tobacco sponsorship clinched it for Rindt; the negotiations were carried out by Ecclestone. Ron Dennis stayed at Brabham and was promoted to chief mechanic. A new man, Neil Trundle joined and after a shaky start the two developed a relationship which was to lead to a business partnership.

Motor racing was an industry in tune with the times, like popular music, film, television, fashion and other talent-based businesses, it was freeing itself from the old order, thriving on being *déclassé*. This mood brought together a group of individuals – all at some time associated with Jochen Rindt – to form the ultimate kit car team, March. Once Ecclestone had arranged for Rindt to drive for Lotus in 1969 the two men started looking to the future and an opportunity to build a whole team around Rindt. They wanted Robin Herd to design a new car based on the Cosworth engine but Herd was much in demand and had only moved from McLaren to Cosworth the previous year. At McLaren he had seen how sports cars he had worked on had been profitably sold on in America and he wanted to benefit directly from his work. Having spent around £30,000 on a single prototype, the momentum had gone out of the Cosworth car. This was largely in the wake of the appearance of wings, a far lighter, cheaper and more effective way of putting the DFV's power

down than four wheel drive. Tests had shown that there was little chance of the car being competitive in 1969, if ever, and when the approaches started, Herd started to think about how to have a stake in his own business rather than working for a salary.

That entrepreneurial spirit was indicative of the times. Herd's school friend Alan Rees, who had tried his hand as a driver, moved to team management in 1968 with Roy Winkleman Racing, effectively the Lotus Formula 2 team which brought him into contact with Jochen Rindt. For some time Rees, Herd, Ecclestone and Rindt flirted with the idea of setting up a team together. At the same time, Rees was talking to another friend, Graham Croaker, an accountant who raced in Formula 3, about setting up a team. The plan was to model themselves on the F1CA teams, building racing cars for sale and promoting the name by running a racing team with direct sponsorship to make the money. At the same time, Herd ran into another old friend and racing enthusiast, Max Mosley, who was a successful patent and trademark lawyer. He spent part of his considerable income on racing a Formula 2 Brabham prepared by Frank Williams. Mosley and Williams had been discussing setting up a team based on long-term sponsorship. Herd and Mosley then started talking about getting together as well.

After Rindt, the central figure in this manoeuvring was Robin Herd who was seen as a winning designer. Ecclestone and Rindt put pressure on him to join them, as did Mosley. He could either be part of Rindt's career, or part of a new alternative, a team based on his friends Max Mosley, Alan Rees and Graham Croaker. At one point they proposed one company to build a car that Rindt would drive in a separate team, which would include Ecclestone to raise sponsorship. Rindt declined, preferring to stay in business with Ecclestone and look for a way to form a team specifically around himself and his needs. The four then decided to go ahead with their idea and put

£2500 each into a new company, March.

Frank Williams had come a long way since his days racing the A35. He shared a flat in Harrow with a variety of well-to-do young men who wanted to get on in motor racing. He became one of motor racing's continental nomads, moving from race to race as a general help, first to Jonathan Williams who raced a Formula Junior Merlyn in Europe. He continued the lifestyle with Charlie Crichton-Stuart and in 1964 he did the same with Anthony Horsley, another regular visitor to the Harrow flat. It was with Horsley, who had two Formula Junior cars, that Frank drove his first races in a single-seater Brabham, in return for looking after the '*équipe*', but without much success.

As a result of his travels in Europe, Frank Williams developed a business acting as an agent for European Formula 2 and 3 owners who wanted to buy spares and communicate with the cars' builders who were all based in Britain. He took the orders, bought the goods, added a profit and shipped them. Before long he started dealing in whole racing cars; in the course of that trading, he acquired an Formula 3 Cooper which he entered for himself. He had one good result, fifth in a race in Skarpnack in Sweden, pocketed the starting money then sold the Cooper on to a Swedish driver for a profit. He kept his spares in lock-up garages around Harrow, expanding his business by becoming a sales agent for Brabham. He gradually forgot about becoming a driver and became a motor racing entrepreneur and entrant as Frank Williams (Motor Racing) Ltd.

Frank Williams and Piers Courage had formed a strong friendship. Courage had been an erratic driver, starting in Formula 3 with a brief Formula 1 career in a BRM for Reg Parnell. Frank Williams believed Courage had real talent and entered him in a Formula 3 race at Brands Hatch in a new Brabham, which he won. In 1968, he entered Courage in Formula 2 races in an unsold Brabham. In 1969 the embryonic Williams team, consisting of Williams, Courage and a mechanic

were made an attractive offer to take part in the Tasman Series and from that it was a small move to Formula 1. In 1969 Williams bought a Brabham BT26, the previous year's car, and set his sights on winning the 1969 World Championship on a shoestring budget.

The last year of the 1960s was the year that Jackie Stewart took the Championship by storm, a demonstration of the power of a small team built around one driver with the right car and engine. He won in South Africa and Spain, then having taken pole and fastest lap in Monaco, retired with a broken drive shaft, giving Graham Hill an opportunity to clinch a fifth victory in Monte Carlo with Piers Courage second, a podium place on only his third outing with Frank Williams. Stewart then took the next three Grands Prix, the Dutch, French and British, and Jacky Ickx, who had left Ferrari where he felt that there was little chance of winning, won the German Grand Prix for Brabham with Stewart second.

Stewart could win the Championship at the Italian Grand Prix at Monza. It was between Jochen Rindt for Lotus-Ford, and Jean-Pierre Beltoise and Jackie Stewart driving Matra-Fords for Ken Tyrell. At the final lap of a fabulous race, coming out of the famous Parabolica corner Rindt and Beltoise took the line for what should have been a duel to the finishing line. But Stewart had anticipated just such a finish and had fitted an unusual gear wheel which allowed him to hold fourth gear while the other two had to change up, giving him just enough advantage to win by 0.008 of a second and clinch his first World Championship.

It was a victory for Matra International, which took the Constructors' title as the official entrant, but it was really a victory for the small team boss, Ken Tyrell, and his partnership with Jackie Stewart. This was further evidence of the superiority of the kit car teams, putting the final touch to the revolution on the tenth anniversary of Jack Brabham's first Championship in 1959. With both Championships decided, Ferrari did not compete in the last three races of the season.

Of the 66 podium places in the 1969 World Championship, Ford-Cosworth DFV engines had powered the cars which took 62 of them, including the first six places at Monaco and the first nine places in the French Grand Prix. Resisting this onslaught and bearing the cost with discreet help from Fiat, was Ferrari. It had been expensive and there was very little to show for the investment. Between 1966 and the departure of John Surtees, to the end of 1969, Ferrari won only two Grands Prix – Scarfiotti in the 1966 Italian Grand Prix and Ickx in the 1968 French Grand Prix. The departure of Surtees had been a bigger blow than expected. It was followed by the firing of Dragoni, the death of Bandini, the arrival of the Cosworth engine and Scarfiotti's death in an accident practising for a hill climb in 1968. The Ferrari team had continued to spiral down, aided and abetted by the Italian press. Ferrari appointed a journalist, Franco Lini, to restore his fortunes through good public relations, rather than face the fact that the cars were not very good.

Mauro Foghieri followed a policy of improving the Tipo 312 by getting more power out of the engine, but Ferrari lacked the services of a really competitive driver. None of the top drivers would go to Maranello. Of the World Champions still racing, Brabham had his own team, Surtees had already fallen out with Ferrari, Hill was recovering from a bad accident but was an unlikely recruit for Ferrari, Denny Hulme was very content at McLaren and an approach to the World Champion Jackie Stewart in 1968, had been swiftly rebuffed. Enzo Ferrari's reputation went before him and the new breed of professional driver was not prepared to put up with the endless intriguing and poor financial rewards of driving for Ferrari. Mario Andretti, an Italian by birth but now an American citizen, the winner of the 1969 Indianapolis 500, had made appearances in Formula 1 in 1968 and 1969 but he had chosen

Lotus rather than Ferrari. There was a pool of talent just below the top level, men who wanted a way in, and who were prepared to work for Ferrari. Chris Amon was taken on in 1967 for paltry wages and left half-way through 1969; Jacky Ickx, taken on in 1968, left to go to Brabham in 1969 where he had a good season, then returned to Ferrari for 1970. Franco Lini left at the end of 1968.

The 1969 season was a low point for Ferrari. He was being hammered by Ford in endurance sports car racing, he was being hammered by Ford-powered cars in Formula 1 and he was being hammered in the Italian press. On 21 June 1969, after a fourth successive Ford victory at Le Mans – a Ford GT40 driven by Jacky Ickx – Ferrari and Fiat announced that Fiat had taken a major stake in Ferrari and would be investing in securing the future. Fiat was the dominant manufacturer in Italy but the cars were pretty shoddy, protected by high tariff walls from foreign competition and they had a poor image overseas. Controlled by the Agnelli family, Fiat had plenty of money and Ferrari had great prestige, albeit waning, and no money, so a deal was done after exhaustive negotiations. Fiat got 40 percent of the company for the equivalent of $11m; the remaining 60 percent was divided with 49 percent to Enzo Ferrari, 10 percent to his illegitimate son Piero Lardi and 1 percent to his long-time friend Pininfarina. The deal gave Enzo Ferrari far less than had been discussed with Ford, but he retained what he wanted most: control of the racing and he now had the money to take on the Cosworth-powered opposition.

The 1969 season was the high point of the kit car revolution, the final victory of the British teams over the grand manufacturers. It was ironic that the financial plan to save Ferrari was announced just a week after the plan to save Cooper, the first of the kit car teams to cause all the problems a decade previously, had failed. In May 1969 the Cooper racing team was closed and on 11 June 1969, the assets of the Cooper business were

Man of the times:
Jackie Stewart became
the man to beat after
the death of Jim
Clark in 1967. He
campaigned tirelessly
for greater safety.

auctioned and John Cooper bought a garage business in Sussex on the proceeds.

The kit car teams revolutionized Formula 1 by developing new technologies and hiring the best drivers, the two ingredients which have always kept them ahead, making it possible to see off comebacks from Maserati and Alfa Romeo, challenges from Honda, Porsche, Matra and Ferrari. They also revolutionized it commercially, and their new financial muscle was beginning to show. At a meeting in Geneva, F1CA agreed new arrangements to cover starting money, casting aside the system by which promoters invited teams to race for whatever fee they felt like offering, to a system of fixed rates for teams and for drivers based on performance and on actual costs of transport and attendance at races.

In September 1969 an article appeared in *Autosport* telling the motor racing world about March. The four friends had set up their factory on a trading estate at Bicester, near Oxford; the factory quickly established itself as a place to be. One result was that a young man called Harvey Postlethwaite, a carbon fibre expert who worked for ICI, wrote and asked to join. Postlethwaite was highly trained and wanted to be part of a small company in tune with the spirit of the times. Max Mosley was in charge of publicity. Robin Herd was busy designing the first March Formula 1 car, the 701, for the coming year and they also planned to be in Formula 2 and Formula 3 with 702 and 703. Graham Croaker was running the business side while Alan Rees was building up the team; he had his eye on a very quick young Swedish driver in Formula 2, Ronnie Peterson, for March's own Formula 2 entries, with Chris Amon for Formula 1. Amon was looking for a team that would be built around him. Rees, however, also talked to Jo Siffert who was being courted by Ferrari, but who was keen to be part of the exciting Bicester scene.

Then the reigning World Champion Jackie Stewart – a man also very much in tune with the times – fell into the March orbit. Lotus, Brabham, BRM and McLaren all wanted to sign him, but he remained loyal to Ken Tyrell. They had no car because Simca had taken over Matra, and Simca, a Chrysler company, was not happy to have one of their cars powered by a Ford engine. Stewart wanted to drive a Cosworth-powered car, so Tyrell contacted March. Mosley promised him a car, even though it was still only on the drawing board, but the deposit which Tyrell paid was a great help to March's small finances.

All that was separate from Mosley's efforts to finance March's own team. That brought him into contact with a man called Bill Dance who was marketing an upper cylinder lubricant, STP. Through that contact, Mosley met Andy Gratinelli, whose team had just won the Indianapolis 500 with Mario Andretti, also sponsored by STP. Andretti wanted to get into Formula 1 and brought STP sponsorship with him. Suddenly the March dream was looking up; it was different from Cooper, Brabham, Lotus and McLaren which had grown out of the motor trade and the aircraft industry, with their own petty hierarchies and attitudes. At March it was long hair, lots of girls, good degrees, fashionable attitudes and coolness. It seemed ridiculously ambitious starting out in three formulae with cars for customers and their own teams, but the World Champion and the Indy 500 winner had faith even though there was still no car.

On 6 February 1970, the lid came off the whole set up at a launch organized by Mosley at Silverstone. It was a stunning success as the cars came out and circled in front of the press: the works team sponsored by STP; a car for the World Champion Jackie Stewart, who was there; another for Mario Andretti, who was also there. It looked as if they had achieved the impossible. Behind the glitter, however, March was stretched to the limits, short of money and with cars in need of more work, but it was borne aloft by the hype and the force of the personalities involved. The old guard muttered that it would all end in tears.

Downforce: Jochen Rindt's Lotus leading Chris Amon's Ferrari at Kylami in 1969, the year that kit car teams used aerofoils to find an edge.

The old order was changing again. Of those who had been around in 1960, Moss was out and Brabham was looking for retirement. Bruce McLaren, whose career dated back to 1958 had his own team and was also rumoured to be thinking of retirement. Phil Hill had retired to sports car racing in 1964 after a bad year with ATS had really finished his career. The glittering career of double World Champion and Indianapolis winner Jim Clark had come and gone in just seven years.

There were four World Champions still driving in 1970: Jack Brabham with three titles; Graham Hill with two; and Jackie Stewart and John Surtees with one each. The top driver was Jackie Stewart; the challengers were Jochen Rindt and Jacky Ickx. Two other very promising drivers who started out in 1970 were Emerson Fittipaldi from Brazil, who joined Lotus, and Clay Regazzoni from Switzerland, who joined Ferrari.

Ferrari had a new car for 1970, the Ferrari 312B, for Clay Regazzoni and Jacky Ickx who returned to Ferrari after a year with Brabham. For 1970 Frank Williams had done a deal with an Argentinian entrepreneur, Alessandro de Tomaso, who was active in Formula 2 in Italy. De Tomaso also wanted to get into Formula 1, so he supplied a chassis while Williams supplied the Cosworth engine and driver Piers Courage. Courage had been made a very attractive offer by Enzo Ferrari but he had turned it down to stay with his friend Frank Williams.

Despite being taken over by Chrysler, Matra

went its own way with the Matra-Simca MS120, and Elf went on supporting Tyrell and his March-Cosworth. Tyrell bought three March 701s but he also started work on his own car, the 001, designed by Derek Gardner who had worked on Tyrell's Matra MS84. Tyrell demanded great secrecy because he did not want to upset March. Gardner went for lightness, and concentrated the weight as low and as centrally as possible, which made for a very nimble car, but one which only the best drivers could hope to drive to maximum capability. The 001 had a Cosworth engine, a Hewland gearbox, and as light a monocoque as could be designed, and it finished up 100lb lighter than the March. A new constructor had been born.

A completely new car started to take shape in the summer of 1969, the Lotus 72. High aerofoils had been banned, but aerodynamically shaped bodies which produced a downforce, acting through much improved tyres, were acceptable. Goodyear, which was locked into competition with Firestone for the attention of drivers, had come into racing as a result of Lotus's success at Indianapolis and it was prepared to put development resources into the pockets of the top teams and top drivers that used its tyres and attracted that attention. The Lotus 72 was designed to maximize the performance of Firestone tyres. Chapman sketched out the idea for a wedge-shaped car with the radiators moved to the side helping to shift weight to the rear, adding to rear wheel downforce. Other improvements included the use of the Hewland gearbox and inboard front brakes. Colin Chapman wanted to retain Jochen Rindt to drive the Lotus 72 in 1970 and Rindt wanted to drive the 72, so after Bernie Ecclestone had negotiated large amounts of money with Chapman, Rindt stayed with Lotus.

The South African Grand Prix was held in early March, but the Lotus 72 was only ready for testing, so Rindt drove an uprated Lotus 49. As a result, the talk of the paddock was March and the five 701s:

one in the hands of the World Champion; another for his team-mate Johnny Servos Gavin; two works cars driven by Chris Amon and Jo Siffert; and Mario Andretti in the STP car. The 701 was heavy but handled well. Sensationally confounding the critics, Stewart promptly put his car in pole position in exactly the same time as Amon – two Marches on the front row of the grid. Jack Brabham was third in the Brabham BT33 ahead of Rindt, then Ickx in the only Ferrari 312B that could be made ready in time for the race.

Stewart and Brabham went into the first corner together as Rindt drove over Brabham's front wheel in a hair-brained attempt to get by which was rewarded by spinning off into the grass. This left Stewart in the lead on lap one of the March 701's first Grand Pix. Brabham was held up by Rindt's intervention, but after checking his car out with two easy laps, he moved up to challenge Stewart, passing him on lap 19 and leading to the end of the race. Hulme also passed Stewart who was third for March, not quite up to the earlier promise but still a sensational result for March on its first outing.

Stewart took pole position in the Race of Champions at Brands Hatch and won from Rindt, March's first victory. Then came the Spanish Grand Prix. The Lotus 72 was ready and there was one for John Miles. Rindt preferred to drive a Lotus 49. The 72 caused a stir with its wedge shape and side radiators, showing the way ahead. The March may have looked a bit old-fashioned but its arrival had increased the number of entrants to the point where there were 22 entrants for 16 places on the grid and the pre-race formalities became a power struggle between the various constituencies. The Spanish organizers had agreed that the first ten places were guaranteed to a combination of the top teams and the five World Champions: Brabham, Hill, Surtees, Hulme and Stewart. That left 12 drivers to compete for 6 places. Two drivers excluded themselves through accidents, 6 qualified, leaving 4 unable to race. Max Mosley intervened and went round the pits area with a petition which would allow them to drive, although they would not share in the starting money and would not be able to gather any points in the World Championship. The organizers agreed and twenty cars lined up for the race. Then the CSI officials returned from lunch and reversed the decision, asking the four drivers to withdraw. They refused and the whole thing started to look ugly when some officials tried to drag Jo Siffert from his car. After a brief spell of acrimony, the four cars were removed by their mechanics leaving the teams and the drivers fuming. The old guard at the CSI had won the day but the way it was handled and the outcome was deeply resented, hardening the divisions between the old and the new. There were only five finishers, three of them March 701s: Stewart, who won March's first Grand Prix, with McLaren second, Andretti third in the STP March, Graham Hill fourth in the Rob Walker Lotus, then Servos Gavin in the second Tyrell-March.

Just two days before the Belgian Grand Prix, on 2 June, Bruce McLaren was testing an M8D CanAm sports car at Goodwood. A section of the rear bodywork that had not been secured properly, flew up at high speed sending the car out of control. It hit an empty marshal's post and Bruce McLaren was killed instantly; he was 33. Like Clark's death two years previously and Senna's in 1994, it was a blow which was felt right through the sport. McLaren had never been in the top league but he was very good, and possibly more important, he was loved. All the McLaren entries for the Belgian Grand Prix were withdrawn.

The Lotus 72 was finally ready to race in the Dutch Grand Prix on 21 June. The challenge to the Stewart-March-Tyrell combination began in earnest from Jochen Rindt, now in the Lotus 72 in which he instantly took pole from Ickx who had made the best start. Rindt passed him on lap two and never looked back, winning by half a minute from Stewart, putting him just one point behind Stewart in the Driver's Championship.

The result hardly mattered. On lap 21, Piers Courage, lying seventh in the Williams de Tomaso-Cosworth, either hit a bump in the notoriously rough circuit or suffered a puncture and crashed into an earth bank. The car burst into flames with Courage trapped inside; he was killed immediately and the huge pall of smoke told the other drivers of the tragedy. Like McLaren, Courage was not a driver who was immediately out of the top rank, but he was highly skilled and highly regarded by the whole Formula 1 community.

Rindt now forged ahead on one of those mid-season rolls which happen when the right driver gets together with the right car and the Lotus 72 was just such a car. He won the French, British and German Grands Prix. The theme of the season was no longer Rindt versus Stewart but Rindt versus a very determined Jacky Ickx, who came second in Germany and stopped Rindt's run of success on Rindt's home ground in Austria with a much-needed Ferrari win. The Lotus 72 had put the March 701 in the shade and Ferrari was improving. March was still leading in the Constructors title, largely because of the number of people driving 701s, and in the Driver's Championship, Rindt had 45 points to Ickx's 23. All Rindt had to do was win the Italian Grand Prix.

There were no special arrangements for the top teams and drivers at Monza for the Italian Grand Prix – all that counted was speed in qualifying – the fastest 20 of the 28 entries would start. Qualifying was fierce; Rindt was very determined to win the Championship in that race and he was driving without the Lotus 72's wing in the hope of squeezing just that little extra speed out of the car. In the final qualifying session, Rindt was approaching the Parabolica and applied the brakes hard; the car started to weave and turned sharply left, straight into the barrier, lifting one of the posts out as it went underneath. Denny Hulme reported the accident to the Lotus pits where Chapman, Ecclestone and Rindt's wife Nina were waiting for news. Ecclestone set off at a run to the Parabolica but Rindt had already been taken to hospital where he was pronounced dead. All the Lotus cars were withdrawn as a mark of respect but also for safety reasons. The race went ahead under a too-familiar pall of gloom following the third violent death among a group of people who however competitive, were for the most part, good friends. In the race, Stewart and Regazzoni fought all the way until Regazzoni took the lead ten laps from the end and pulled ahead to the flag for a very popular Ferrari win, six seconds ahead of Stewart's March.

Lotus had lost a second star driver in two years. The cause was never fully established, but one possibility was that a shaft carrying the right inboard brake failed. Another possibility was that the tyres were not warm or were unbalanced in their degree of warmth, and John Miles has said that when he tried the car without the wing it was very difficult. Emerson Fittipaldi, who had only joined the Lotus Formula 1 team that year, was thrust into the role of team leader in the same way that Graham Hill had been in 1968.

Lotus missed the Canadian Grand Prix which Ickx won with Regazzoni second, a Ferrari 1-2, then Lotus was back at Watkins Glen for the US Grand Prix. There was a mood among the kit car teams to try and preserve the title for Rindt: Chapman told Fittipaldi that he had to finish in front of the Ferraris and he agreed to do what he could. Stewart, now driving the Tyrell 001, was also determined. Ickx took pole, then Stewart, then Fittipaldi, and Stewart took the lead with Ickx in second place. Half-way through the race, a fuel pipe on Ickx's Ferrari broke and his trip to the pits put him out of the running. Then Stewart's car failed, 23 laps from the end and Fittipaldi took the lead with Ickx on a charge a lap behind but gaining inexorably. Fittipaldi held his position to the end and won, ensuring a posthumous title for Rindt.

Ickx won the final race of the season, the Mexican Grand Prix. It was Jack Brabham's last race in Formula 1, bringing the curtain down on a career which had seen him lose a number of close friends, especially Bruce McLaren, his team-mate at Cooper in the 1950s. Bruce McLaren was 33, Piers Courage was 28, the same age as Jochen Rindt. All three had special relationships, even closer than the close friendships which are normal in the Formula 1 family: McLaren with Teddy Mayer, Piers Courage with Frank Williams and Jochen Rindt with Bernie Ecclestone. Their deaths evoked memories of other great friendships – between Chapman and Clark, Teddy Mayer and his brother Tim, and further back between Ecclestone and Stuart Lewis-Evans. The World Championship contained many friendships, but those bonds had been particularly special, playing an important part in the sense of camaraderie which had shaped an era of youthful struggle and radical change.

Power broker: Bernie
Ecclestone made
Formula 1 a business.

4

IT PAYS TO
ADVERTISE

The death of three star drivers in a single season was, even by the standards of the time, tragic. The deaths cast a shadow over the whole sport but they also underscored the importance of safety. The deaths also highlighted the importance of the personality of the driver as the focus of the sport, something beyond the engineering excellence, mystique and personality of the racing car. This was the 1960s, when images of pop stars, TV personalities, film and sporting stars became powerful cultural and economic tools. The handsome young men in racing with talent became commodities to be marketed and the greater the exposure the higher the price.

The late Bruce McLaren, Graham Hill and Jack Brabham belonged to a different age. With the turn of the decade there was change in the look and feel of Formula 1. Like everything else it had been subjected to the pressures of the 1960s. Graham Hill was on his way down. Brabham retired at the end of 1970 and sold his shares in MRD to Ron Tauranac.

Rindt's death also brought to an end the plans harboured by Bernie Ecclestone to run a Formula 1 team with Rindt as driver. Ecclestone redoubled his efforts to find a way into Formula 1 and cast his eye towards Brabham. Ron Tauranac knew he was not the best person to raise sponsorship and he discussed the prospect of a partnership with Ecclestone at the 1971 Monaco Grand Prix. This would allow him to concentrate on designing and building cars while Ecclestone ran the business.

Ron Dennis had left Brabham to form a Formula 2 team, Rondel Racing, with Neil Trundle. Ron Tauranac, with whom Dennis had formed a strong relationship at Brabham, leased two Formula 2 chassis to his two former mechanics. They bought six FVA Cosworth engines in a poor state from Bernie Ecclestone, then rebuilt them. Dennis had the services of Tim Schenken, an Australian driver with Brabham, but when a young French driver, Bob Wolleck arrived with sponsorship from the French Motul oil company,

Rondel signed him up. Dennis met Graham Hill casually one day at the Brabham factory and asked him to drive for Rondel in Formula 2; Hill agreed. Dennis and Trundle raised some sponsorship from Tony Vlassopoulos, a ship broker with an enthusiasm for racing. The team was always immaculately turned out at a time when motor racing was generally more a matter of grubby garages; Dennis insisted on sparkling cleanliness and clear surfaces. Rondel swiftly established itself on the Formula 2 circuit: Hill came second in the first Formula 2 race of the season at Hockenheim, then he won the Jochen Rindt Memorial Trophy at Thruxton on Easter Monday, giving the new team a wonderful start; Ron Dennis was 23.

After the death of Bruce McLaren, McLaren Racing continued in Formula 1 and in sports car racing. In Teddy Mayer, McLaren had a manager with racing nous built up over a decade; in Denny Hulme it had a recent World Champion, and in Ralph Bellamy, who joined to design the M19, it had a new designer and a promising car for 1971.

Frank Williams' team was evolving. He bought a March 701 and took on French driver Henri Pescarolo, who came with £38,000 of sponsorship from Motul, and Carlos Pace from Brazil who brought another £10,000 for a Formula 2 drive. He had a further £10,000 from Ted Williams, a machine tool manufacturer and great personal supporter of Frank Williams, plus another £10,000 from Politoys.

At March, the impact of the Lotus 72 and the cold facts of economic life had taken hold. After a fantastic start in 1970, March cars had become the benchmark in Formula 2 and Formula 3 and sold well. They made a profit of £3000, but once the car-selling season was over it was woefully short of cash to keep going. Robin Herd and Max Mosley had to arrange for £20,000 to be invested through their families. Mosley wanted control of the purse strings and said he would go unless he could turn March from a lifestyle business into a proper business. In doing so he brought in his half-brother

Partnership: Jackie Stewart and Ken Tyrell, one of the great winning relationships, which won 3 World Championships, in 1969, 1971 and 1973.

Jonathan Guinness, a merchant banker, who bought Graham Croaker's shares. Croaker left, taking a Formula 3 car by way of severance. STP stayed on as a sponsor but the amounts of money were not enough to support the Formula 1 team which continued to rely on the production side of the business. Tyrell was now making his own cars, so was no longer a customer.

Alan Rees wanted to lose Chris Amon because he was expensive and was not World Champion material, while their Swedish Formula 2 driver, Ronnie Peterson, clearly was. Colin Chapman had approached Ronnie Peterson following the death of Jochen Rindt, but Peterson stayed at March where he liked the atmosphere and Rees signed him up for Formula 1. Amon was not happy because he felt that the resources were spread too thinly and wanted more attention focussed on him alone, so he left for Matra, still owed money by the cash-strapped March. The dream was over.

Ferrari had invested heavily in plant and test equipment and the production car side of the business was firmly under Fiat management which suited Enzo Ferrari. Production had risen from just over 600 cars in 1969 to over 1000 in 1971, leaving Ferrari free to exercise his autocratic management style on the racing division alone.

Ken Tyrell had the backing of Elf and Goodyear and the team was called Elf-Team Tyrell in its first real season as an independent constructor. A second car, 002, was built for François Cevert, made slightly longer, to accommodate the Frenchman's lanky frame, but the team was built around Stewart in the same way that Rindt had wanted to operate with Herd before the advent of March.

Stewart took pole position in the South African Grand Prix of 1971 in the Tyrell 001, but Denny Hulme led from Mario Andretti's Ferrari until the rear suspension on his McLaren M19 gave way and he had to slow down. Andretti gave Ferrari a good start to the season by winning his first Grand Prix with Stewart second, proof, if it were needed

of the value of a top driver like Andretti. Ickx put Ferrari on pole in the Spanish Grand Prix with Regazzoni second, then Amon and Stewart, but Stewart managed to get past both of them to be second at the first corner. On lap six Ickx left just enough room coming into the finishing straight and Stewart went through into the lead which he held despite constant pressure from Ickx.

The two Tyrells appeared in the Dutch Grand Prix with air scoops above the drivers' heads, channelling clean air straight to the carburettor air intakes in a sealed box. They passed scrutiny but were not used in the race. Stewart's car had a new nose cone which deflected the airflow from the front wheels, killing the tendency for the wheels to generate lift. Stewart's record slipped in the Dutch Grand Prix where Ickx won for Ferrari.

Ronnie Peterson was fourth at Zandvoort in a works March-Cosworth. Alfa Romeo had offered March the use of their engines instead of the Cosworth, a huge financial benefit in kind which Mosley wanted to accept, but Alan Rees wanted to give Peterson a chance of winning and wanted to stick with the Cosworth. The Alfa V8 engines were tried and Peterson had qualified using one, reverting to Cosworth power for the race.

The French Grand Prix was held at Paul Ricard, a new specially built circuit as Le Castellet, just north of Marseilles, designed for safety with big run off areas. Stewart took pole and he and Cevert finished first and second. Peterson drove a March-Alfa at Paul Ricard but retired after falling back steadily, and after that he went back to Cosworth for the rest of the season. Stewart won the British Grand Prix and in the German Grand Prix at the much improved Nurburgring, the Tyrells were on form again, Stewart taking pole position and winning with Cevert again second.

There were four races left, and while technically Ickx and Peterson could overtake Stewart, it depended on Ickx winning three Grands Prix and one second place while Peterson would have to win four times with Stewart gaining no points at all. Jo

Siffert took pole position for BRM at the Ostreichring and the lead. Stewart was experimenting with narrower tyres which was a mistake, and although he held second place for a time, eventually Cevert passed him. Several laps later, Stewart's car lost a rear wheel when a stub axle broke. While he was walking back to the pits, he effectively became World Champion for the second time when Ickx's Ferrari gave up under the pressure. Tyrell had shown what a small dedicated team could do with the right driver, and for that matter so had March.

The new faces, the pace and fierceness of the competition, the drama of the Championship and the increased financial rewards for those who were successful created a great deal of interest. Formula 1 looked like a real business opportunity for big sponsors, small entrepreneurs and talented drivers. This mood triggered attempts by British, Japanese, Italian, German and Brazilian businessmen to start teams, build cars and join the attractive world at the top of the sport; they had varying degrees of success.

John Surtees had retired from active racing and he moved into Formula 1 as a constructor with Tim Schenken and Mike Hailwood as drivers. His team was rather awkwardly titled Brooke Bond Oxo-Rob Walker-Team Surtees after its sponsors and the remnants of the last of the great privateers. Peter Connew, who had worked as a draughtsman for Surtees in 1970, started to build a Formula 1 car in a lock-up garage in Essex with sponsorship from a French seafood company, Darnval. It only made one appearance, in the 1972 British Grand Prix, but driver François Migault failed to qualify when the suspension collapsed. The Pederzani brothers started the Tecno team in Bologna with sponsorship from Martini & Rossi which backed them for two seasons.

Frank Williams had backing from Motul which enabled him to buy two March-Cosworth 711s for Henri Pescarolo and Carlos Pace whom he signed up on a 50-50 deal for starting and prize money.

The American tobacco giant Philip Morris, sponsored BRM with its Marlboro brand, calling the cars Marlboro-BRMs for the 1972 season. The sponsorship coup of the moment, however, went to Lotus where the Lotus 72 changed its livery completely, to become the John Player Special, its whole body painted in the black and gold livery of the cigarette packet.

Bernie Ecclestone had been trying to get into the charmed circle at the top since the late 1950s; in November 1971, he did it by acquiring 100 percent of Brabham from Ron Tauranac. Ecclestone wanted control and when he offered Tauranac a reported £200,000 for the business, Tauranac took it. Ecclestone brought in Ralph Bellamy from McLaren at the end of 1971 to assist Gordon Murray, the South African designer who had joined in 1970. Tauranac stayed to run the workshops and supervise the designers, but Ecclestone was set on transforming the Brabham business along his own lines, starting with his preoccupation with order and cleanliness. First he moved the production of cars for private customers to other premises. Then he brought in Keith Greene as team manager to transform Brabham into a team which built cars purely for the team to race under sponsorship. These moves were in line with the way Formula 1 was developing as a business but were not the way things had been at Brabham under Tauranac. The relationship between Ecclestone and Tauranac began to sour quickly.

Ecclestone inherited Graham Hill with the team, a driver who was still highly respected but also seen as well past his best as a driving talent. Ecclestone brought in a new driver, Carlos Reuterman, who had yet to drive in Formula 1. Reuterman was the son of a cattle rancher in Santa Fe and came with sponsorship money from the Argentine state oil company, YPF and Argentine Meat.

March was trading at a loss, its deal with STP falling far short of the funds needed to run a

Young blood: Emerson Fittipaldi became the youngest World Champion at 25 and inspired a generation of Brazilian motor racing drivers.

Formula 1 team. There were two philosophies developing in the company: the dedicated Formula 1 team route, looking to achieve success to attract the money, which was favoured by Alan Rees, while Robin Herd and Max Mosley favoured continuing to manufacture cars to sell as the basis of the business. March produced 60 racing cars in 1971, mostly for Formula 2 and Formula 3 customers, but had lost £73,000 doing so. Ronnie Peterson had won the European Formula 2 Championship, and that was the base from which Herd and Mosley wanted to build, and their view prevailed. Rees, who had originally spotted Peterson, departed, the second of the four men whose names adorned the masthead to go. Mosley then signed up Niki Lauda as a pay driver. Lauda had driven a March in his one and only Formula 1 race, his home Grand Prix in Austria in 1971, and for 1972 he came to March

with £35,000 which he had managed to borrow, against the wishes of his family, to drive for March. The money came just in time.

Against the kit car teams and their sponsorship deals, Ferrari had his deal with Fiat. Mauro Foghieri had developed the Ferrari 312B2 and had managed to give the new car around 33 percent more raw power than the Cosworth. The drivers, Ickx, Regazzoni and Andretti, preferred the previous car but Foghieri was blamed for the results and was moved away from the Formula 1 racing department. His role was taken over by Sando Colombo who swiftly upset the old guard by ordering three chassis fabricated in England.

The influx of South American drivers had rekindled interest in the region and the Argentine Grand Prix reappeared after an absence of twelve years. Carlos Reuterman put the BT34 on pole

New record: Jackie Stewart's 25th victory at
Monaco in 1973 equalled Jim Clark's record;
victories in Holland and Germany raised it.

position ahead of favourite Jackie Stewart, much to
the delight of Bernie Ecclestone and the local
crowd, but the World Champion asserted himself
in the race and won.

Emerson Fittipaldi showed his Championship
form in Spain, winning against determined
opposition from Ickx and Regazzoni after Stewart
retired following a crash. Fittipaldi won with a fuel
leak which required him to drive super-
economically. At Monaco, Jean-Pierre Beltoise
gave Marlboro-BRM a much appreciated first win
in its new colours, in what turned out to be the last
BRM victory. Then the season settled down to a
theme: Lotus versus Tyrell. Stewart did not race in
the Belgian Grand Prix because of a stomach ulcer,
so Fittipaldi won with Cevert second. Stewart was
fit for the French Grand Prix, which he won from
Fittipaldi, then Fittipaldi won the British Grand
Prix with Stewart second, putting Fittipaldi on 43

points and Stewart on 27. The British race saw the
debut of the first Williams-constructed car, the
FW03, in the hands of Henri Pescarolo, but he
retired on lap 7 with suspension failure.

Jacky Ickx led the German Grand Prix from
start to finish. On the last but one lap, Regazzoni,
who was lying second, went wide on a corner and
Stewart nipped inside him on the racing line.
Regazzoni forced his way back on to the line,
Stewart crashed and Ferraris finished first and
second. Fittipaldi won in Austria, with Stewart out
of the points again, and the Brazilian, now with 52
points, could take the Championship in the Italian
Grand Prix. Stewart's Tyrell failed on the grid and
Ickx, Regazzoni and Fittipaldi had a close battle at
the front until Regazzoni came upon Carlos Pace's
March, stationary in a chicane. Going faster than
the yellow flags indicated, he hit the March and
tore off a wheel. Ickx then took the lead. Fittipaldi

Swan song: Ronnie Peterson's last race for March,
fourth in the 1972 US Grand Prix. He went to
Lotus but returned to March in 1976.

could take the Championship with a second place, but he was determined to do it in style. He put pressure on Ickx, trying to out-brake him into the chicanes but failing each time, then suddenly the Ferrari's engine failed and up went Ickx's arm. It was a fairy-story ending: Fittipaldi was 25, the youngest driver to take the Championship, and the first from South America since Fangio.

During the 1970s, Formula 1 struggled to make racing safer, with new regulations for cars and circuits. Fire had been a great killer, and a popular new regulation introduced from the 1973 Spanish Grand Prix, stipulated that all cars would have deformable structures to protect the fuel tanks from rupturing. All designers turned their skills to achieving it with minimum effect on performance.

Ralph Bellamy left Brabham to go to Lotus. Ron Tauranac had suggested that he get rid of Bellamy's assistant, Gordon Murray, but instead

Ecclestone told Murray to design a completely new car based on the Cosworth engine. Murray was a highly trained designer, like Chapman, with a degree in engineering from Natal University. He had tried to work for Chapman when he arrived in Britain in 1970, but there were no vacancies. Now, three years later, Ecclestone had given him the job of designing the challenger to Lotus domination, the BT42, and he had just four months to do it.

At McLaren, Gordon Coppuck had a similar brief, seeking to accommodate the new fuel tank regulations in the M19C which was heavy and slow on the straights but handled well. The McLaren M16 Indy Car was designed for constant high speeds, so Coppuck started by putting the front end of an M16 and the rear end of an M19C on the floor of the workshop to see if a compromise would work. The new McLaren M23 evolved from that experiment, progressing with the development of side pods for the radiators, like the Lotus 72 and a big air scoop like the Tyrells. The side pods were an integral part of the monocoque and acted as deformable structures protecting the fuels tanks.

At March the finances were no better, and when STP withdrew its support, it looked like disaster. STP then came back with a smaller sum and the Formula 1 team survived in reduced form. Ronnie Peterson had made the 721 look better than it deserved and March depended on him, but his three-year contract came to an end in 1972. As early as the 1972 French Grand Prix, he had been approached by Colin Chapman to drive for Lotus, and although he was very much part of the original set-up at March and still loved it there, he decided to go. When he told Herd and Mosley, they were shattered. They had all hoped that the partnership would produce a Championship victory which would launch March and Peterson as serious challengers, but had to admit that there was no immediate prospect of doing so. From March's point of view, it was a disaster; it had little hope of attracting another driver of Peterson's calibre. Lauda was promising, and he had won the John Player Formula 2 Championship in Britain, but he was not quick enough. Although he thought he had done well enough to justify a works drive, there was not enough money, so when BRM offered him a drive for 1973, he took it. Mosley decided to run one car in 1973, for Jean-Pierre Jarier.

The March Formula 3 team showed signs of the financial strain and folded at the end of the year leaving driver James Hunt looking for a new home. He found it with Lord Alexander Hesketh. Hesketh was a *bon viveur* but no *dilettante*, and with Hunt on board, he started to think about Formula 1. When Hunt came third in a Surtees in the 1973 Race of Champions, Hesketh not only bought a March 721, he tempted Harvey Postlethwaite away from March to form a small dedicated Formula 1 team around Hunt.

Another new name for 1973 was Shadow. It was financed by American Don Nichols, a former US Army officer and a veteran of US sports car racing, whose driver since 1970 had been Jack Oliver. Nichols' sponsor was Universal Oil Products, a US chemical company, and he set up shop in Northampton having lured Tony Southgate away from BRM.

Bernie Ecclestone started appearing at F1CA meetings in 1972. The meetings were very informal, usually held in a room at the Excelsior Hotel near Heathrow. The members were Lotus, Tyrell, Williams, McLaren, Brabham, March, Surtees, Ferrari, BRM and Matra. There was no formal structure, but Ken Tyrell took a leading role in the discussions and any action decided on was usually followed up by most of the members going along to any further discussions because they all wanted to be there to protect their interests. By the end of 1972, Andrew Ferguson had been removed, and an Ecclestone nominee, Peter Mackintosh, had been appointed to replace him. Mackintosh worked closely with Ecclestone.

During 1972 there was a struggle going on between F1CA and a new organization, Grand Prix International, formed to promote the interests of race organizers. The new body proposed a total prize fund of half a million Swiss francs for each Grand Prix, around two-thirds of what the teams wanted, and as part of its negotiations, threatened to seek the sanction of the CSI for Grands Prix to be run using Formula 2 cars if the teams would not agree. Ferguson and F1CA dealt directly with the race organizers and persuaded them that it would be a folly. The race organizers backed off, and the following year a new body representing the race organizers, backed by the CSI, agreed terms with F1CA involving sliding scales for each team based on performance.

Clay Regazzoni took the first pole position of the season in the Argentine Grand Prix. In the mêlée at the start, François Cevert shot through from the third row of the grid into the lead only to be passed by Regazzoni on the first lap, then came Emerson Fittipaldi and Ronnie Peterson. Stewart

Special moment: Lotus gave John Player 3 Driver's and 4 Constructors' titles in the 1970s, each greeted with jubilation by Colin Chapman.

started working his way up from eighth place to join the leaders; Regazzoni fell back having used up his tyres, leaving Cevert leading with Stewart second. Much to the delight of the crowd, Fittipaldi challenged Stewart, then Cevert and won. The victory set São Paulo alight during the two weeks leading up to the first Brazilian Grand Prix at Interlagos. The two Lotuses were on the front of the grid but the race came down to a duel between two World Champions, Fittipaldi and Stewart, his only real challenger. Fittipaldi won and Brazil went into raptures.

The first Shadow appeared in South Africa where Hulme was driving the first McLaren M23. Fittipaldi led at the start, but Hulme overtook him on lap 1. Stewart won and Hulme finished fifth in the M23, serving notice of its competitiveness. Fittipaldi won the Spanish Grand Prix after Stewart dropped out with brake failure, then

Stewart won in Belgium and Monaco, evening up the title race with Fittipaldi still ahead on 41 points, Stewart on 37 and Cevert on 21. In Sweden, the local hero, Peterson, led from the start, with Fittipaldi second, until lap 70 when Fittipaldi's gearbox failed and Stewart moved up to second place. His brakes started to fail and he slowed and Hulme took over second place. Then on the last lap, Peterson had a puncture which forced him to slow down, giving Denny Hulme the opportunity to pass, and giving the McLaren M23 its first victory, much to the disappointment of the crowd. In France, another McLaren M23, driven by a young South African, Jody Scheckter, whom Teddy Mayer had signed up, led from the start until he crashed on lap 43. Peterson won with Cevert in second place, Reuterman third, Stewart fourth, Ickx fifth and James Hunt sixth, his first Championship point. Stewart's three points put

Revival: Mauro Foghieri gave Ferrari 3 Driver's
and 4 Constructors' titles in the 1970s, with help
from Niki Lauda and Jody Scheckter.

him one ahead of Fittipaldi, who crashed.

Jody Scheckter had a reputation as a charger, and taking him on was a move designed to put some pressure on the two older McLaren drivers Hulme and Revson. In the British Grand Prix, Scheckter shot off from the third row of the grid, challenging Peter Revson for the lead by trying to take him on the inside at Woodcote corner. He was too fast and went wide, spun across the track and bounced back from the barrier into the oncoming pack. Revson just managed to get through, having clipped his team-mate, but behind him there was carnage; 9 cars were put out of the race, including the whole Surtees team, and it was stopped. The only serious injury was a broken ankle for Andrea de Adamich. Peterson took the lead in the restarted race until it rained and Revson overtook him, giving the McLaren M23 a second victory.

Stewart won the Dutch Grand Prix with Cevert second, putting him 10 points ahead of Fittipaldi, a victory which made him the leading race winner in the history of the Championship with 26 victories, 1 more than Jim Clark. But any celebration was swiftly abandoned because of another fatality. Many felt that the race should have been stopped when Roger Williamson, driving Tom Wheatcroft's March, crashed and burst into flames; no marshals were on hand to help and no fire tender was sent. David Purley, also in a March, stopped and tried heroically to get Williamson out of the burning wreakage, but he failed and Williamson died in the flames. Purley was later awarded the George Medal.

Stewart could take the Championship with fourth place at the Italian Grand Prix, provided that Fittipaldi did not win. Fittipaldi could keep his hopes of the Championship alive if Stewart failed to get the right number of points, and expected Peterson to agree to give him the lead in that event. Peterson was also in a position to win the Championship – just – and had other ideas. Peterson led the race from the start with Fittipaldi second, Hulme third and Stewart fourth. Stewart then had a slow puncture and went into the pits, rejoining in twentieth place on lap 9 with Peterson and Fittipaldi nearly a lap ahead. Stewart started to push to the front and by lap 36 was in seventh place, then he passed Hailwood for sixth place. Four laps later he had passed Reuterman to take fifth, behind Cevert, who gave way immediately. Stewart was now in a position to win the Championship, provided Fittipaldi did not win the race. He started to reel in Revson in third place, and was in sight of him as they started on the last lap. Out front, Peterson was still in the lead and showed no sign of giving way to Fittipaldi. In the pits, Chapman and Peter Warr decided not to intervene. To have done so would have meant that they would have to arrange to give Fittipaldi the next two races as well. Peterson won, giving Stewart the title. Fittipaldi decided to leave Lotus there and then.

Peter Revson won the Canadian Grand Prix in the McLaren M23, then Peterson won the US Grand Prix. Stewart did not take part in the last race of the season at Watkins Glen because in practice his great team-mate François Cevert crashed and was killed; Ken Tyrell withdrew the entry. Jackie Stewart was Champion for the third time, joining Jack Brabham on three, the only men except Fangio to pass the two mark, but it was a sad Stewart who made his way home into retirement.

Peter Revson had a good year at McLaren but he and his long-standing colleague, Teddy Mayer, had their fair share of rows. Mayer was super-competitive and gifted, but he was a rather uncompromising figure to lead the team. He could be very abrupt with people when they needed encouragement, and while Bruce McLaren had

been alive there had been a softer edge to the team. The more easy-going spirit of the 1960s gave way to the realization that it was a business, a tough business. Mayer was at a crossroads; there was a huge sponsorship deal in the offing but he would have to put business before sentiment to accept it. The Yardley sponsorship deal had been for three years but it was not enough for Mayer's ambitions. He wanted Emerson Fittipaldi, and with him he knew he could get the backing of Texaco and Marlboro which was looking to move from BRM. The discussions took place in great secrecy, but there was an awareness that Marlboro was looking for a big deal involving Fittipaldi, to put one team in a truly winning position. The fiercest competition to land the deal came from Bernie Ecclestone at Brabham, who was equally determined, but Mayer managed to clinch it, a rare example of Ecclestone being bested. The total sponsorship amounted to £500,000 to run a team with Fittipaldi and Hulme as Marlboro-McLaren.

Marlboro's sponsorship of McLaren was the start of a long relationship, one in which Marlboro became a huge backer, not only of McLaren, but of motor racing in general on both sides of the Atlantic. Marlboro had been conceived as a cigarette for women, but it had been a marketing failure. Philip Morris had been influenced in its decision to get into Formula 1 by the tremendous success of the John Player Special Lotus cars in the complete livery. Philip Morris began to buy into the whole structure of the sport, taking advertising space at circuits and moving into the lower formulae, into rallying, into motor cycling and into Indy Car racing in the US. Marlboro was to become the world's leading brand of cigarette, a marketing masterstroke built largely on the image first created by Formula 1 and the World Championship.

The growth of Formula 1 in 1973–4 was completely counter to the economic climate of the time. In October 1973, the Yom Kippur War and the resulting oil crisis shook the world economy;

whole economies had to change direction and many businesses had to make major adjustments to the way they traded just to survive. Not a single Grand Prix was cancelled; the mass attraction of Formula 1 and its growing international status made it ideal as a promotional tool, and the big established teams continued to grow. John Player continued to sponsor Lotus where Peterson was joined by Ickx from Ferrari. Embassy cigarettes continued to sponsor Graham Hill's team when he switched from Shadow to Lola as a supplier.

Ferrari did feel some aftershocks from the economic earthquake. It had been a disastrous racing year again – Jacky Ickx and Arturo Merzario had only managed three fourth places between them. Fiat provided the services of a member of the Agnelli family, a lawyer, Luca di Montezemolo, as the management supremo. Enzo Ferrari could be outflanked because di Montezemolo could bypass him and go straight to the top of Fiat if he needed to, but he was a deft enough manager to handle Enzo Ferrari carefully while implementing long overdue change. Ferrari had been eclipsed at Le Mans, first by Ford, then Porsche, then Matra, absorbing huge amounts of money since the last victory in 1965, and Enzo Ferrari was forced to give up endurance sports car racing. Colombo had failed to improve the Tipo 312 and Mauro Foghieri was brought back from obscurity to prepare the 312B3 for 1974. Shell pulled out of Italy, selling its assets to Agip which picked up the sponsorship of the team. This signalled another change; previously the all-red Ferraris had carried only a Prancing Horse emblem and now had to carry the commercial logos of its sponsors and suppliers. Enzo Ferrari had always resisted this but financial realities made it inevitable; some were even foreign – Goodyear, Ferodo, Champion, Heuer.

The biggest change was in the drivers. Ickx had become increasingly frustrated with Ferrari in 1973 and left before the end of the season, driving for McLaren and Williams before settling with Lotus.

Enzo Ferrari had seen how Regazzoni had fared at BRM after he had left Ferrari, regularly being bested by his team-mate Niki Lauda, so a test was arranged for Lauda at Maranello followed by a meeting with Enzo Ferrari. Lauda was not impressed by the car and said so, in English, pointing out that the front suspension needed changing. Piero Lardi was translating and told Lauda he could not say that, softening the point to his father. Enzo Ferrari asked Foghieri how long the changes would take and invited Lauda back to test the car again. He did, and the car was a second faster; Lauda agreed to drive for Ferrari. The package was complete – di Montezemolo was in charge, Foghieri was back at the drawing board and Lauda was there not only as a talented and mature driver, but with the confidence to speak out openly about deficiencies in the car. Ironically, Regazzoni was taken back to partner him.

Bernie Ecclestone had signed Carlos Pace who was a far more outgoing character than Carlos Reuterman. As he brought Pace closer into the Brabham team it caused a certain tension with Reuterman. Following his abortive attempt to get Marlboro sponsorship, Ecclestone had a fortunate break when Martini switched its backing to Brabham for 1974 when the Tecno team folded.

The network of engineering businesses in Britain grew both in size and expertise. Ron Tauranac joined Trojan, which manufactured McLaren production sports racing cars, to design a Formula 1 car for his protégé Tim Schenken. The first Japanese attempt at a Cosworth-based kit car was named Make, which built one car, the F101, for Howden Ganley. Ron Dennis and Neil Trundle had a good year in Formula 2, Henri Pescarolo won the prestigious International meeting at Thruxton and Bob Wolleck finished sixth in the European Championship. Their car, the M1, was designed by Ray Jessop, the M standing for Motul, their French backer and it was building the first chassis which began to turn Ron Dennis's mind to Formula 1. Rondel started out as a Formula 1

Dream team: March's future looked golden
in 1970 but it never gelled as a team and
pulled out of Formula 1 in 1978.

project, Token, with Ray Jessop as designer, but
Dennis knew the company could not finance it and
sold it on to Tony Vlassopoulos.

The reputation of the British racing car builders
spread across the Atlantic. Roger Penske, who was
becoming something of a legend at Indianapolis
and in US sports car racing, was steadily building a
huge corporate empire based on his racing success.
To supply cars for it, he started a factory in Poole,
Dorset hiring Geoff Ferris, who had worked at
Brabham with Ron Tauranac, to build sports cars
and Indy Cars. At the same time, he moved into
Formula 1 with his long-time friend Mark
Donohue. Parnelli Jones, another Indy Car man,
also started to build Formula 1 cars in Britain.

Commercial pressures made it quite difficult for
new entrants to get in. There were fifteen races in
1974, pushing up the cost of taking part, and the

F1CA teams sought to protect their positions by
securing the lion's share of the starting money for
themselves, so new teams had an uphill struggle.
Television was beginning to take a serious interest
and the sponsors wanted the effort concentrated
where it could be guaranteed the greatest exposure.
This, obviously, was not at the track where the true
enthusiast went, but at home, and slowly a new
breed of armchair fan started to emerge. These
developments accelerated the decline of two great
historical elements of Formula 1: the private
entrant and the non-Championship race. Taking
part was fun, but winning was all and as the
rewards for winning grew, so did the costs, adding
to the spiral of forces for change.

The growing commercial possibilities in
Formula 1 were clear to Bernie Ecclestone. He
could see that, through F1CA, the teams really

Contact: Denny Hulme, No. 6 and Jean-Pierre Beltoise, No. 14, collide on lap 1 of the 1974 Grand Prix; the mêlée took out 5 other cars.

could use their commercial muscle to prise more starting money out of the track owners and demand a greater share of the television revenues which, at the time, went to the track owners. His vision was no longer of 15 separate races but of a single World Championship, controlled by F1CA in the interests of the teams. He wanted to commercialize the sport as a whole rather than team by team and race by race, and the key to that was a mutually advantageous alliance between the constructor teams, their sponsors, in particular tobacco, and television. To achieve it, Ecclestone needed a platform, a constituency, and that was F1CA which he increasingly made his instrument.

Ecclestone was unlike the other team owners in that he had other business interests, but in April 1973 he reportedly sold all his other businesses in a

single deal. The reason he has since given was the introduction of VAT which followed Britain's entry into the Common Market. His reason: he was not prepared to be a tax collector for the government. From 1973 he did become increasingly focussed on his vision of Formula 1 as a single entity, negotiating from a position of strength with track owners, broadcasters and even governments.

Reuterman made a superb start at Interlagos in the Brazilian Grand Prix but his tyres let him down and he finished seventh while Emerson Fittipaldi gave McLaren a second victory. Peter Revson was killed in pre-qualifying for the Spanish Grand Prix when the suspension in his Shadow failed and he hit the barrier hard. Lauda took pole and went into an early lead, but the BT44 was a match for the Ferraris in straight line speed, and Reuterman was able to outbrake Lauda on lap 10 to take the lead and win, the first victory since Ecclestone had bought the team. Peterson won the French Grand Prix, with Lauda second and Regazzoni third; Fittipaldi retired with engine failure, so the two Ferrari drivers were suddenly leading the title race, Lauda with 36 points and Regazzoni with 32 to Fittipaldi's 31.

The last race was the US Grand Prix. Mario Andretti was fastest in practice in a Parnelli, but Reuterman took pole position with James Hunt second in a Hesketh, then Andretti. Reuterman led with Hunt second and the two pulled away from the rest with Pace and Lauda ahead of the three title contenders, Scheckter fourth, Fittipaldi fifth, and Regazzoni sixth. Regazzoni slipped back to ninth place so Fittipaldi knew that as long as he stayed ahead of the Ferrari, the title was his. That is what happened: he finished fourth behind Hunt, Pace and Reuterman, who won.

It was Fittipaldi's second World Championship and McLaren's first, and for good measure they took the Constructors' title as well. Marlboro was delighted with the result, but McLaren's stalwart driver, the former World Champion Denny Hulme, who had been at McLaren since 1968, took this moment to retire.

Winning the title had been no pushover for McLaren in the face of very stiff competition, especially from a revitalized Ferrari. McLaren had won both titles, but Regazzoni had nearly won the Driver's title and Ferrari was second in both, a huge improvement on the previous year. Lauda had more than shown his mettle and under Luca di Montezemolo's careful, firm management, there was a renaissance rather than a revolution going on at Maranello. Mauro Foghieri worked flat out in the winter of 1974–5 to improve the 312 engine which was giving 440 bhp, and there was a new, five-speed gearbox mounted transversely across the rear of the car, giving it a new designation, 312T, for *transversale*.

There was a minor revolution going on at

Brabham too. Ecclestone and the team could see that the flat 12 engine was giving the Ferrari drivers more power than the Cosworth, and that greater power was playing a part in the revival of Ferrari's fortunes. Early in 1975 he contacted Alfa Romeo, which was developing a flat 12 engine with Autodelta and the Ferrari renegade Carlo Chiti, whose team claimed a power output of 510 bhp compared with 500 bhp for the Ferrari. Ecclestone did a deal with Autodelta and Gordon Murray was sent down the power route to victory with a completely new Brabham-Alfa BT45. Like Cooper-Maserati, another famous name from the past was back in the World Championship in a curious marriage with a kit car team.

Ferrari was on the up, but Lotus was on the way down: the sports car business lost nearly £500,000 and Ronnie Peterson was not happy. Ralph Bellamy's Lotus 76, a lightweight derivative of the 72, had not been successful and Peterson and Ickx had raced Lotus 72Es with the new cars often relegated to spare status. Chapman started looking for radical solutions to make progress in Formula 1. The idea behind the Lotus 77 was adjustability, the ability to tailor the car to the individual characteristics of each circuit, longer wheelbase and narrower track for faster, straighter circuits and shorter wheelbase and wider track for the shorter, twisty circuits. Chapman described this as a 'variable geometry car'. Beyond that the Lotus 78 was started in great secrecy, another of Chapman's great new ideas: using aerodynamics to stick the car more firmly to the track, not using wings above the car, but using the airflow under the car, to suck it to the track.

The new kit car teams were having mixed fortunes: Tecno, Trojan and Amon had given up; Surtees signed up John Watson from Hexagon Racing for a single car team; Graham Hill was persevering with Lola but with little to show for it; Shadow was running two DN5 cars for Tom Pryce; and Jean-Pierre Jarier and Williams had signed Arturo Merzario and Jacques Laffite to drive the

Best men: James Hunt, World Champion 1976,
with Lord Hesketh at Hunt's wedding. Hunt
became a BBC commentator and died in 1993.

FW04. Wilson Fittipaldi had formed a team with backing from one of Brazil's huge state sugar corporations, Copersucar, driving the Cosworth-powered FD03 himself. At Hesketh, Harvey Postlethwaite had designed a new car, the 308, for James Hunt, and Rob Walker bought one to enter a tough Australian driver, Alan Jones. The two American teams were getting a foothold: Roger Penske was running Mark Donohue in a March 751 until his own cars were ready and Parnelli had signed Mario Andretti to drive his VPJ4. Ron Dennis opened a new factory at Woking for Project Three Racing, with Formula 1 ambitions.

In 1974, Marches won all 11 races in the European Formula 2 Championship, but Formula 1 was draining the money away. At one point March almost decided to get out of Formula 1, but came back in when an eccentric Italian, Count Googhie Zanon, who had supported a number of racing drivers, including Ronnie Peterson, put up £50,000 if they would take on Lella Lombardi, an Italian woman driver who had come fifth in the European Formula 5000 Championship. Vittorio Brambilla stayed.

The line-up for the first race of the season in Argentina saw Wilson Fittipaldi right at the back of the grid with his brother, Emerson, on the third row in the latest M23 behind Jean-Pierre Jarier who had surprised everybody by putting the Shadow DN5 on pole. Jarier's car broke down on the warm-up lap, leaving pole position empty; Reuterman went straight for the gap and led from Pace, Lauda, Hunt and Emerson Fittipaldi. On lap 12 Wilson Fittipaldi crashed and caught fire. Fortunately he was unhurt, but Emerson was a little slower until he knew his brother was safe. Hunt and Fittipaldi then moved up to put pressure on Reuterman and both passed him, then Fittipaldi passed Hunt to win.

Carlos Pace won in Brazil for Brabham, with Fittipaldi second, and Scheckter won for Tyrell in South Africa where Lauda and Regazzoni gave the Ferrari 312T its debut and Lauda finished fifth. The safety campaign by drivers reached a landmark at the Spanish Grand Prix when they inspected the circuit and found that the barriers were inadequate, with many of the bolts loose. They went on strike, refusing to practice on the Friday and Saturday morning. Emerson Fittipaldi, who was leading the Championship, led the strike and even when others returned once the organizers had tightened everything up, he refused to drive and went home. The two Ferraris were on the front row of the grid, then James Hunt, then Andretti in the Parnelli. Lella Lombardi was at the back of the grid in her March. Lauda made a great start, only to collide with Regazzoni at the first corner, putting both Ferraris out, although Regazzoni rejoined well down the field. Hunt was leading from Andretti when, after one lap, Merzario and Wilson Fittipaldi stopped in further protest at the safety of the circuit. Hunt then crashed, then Andretti followed him when his suspension gave way from damage sustained in the earlier accident with the two Ferraris. Other crashes included Depailler, Donohue, Jones, Wunderink, Pryce and Peterson, then Regazzoni retired. On lap 25 Rolf Stommeln was leading in the Hill 371 when his rear wing fell off. The sudden loss of downforce caused him to crash into the barrier, bounce back into Pace's Brabham, who was lying in second, then back into the crowd, killing five spectators and a fire marshal. Stommeln was badly injured. The race was stopped with Jochen Mass for McLaren in the lead; Lombardi was lying sixth, two laps down in the depleted field, gaining the first World Championship points by a woman. It was a Grand Prix most would rather forget.

Niki Lauda led the French Grand Prix at Paul Ricard from pole position to the flag in one of his best drives, but his Championship lead narrowed when Emerson Fittipaldi won the British, and Reuterman won the German Grands Prix. The Austrian Grand Prix took place in heavy rain, weather which matched the mood of the day. Mark Donohue had had an accident in practice in the Penske March 751 which killed a marshal; Donohue was in hospital with serious head injuries from which he died three days later. The weather looked set to clear for the race and most of the teams set their cars up for dry conditions, but Vittorio Brambilla set his works March 751 up for the wet. Lauda took the lead with Hunt second and Brambilla third. The rain stooped, then started again in earnest and Lauda's Ferrari was not handling well in the conditions. Hunt and Brambilla who was good in the wet, passed him, then Brambilla passed Hunt and started to pull away. On lap 29, with Brambilla leading, the race was stopped and March won its first Grand Prix.

The *tifosi* could see the prospect of Ferrari winning both World Championships, their first real taste of either title for 11 years, and Lauda could clinch both at Monza. The weather at Monza was very wet, but after Lauda took pole position with Regazzoni beside him at the front of the grid, nothing could dampen the emotional atmosphere across Italy. Regazzoni took the lead with Lauda second and Jochen Mass third. At the end of lap 1 Mass misjudged his braking point going into a new chicane right in front of the grandstand and suddenly cars were spinning in all directions. The two Ferraris forged ahead with Regazzoni pulling steadily away from Lauda while the mess at the chicane was sorted out and the track cleared. Fittipaldi had made it through the mêlée and gained on Lauda for the remainder of the race. Lauda was more intent on preserving his car and winning the Championship than winning the race and six laps before the end, Fittipaldi passed him. Regazzoni won the race and 23 seconds later Lauda won the Championship, releasing 11 years of pent-up emotion and expectation from the crowd. To be Italian at Monza that Sunday was sheer bliss; the name Niki Lauda was on every pair of lips and by the end of the day he had been catapulted to superstar status giving Ferrari its first Driver's Championship since 1964 and its sixth since the Championship started in 1950.

In November 1975 Graham Hill crashed his own aircraft in fog near Elstree airfield and all on board were killed. Hill's driving career had finished that year at Monaco, the site of his first-ever Grand Prix 17 years earlier in 1958 and a race he won five times. He failed to qualify in 1975 and retired. His death so soon afterwards, on the brink of a second career as a team owner, was a huge blow to British motor racing.

Another name from the pioneering years of British motor racing also disappeared in 1975. Sir Alfred Owen had withdrawn his support for BRM at the end of 1974 and the Motul sponsorship disappeared at the same time, as did Jean-Pierre

Beltoise, the driver who had given the team its last Grand Prix win. It survived as Stanley-BRM with a single car team for the Formula 5000 Champion Bob Evans, but it was a shadow of its former self. Other than Ferrari, it was the only other team which could trace its history back to the start of the World Championship in 1950. While Ferrari had managed to haul itself back to the top, BRM, despite efforts by a great many people, finally died.

McLaren was the best managed team of 1974, the year Fittipaldi won its first Championship. He came second in 1975 and gave Teddy Mayer and Marlboro a whiff of consecutive titles. Teddy Mayer wanted Fittipaldi to stay, but he moved to Brazil to drive for his brother's team, Copersucar-Fittipaldi. Wilson Fittipaldi was working hard to build a team on British lines in Brazil and the services of a double World Champion were useful as a driver and for sponsorship. Teddy Mayer approached James Hunt, who had driven the Hesketh to great effect, winning one race, coming third three times, and coming fourth in the Championship. When Mayer offered Hunt a retainer of £40,000 per annum for 1976, Hunt took it.

Lord Hesketh, who did not have sponsors, was feeling the financial strain. After three years in Formula 1, having produced a promising car in the 308, he was approached by Austrian oil prospector Walter Wolf, who had made money in Canada. Wolf had a penchant for racing and when he met the cash-strapped Frank Williams in 1975, Williams had proposed a team based on buying out Hesketh and built around the 308C. Wolf bought Hesketh's assets for a reported £450,000 and a 60 percent stake in Frank Williams' team to form Wolf with Harvey Postlethwaite as designer and Peter Warr from Lotus as team manager. The cars were renamed Williams, but Frank Williams was consigned to seeking sponsorship and, with Patrick Head, who had joined Williams in 1975, was effectively sidelined.

At Brabham, the BT45 Brabham-Alfa was

rolled out to great fanfares in the colours of Martini-Rossi. It was very heavy and complicated and Gordon Murray rued the day that they had stopped developing the Cosworth-based BT44B. Carlos Reuterman still hankered after the old Cosworth cars too, so Ecclestone sold them to John MacDonald, a north London garage owner who was forming his own Formula 1 team, RAM, which had fielded Alan Jones in Formula 5000 and was now moving up to Formula 1.

Alan Jones was driving for John Surtees, whose sponsors had been many and varied, but for 1976 he did a sponsorship deal with Durex, the condom manufacturer. This caused outrage among some of the bigger wigs at the BBC, which withdrew coverage from some non-Championship races.

At Lotus, the financial situation was dire. John Player was being tight with the money because of the lack of success and at one point, Peter Warr even tried to sell Ronnie Peterson's contract, one of the company's more valuable assets. Ickx left to go to Wolf following the 1975 French Grand Prix, and Ronnie Peterson, who had never had a good relationship with Chapman, wanted to leave and started discussions with Shadow and March.

March was still producing its Formula 2 and Formula 3 cars but they had been less competitive in 1975. Brambilla was having great success in Formula 2 with Ron Dennis's Project 3 team in a March 752. Peterson was still not happy: he could drive the right car very fast, but he could not interpret the car's performance to engineers as Lauda and Fittipaldi could. He was still close to Alan Rees who had spotted him first and Rees was now at Shadow where Jack Oliver had virtually retired from racing to raise the sponsorship.

A French kit car team was established in 1975 by Guy Ligier, a former rugby player who had made his fortune in construction and raced in Formula 1 briefly in the late 1960s for Matra and in a Cooper-Maserati. He came second at Le Mans in 1975 sponsored by the French tobacco giant, Gitanes, and was then persuaded to move into

Formula 1, virtually as a French national team. Matra had pulled out of Formula 1 but Ligier persuaded it to go on producing the V12 engine and he signed Jacques Laffite, a highly successful Formula 2 driver. The cars all carried the prefix JS in memory of his great personal friend Jo Schlesser who had died in the Honda in 1968.

Ferrari was slipping again. Luca di Montezemolo had gone back to Fiat, leaving the team in the hands of Daniel Audetto who lacked di Montezemolo's management skills and was also not as focussed, disciplined and dedicated.

The World Championship was contested over 16 Grands Prix in 1976, more evidence of the commercial success. The additions were a second US Grand Prix and the first Japanese Grand Prix. The prospect of another season of close battles between the Ferrari 312T and the McLaren M23, driven by the reigning World Championship Niki Lauda and the new British hope James Hunt, was a personality clash tailor-made for television. Up to that point, the BBC would usually cover the British Grand Prix live and possibly Monaco, but it would only show highlights of the other Grands Prix. It had been eight years since Jim Clark had been a British racing hero and the prospect of Hunt becoming Champion raised British interest considerably. Television technology was not what it is today and enthusiasts followed Formula 1 in the specialist press and in newspapers. It was ironic that just as sponsorship was becoming the paymaster of the sport, the BBC started to pick up on the interest created by James Hunt.

Full television coverage was expensive to mount along several miles of closed roads. The move from closed public road circuits to so-called 'artificial' circuits such as Silverstone, which had initially started for safety and commercial reasons, helped television. The last race on closed roads at the great Reims circuit had been in 1966, at Rouen in 1968 and the twisting road circuit at Clermont-Ferrand, practically a mini-Nurburgring, was used for the last time in 1972. There had been no Belgian Grand Prix in 1969 because Spa was thought to be too dangerous and a great deal of work had been carried out for 1970, but it was cancelled again in 1971 and the race was moved to much less demanding circuits at Nivelles and Zolder. It was the same at the Nurburgring, which gave way to Hockenheim in 1970 while improvements were carried out. The first purpose-built circuit in France was Paul Ricard, first used in 1972.

To drivers the move to artificial circuits was about safety, to race promoters it was about being able to control access and concentrate advertising, to television it was about having a smaller, more controllable circuit to cover. To traditionalists the move was symptomatic of the commercial tail wagging the sporting dog, it was about the loss of the romantic amateur sporting history of Grand Prix racing. There was concern that if Formula 1 lost its image as the pinnacle of motor racing, then the status of the World Championship would be diminished. The stakes were getting higher; commercialism was no longer creeping but rushing into the sport. Money was increasingly the objective and the top talent was attracted to the money, making it very difficult for the newcomer to get a foothold.

The Argentine Grand Prix was abandoned because of political unrest following the return of Juan Perón in 1973 after 18 years in exile. He died in 1974, a military dictatorship took over and the 'dirty war' started. There were also financial and political problems in both Argentina and Brazil which resulted in sky-high inflation. Brazil had been in the grip of incompetent military rulers since 1964 and the economy was perpetually on the verge of bankruptcy, but the cash was found to stage the race that would see Brazil's double World Champion Emerson Fittipaldi drive a Brazilian-backed car built at Interlagos. James Hunt gave McLaren and Marlboro a good start by claiming pole position at Interlagos by 0.2 of a second from Lauda who won. Emerson Fittipaldi finished 13th, three laps behind Lauda.

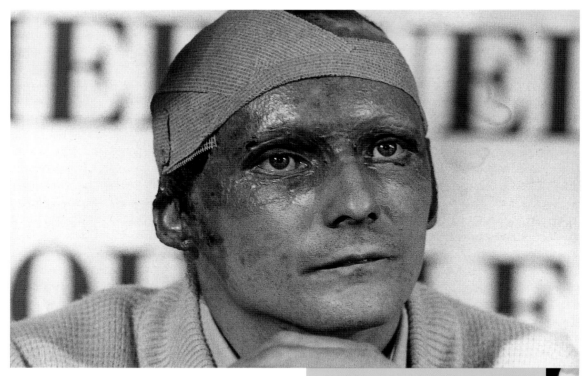

Commitment: few believed Niki Lauda would
be back after his accident in 1976, but he was
driving 5 weeks later, missing the title by 1 point.

The relationship between Chapman and Peterson had soured beyond repair. Peterson had been in discussion with Alan Rees at Shadow and Robin Herd at March. The deciding factor was Count Zanon who was still paying March £50,000 a year for Lella Lombardi's drive; when he offered to switch the money to Peterson, March agreed.

The Ferrari revival continued at the US (West) Grand Prix at Long Beach. It was a street circuit, not what the drivers liked, but the promoters offered huge sums of money. Regazzoni won, Lauda was second.

The owners of Brands Hatch held a charity night at the Albert Hall to promote the move of the British Grand Prix to their circuit which had been refurbished at great cost. But because of the Durex advertising on the Surtees cars of Alan Jones and Brett Lunger, the BBC withdrew its coverage. McLaren was sponsored by Marlboro cigarettes but that did not seem to matter as much as the thought of condoms. The television audience was consequently deprived of great drama, great controversy and a great race. Lauda started from pole, just 0.6 of a second ahead of Hunt. He made a good start, but entering Paddock Bend the two Ferraris touched and ricocheted into Hunt's McLaren which was launched into the air. Hunt continued for a short time then parked. The stewards stopped the race and decided that any car which had not completed the first lap would be excluded and that no spare cars could be used. That ruling included Regazzoni, Laffite and Hunt but all three appeared for the restart. Hunt was in a spare car, so he was ordered off to howls of disapproval from the British crowd. Then Hunt swapped the spare car for the original which had been repaired and the stewards capitulated on the basis that Hunt's car had been moving at the time the red flags had been put out stopping the race. Ferrari and Ligier simply started in their spares and decided to argue the rules after the race. Lauda led for most of the race with gearbox problems but Hunt started a charge on lap 45 and overtook him, winning a rapturous victory.

Ferrari, Tyrell and Copersucar objected to Hunt's restart although the latter two withdrew their protests after viewing film of Hunt stopping. Luca di Montezemolo decided otherwise and lodged an appeal, despairing at the British organizers, and the result was referred to the CSI for adjudication. On the basis of the result on the track Lauda moved up to 58 points to Hunt's 35.

There was more controversy at Nurburgring for the German Grand Prix when Lauda was critical of the safety arrangements. In the race he started on wet tyres and had to stop to change. Driving to catch up on a long left hander, the back of the car kinked away to the left, an odd movement which sent the Ferrari spinning across the track into the barrier on the far side, through it and into a wall, which burst the fuel tanks, finishing up a ball of flame. There were no marshals immediately to hand and the first on the scene were three drivers who skidded to a halt nearby. Brett Lunger, Guy Edwards and Arturo Merzario struggled to get Lauda out and succeeded with the help of a marshal. Lauda had inhaled a great deal of smoke and toxic fumes and was very badly burnt, especially around the face because the crash had torn his helmet off. He was rushed to hospital where he was expected to die and a priest was summoned to give him the last rites. Lauda woke up during the process, realized what was happening and fought for his life. Hunt won the race with Scheckter second.

It was the last Grand Prix at the old Nurburgring. Although disappointing for the romantic tendency, it delighted drivers who wanted Grands Prix to be made much safer. After a campaign led by Jackie Stewart even though he had retired, the German Grand Prix was moved to the artificial circuit at Hockenheim, marking the end of true road racing.

It was also the end of the period of fragile stability at Ferrari. Once again blame was heaped on Ferrari for the near death of another driver with suggestions that the car was at fault, the ultimate insult to Ferrari. The next Grand Prix was in Austria, on Lauda's home turf, so the *scuderia* tactfully withdrew. John Watson won at the Ostreichring for Penske with Hunt fourth.

There were three Ferraris entered for the Italian Grand Prix for Regazzoni, Lauda and Reuterman. The internal view at Ferrari was that Lauda's career was over, but they had reckoned without his iron will. Lauda reappeared at Monza, his head swathed in bandages with patches of burnt flesh still visible and bleeding. Hunt started from the back of the grid when the fuel that McLaren was using was found to be of too high an octane. Ronnie Peterson won for March after taking the lead on lap 11, a determined victory which only happened after holding off repeated attempts by Regazzoni to pass him. It was a dream result for March, but the biggest cheers were for Lauda who was fourth, keeping him ahead of Hunt by 61 points to 56. On 24 September, the CSI upheld Ferrari's appeal against Hunt's restart at the British Grand Prix because Hunt's car had been repaired during the period between the crash and the restart. Many believed that the decision was in part to pay Ferrari back for the decision at the Spanish Grand Prix which had reinstated Hunt over Lauda. This had the effect of increasing Lauda's points by 3 to 64 and reducing Hunt by 9 to 47.

The Championship would be settled in the last race of the season, the first Japanese Grand Prix at Fuji. Hunt needed fourth or better because he had

6 wins to Lauda's 5 so he would win in a tie. Magically, there were no Durex logos in sight; Surtees was running with Theodore sponsorship for the first and only time that season. With the prospect of a British World Champion and a huge audience in Britain even if it was in the middle of the night, the BBC got its act together in spectacular form using a satellite link, still something of an innovation in 1976, to transmit the race live not only to Britain, but providing a feed which could be taken up by other broadcasters worldwide.

It poured with rain on race day but it was decided to go ahead. Hunt went into an early lead, the only driver with a remotely clear view. Lauda, lying tenth on lap 2 in the middle of the pack had very poor visibility and he decided that Championship or no Championship it was too dangerous. He slowed down, drew off the circuit, parked his Ferrari and retired. Carlos Pace did the same on lap 5 and Fittipaldi followed suit two laps later while Hunt raced on in the lead. Then the rain stopped and everybody was on the wrong tyres. Hunt had to slow down to preserve his tyres and Andretti came through, taking Depailler, then Hunt, whose front left tyre then deflated with twelve laps to go. Fortunately it was just before the pits and he pulled in easily only to find that the jack would not fit under the car because of the deflated tyre. The McLaren mechanics lifted the car bodily to get the jack underneath, watched by Lauda, then Hunt rejoined in fifth place behind Alan Jones and Regazzoni. He did not know where he was, so he charged, taking Jones and Regazzoni in the murk to finish third behind Depailler and the winner, Andretti.

James Hunt was World Champion by one point, although he did not know it until he returned to the pits and he did not believe it fully until he was on the podium. It was the second World Championship for McLaren and Gordon Coppuck's M23. Lauda would have taken the Championship with fifth place and Mauro Foghieri offered him the opportunity to claim that the car

had been faulty, an offer Lauda declined, telling the truth at his press conference and saying the same thing to Enzo Ferrari on the telephone. Ferrari was supportive in public, but in private he was what Lauda later described as 'less than dignified'. In fact he was furious at seeing one of his cars parked in a Grand Prix, especially one which could have won the Championship; it was not what he expected of his drivers. The relationship between Ferrari and Lauda was irrevocably scarred.

At Ferrari, Daniel Audetto had returned to Fiat to run the rally team and a new team manager was installed, Roberto Nosetto, a Ferrari insider of some 20 years. The new 312T was competitive in spite of being a little long in the tooth. Lauda was back after a winter of plastic surgery, but Ferrari was convinced that he had lost his edge, and suggested that he move into a management role, essentially a ploy to keep him away from other teams. Lauda pointed to the contract under which he had driven for Ferrari for three years saying that if Ferrari wanted to end it, then Lauda suggested doing it then, leaving him free to drive for other teams. He wanted to drive, he wanted to win the Championship especially after losing it so narrowly the previous year. Ferrari backed down and to make way for Carlos Reuterman – who had been intended as a replacement for Lauda – Regazzoni was let go, leaving Reuterman and Lauda as team-mates. When asked whether he thought of Reuterman as a team-mate or a rival, Lauda famously replied, 'neither'.

Colin Chapman's latest technical revolution, the development of the ultra-secret Lotus 78 'wing car' was going well. Lotus had been in the doldrums since 1975, the sports car division was losing money again and the lack of success in Formula 1 had made John Player more circumspect about the money it put into the team. Chapman came up with an idea which sprang from sports car racing in the US where he had seen fans used to create a low pressure area under the car, effectively sucking it to the track, giving more grip. It was the same theory

Six pack: Peterson in a Tyrell P34; designed to reduce frontal area and improve braking, it worked until eclipsed by wing car aerodynamics.

as the wings mounted above the car which pushed the car down, but by inverting the aerofoil and putting it in the airflow under the car, it would be much more efficient, creating less drag for the equivalent downforce. Chapman wrote the whole idea down in a paper which he then delivered to Tony Rudd who developed it. The development team was set up at Ketteringham Hall, a country house near the factory at Hethel airfield. They built quarter-scale models which they took to the wind tunnel at Imperial College London for 400 hours of testing. The prototype was ready in August 1976 and Mario Andretti tested it at Hethel, then at Snetterton where he found that while it only lived up to 75 percent of the expectations, it was a truly fantastic drive. They decided that though they could have used it for the rest of the 1976 season, it was better to keep it secret so that the other teams would not have the whole of the winter to

copy it. It was unveiled to the press on 21 December 1976.

Frank Williams lost his F1CA membership when he sold out to Walter Wolf because he was no longer a constructor. He was not happy with the arrangements with Wolf and when he discovered that he was to be left in Britain for the first race of the 1976 season, he decided to leave and Patrick Head decided to go with him. They had nothing except a new name: Williams Grand Prix Engineering, 99 percent of the shares in Frank's name and 1 percent in his wife Virginia's name. For 1977 he signed Patrick Neve, bought a March 761 for £14,000 and four second-hand Cosworth engines, and set up in a run down factory in Didcot in Oxfordshire. Patrick Head set about designing a new car, the FW06, and Frank Williams went looking for sponsorship.

Roger Penske decided to leave Formula 1 at the

end of 1976, his departure marking the end of the US involvement in Formula 1 at constructor team level. Formula 1 was the sideline for Penske, his main business being in America. He kept the factory in Poole to produce cars for America. Penske's decision left John Watson without a job, but he was signed up by Bernie Ecclestone to partner Carlos Pace.

Ronnie Peterson knew that Robin Herd would never be able to provide him with a really competitive car, and although he loved it at March, when an offer came from Tyrell to replace Scheckter who had gone to Wolf, he took it. Brambilla left and went to Surtees. The Shadow team had not done well for Don Nichols and his sponsor Universal Oil Products; a couple of pole positions were all they had to show for their efforts and as a consequence UOP pulled out at the end of 1975. Tony Southgate had gone to Lotus and Jack Oliver had turned from driving to raising sponsorship, and he was successful with Tabatip cigarillos and with an Italian financier, Franco Ambrosio.

Following the coverage of the 1976 Japanese Grand Prix, the BBC started to take Formula 1 much more seriously. Jonathan Martin, a BBC sports producer with a love of the sport, worked with Ecclestone in his capacity as the head of F1CA to make motor racing more of a TV spectacle. The BBC initiated a significant change when it replaced Raymond Baxter, the rather upper-class, somewhat detached if not actually aloof outside broadcast presenter for the more racy, pure enthusiast commentator Murray Walker. It was an inspired move, bringing the sport increasingly into line with the mood of the times, a long overdue cultural change.

The calendar had grown to 17 Grands Prix, the first in Argentina. James Hunt gave a World Champion's performance in qualifying, putting the M23 on pole position from John Watson, Depailler for Tyrell and Lauda, but all four retired in the race with mechanical problems. Jody Scheckter won in

the Wolf followed by Mario Andretti in the Lotus 78, its first outing. Andretti nearly did much better, for he had been disputing second place with Pace when a wheel bearing collapsed. The Lotus 78's undercar wings were contained in wide side pods on the car, but those caused little comment in the pits and paddock.

Before the start of the European rounds of the World Championship, Carlos Pace was killed in a light aircraft accident in Brazil, a personal blow to Bernie Ecclestone, which also left Brabham without a No.1 driver. Ecclestone replaced him with Hans Stuck from March, but soon afterwards he started very secret discussions with Niki Lauda for 1978. What was sauce for the Ferrari goose with Reuterman in 1976, was sauce for the Brabham gander in 1977.

In the US (West) Grand Prix at Long Beach, Scheckter led most of the race, once again showing his class, until a slow puncture made the Wolf unstable. Mario Andretti and Gunnar Nilsson had shaken the Lotus 78 down and just before the flag Andretti passed Scheckter in the 'ground effects' car to win its first race. Andretti followed that up by taking pole in the Spanish Grand Prix, then leading from start to finish. Slowly it started to dawn on people that Colin Chapman had once again come up with something special.

The entry for the British Grand Prix was 41, and for the first time, a pre-qualifying process was introduced to sort out the no-hopers. One driver who passed the pre-qualifying and went to ninth on the grid in his first Grand Prix appearance was young Canadian driver Gilles Villeneuve, driving for McLaren. James Hunt won with Lauda second. Lauda then won in Germany, with Scheckter second. In Austria Lauda was second to Alan Jones who gave Shadow its first victory. Lauda won in Holland too, making it very clear that he was far from past his best as Ferrari had speculated. Enzo Ferrari had a very good intelligence system and he got wind of the deal between Lauda and Ecclestone. Just after the Dutch Grand Prix the

Breakthrough: James Hunt in the M23 McLaren
in 1976, making it the fifth kit car team to win
the Driver's Championship.

deal was announced, with Parmalat, an Italian dairy products company footing the bill. There was nothing Ferrari could do about it except ask young Gilles Villeneuve to come to Maranello to discuss signing for 1978.

Mario Andretti won the Italian Grand Prix at Monza with Lauda second. Ferrari had not signed Villeneuve and now wanted Andretti, a hero for Italian fans because of his Italian origins. But even in the new commercial world, Andretti's relationship with Chapman was stronger than the inducements Ferrari offered with promises of huge financial rewards. Andretti stayed at Lotus.

The heated speculation about Lauda's replacement at Ferrari swirled around the deciding race, the US Grand Prix, where Lauda needed just one point to take the Championship. Ferrari was outraged at Lauda's decision to leave the *scuderia*

and he tried to bully Lauda, to no avail. In his anger, Ferrari even phoned Lauda's mechanic, the hugely popular Ermanno Cuoghi, to ask if he was leaving with Lauda. When Cuoghi honestly said he was thinking about it, Ferrari fired him on the spot. For Lauda the race was simply a matter of getting enough points to take the Championship. James Hunt was on pole, then Stuck, Watson, Andretti, Peterson and Reuterman ahead of Lauda. Hunt won with Andretti second, Scheckter third and Lauda fourth, making him Champion for the second time in three years. Ferrari was delighted with the victory but Lauda was so disgusted with Ferrari's treatment of Cuoghi that he told Ferrari that he would not compete in the last two races of the season, making Ferrari even more furious. So the man who more than any other had restored the Ferrari fortunes with two World Championships

Sponsor-free zone: the privately financed Hesketh team was as professional as any on the grid. Hunt took 4th in both title races in 1975.

after a decade in the doldrums, left amid great acrimony.

Ferrari brought forward the signing of Gilles Villeneuve for the Canadian Grand Prix. He was just the kind of driver Enzo Ferrari liked, fearless to the brink of destruction, committed to winning at all costs, a racer. Scheckter won in Canada and Hunt won in Japan, but the season ended on a sad note when Villeneuve went off the track at Fuji and killed two spectators. Ferrari had won both titles but Mario Andretti had won four Grands Prix in 1977 in the Lotus 78 to Lauda's 3 and Scheckter's 3, and Lotus was second in the Constructors' Championship. The Lotus 78 had been the car of the year, with Andretti leading more laps in the whole season than any other driver, prompting his most famous remark about the car, 'it feels like it's painted to the road'.

Shadow reached a parlous financial state in 1977 which led to a split in the team. Tony Southgate had returned, only to join the exodus to form Arrows, a team like March, whose name came from the men who were behind it: Franco Ambrosio, Alan Rees, Jack Oliver, Dave Wass and Tony Southgate, both designers. The A1 cars were painted gold, the colour of its sponsor, Warsteiner beer. During 1977 Gunnar Nilsson had been diagnosed with stomach cancer and he left Lotus; he signed for Arrows but was never well enough to drive and died in October 1978. The team took on Riccardo Patrese instead. No sooner had Arrows produced its first car than Don Nichols of Shadow issued a High Court writ claiming damages arising from the similarity between the new Arrows and the most recent Shadow, which had come from the same design team. Nichols was successful in his action and the Arrows team had to go back to the drawing board. Ambrosio was later jailed for fraud in Italy.

Chapman replaced Gunnar Nilsson with Ronnie Peterson although Andretti had serious misgivings about Chapman's choice. Two drivers going for the Championship in the same team would spread resources too thinly, could cause friction, and could conceivably lead to accidents as had happened in Brazil in 1976 when the two had been in the team together for just the one race.

Chapman was already at work on the Lotus 79 for 1978, taking the idea of the 'ground-effect' car even further. However, progress was slow and it was not ready for the first part of the 1978 season, so Andretti and Peterson had to use the Lotus 78 instead.

Undercar aerodynamics was just one revolution taking place in 1977; the other was turbocharging, which had been used at Indianapolis, particularly in qualifying, since 1967. Turbocharging involved placing a small turbine in the exhaust gases, which was used to force fuel into the engine under pressure, increasing power. Renault, which had won the first ever Grand Prix in 1906, had re-entered motor sport in the 1970s through rallying. It had developed a 1.5-litre V6 engine which had carried it to dominance by 1976 and its engineers were looking to develop a turbo version of the engine which could also be suitable for the supercharged category in Formula 1. Renault started its Formula 1 programme in 1975 and by 1978 it had a Formula 1 team based on the Renault RS01 car fitted with a Renault-Gordini EF1 turbo engine with André de Cortanze and Jean-Pierre Jabouille as drivers.

Williams had not done well in 1977. The accounts showed that the company turned over £487,000 in 1977 on which it made a profit of £593, but in December Frank Williams unveiled the FW06 in a blaze of publicity to please his new sponsor, Saudia, the Saudi Arabian national airline which had contributed £30,000. The deal had

been initiated through the airline's advertising agency in London where a friend of Williams' worked. It was Frank Williams who had worked very hard to make it happen, building up a strong relationship with Sheik Kemel Sinahi, the president of Saudia, who was there to celebrate the deal. It turned out to be the catalyst which put the Williams organization on a sound financial footing. On the strength of the sponsorship he had taken on Alan Jones at a salary of £40,000 a year.

The Saudi connection expanded when Charles Chrichton-Stuart, one of the fun-loving young men with whom Frank Williams had shared a flat in the early 1960s, who was now selling top-of-the-range cars in Kensington, sold a Ferrari to a member of the Saudi Arabian Royal Family, Prince Sultan bin Salman in January 1978. Frank Williams met Prince Sultan and suggested a sponsorship deal. Following this, Frank was invited to Saudi Arabia where he met the son of King Fahd, Prince Mohammed bin Fahd, whose large business interests were managed through a holding company called Albilad. Williams explained what he felt sponsorship could do for the Prince and his company and left for England. Nothing happened for some time, then Jonathan Aitken MP contacted Williams on behalf of Prince Fahd asking to see him. They met, and Aitken explained that the Prince would be coming to London soon and would Williams come to meet him again at the Dorchester Hotel. Williams did better than that – he dressed an FW06 car in Albilad livery and delivered it to the Dorchester on a transporter for the Prince, who was delighted. The next stage was to arrange for the Prince to visit the World Championship's own piece of high society action, the Monaco Grand Prix.

As Williams' finances improved, so March continued to hover near crisis, and Max Mosley decided after seven years that the endless struggle between finance and motor racing was an unequal one. They had gained no points in 1977 and Formula 2 sales were down because the March was out of date. The same prospect loomed in Formula 1 where Colin Chapman had come up with a new, technical revolution which was going to be very costly to emulate. Mosley had developed a strong and close relationship with Bernie Ecclestone at F1CA and in 1978 he decided to quit March and join Ecclestone full-time, selling his shares to Herd, the only one of the original four left.

Ecclestone had cultivated his relationship with Jonathan Martin at the BBC, and in 1978 the BBC sports department finally decided to show the whole racing season. It could not transmit all the races live, partly for reasons of cost, but also because it could not accept the technical quality of the broadcasts from some of the overseas broadcasters. They decided to use Murray Walker to do the commentary as the race happened, then put the race out as an edited package later in the day. It was a breakthrough – a major broadcaster had accepted that showing the whole World Championship was a good idea. The Championship was on its way to becoming an international television event, exactly what Ecclestone wanted.

The mid-1970s saw a sea-change in the relationship between the teams and the track owners. This was down to Bernie Ecclestone who bound his fellow constructors together in the common cause of extracting more money out of each race. First he made all the F1CA teams agree to commit to appearing at all Grands Prix, then by guaranteeing the track owner the top teams and the top drivers from F1CA's ten members, they could promote the races more heavily. In exchange he asked for and got around $500,000 from each track owner. Where entries exceeded the size of the grid, 22 places were reserved for F1CA members and Ferrari, after which pre-qualifying came into force and the best of the rest had to compete for the remaining places. The arrangement not only increased the money coming into the teams through F1CA, it increased its power in relation to the FIA and the CSI, a shift of power of immense significance to the structure of the World Championship.

In the opening of the European leg of the Championship at Monaco Frank Williams' guests arrived from Saudi Arabia. They included Prince Sultan, Prince Mohammed and a young Franco-Saudi, Mansour Ojjeh, whose father owned Techniques Avant Garde (TAG), a high-technology research and development company with many government contracts which acted as a go-between in defence contracts between Saudi Arabia and France. Mansour Ojjeh was enchanted with Formula 1, and following the race he spoke with his father; and Frank Williams was soon making more trips to Saudi Arabia. The trips produced sponsorship from a string of businesses, some of which did not benefit directly from involvement with Formula 1 but were part of the Prince's network of business associates. Bin Laden was in road building, Baroom was in steel and Dallah serviced aircraft. Albilad put in £200,000, Saudia raised its contribution to £100,000, and between them, with Goodyear providing Williams with the latest soft compound tyres, the sponsorship amounted to £500,000. This was Williams' budget to compete in all the races, which gave him back his F1CA membership at the end of 1978, making a challenge for the Championship possible.

Patrick Depailler won Monaco for Tyrell, then Chapman brought the Lotus 79 in from testing for the Belgian Grand Prix. Andretti took pole, and led from start to finish, pursued at first by Villeneuve until Peterson passed him to finish second. It was another landmark, not only for Lotus, but for Formula 1. Like the Lotus 25, the Lotus 49 and the Lotus 72, when Chapman got things right they worked superbly. Andretti and Peterson were together again on the front row of the grid in Spain and, after some harassment from Hunt, gave Chapman a second and consecutive Lotus 1-2, and this time Andretti took fastest lap. The Lotus 79's performance had been noted by all the teams. It was not difficult to copy, but the detail had to be

Pit stop: Bernie Eccleston of Brabham and Max Mosley of March confer in 1977 before they joined forces at F1CA.

meticulously researched and would take time, but most of the teams started doing so.

Gordon Coppuck's Brabham-Alfa BT46B Fan Car made its debut at the Swedish Grand Prix at Anderstorp and it drew a lot of attention. It was designed to achieve the same ends as the Lotus 79 but by different means, the fan doing the work of the wings. The fan was said to be 70 percent for cooling and 30 percent for suction, but it was not ducted to the radiators, undermining that argument and five teams protested before the race, to no avail. Lauda won, breaking the Lotus run, and Colin Chapman and Ken Tyrell both protested to the CSI after the race. Ecclestone tried to get an agreement through F1CA that it would be abandoned at the end of the year, but the CSI said no, despite having passed the system in the development stage and it had to go, although in the curious logic of Formula 1, the result of the contentious race stood.

The runaway Lotus success was too much for the motor racing establishment and on the Saturday before the Dutch Grand Prix an announcement by the FIA set the scene for a power struggle which would dwarf all others in Formula 1. Jean-Marie Balestre, the newly elected president of the FIA and the CSI, announced that skirts could remain for the rest of the season, but that from 1979 they would be banned. The F1CA teams, which had all invested so much in developing the system and saw it as the only way to counter the potential superiority of the turbo engine over the Cosworth, met and announced they would ignore the ban.

James Hunt had only 8 points to show for the season and before the Italian Grand Prix, Teddy Mayer told him that he would not be renewing his contract for 1979. Andretti was on pole at Monza but the new Ferrari star, Gilles Villeneuve, was alongside him, then Lauda, the former Ferrari star. Peterson could keep his Championship hopes alive by winning, but he had switched to a spare car, a Lotus 78 after crashing the 79 in practice.

The start was a shambles; the lights were turned to green as the back markers were still driving on to their grid positions. When those at the back saw Villeneuve away first, they got going again, bunching up the middle of the grid where Peterson, Hunt and Riccardo Patrese, the second McLaren driver, touched. Peterson's Lotus bounced into Brambilla's Surtees, then into the barrier, then back on to the track in flames. Regazzoni, Hunt and Depailler were out of their cars in seconds and dashed into the flames to pull Peterson out. They laid him down on the track suffering serious injuries, including two broken legs. Out went the red flags, but when Villeneuve and Andretti arrived at the end of the first lap, the crowd gave a cheer to see a Ferrari in the lead. It took an ambulance 20 minutes to arrive to take Peterson and Brambilla to hospital.

Of all the people in Formula 1, Peterson was one of the most agreeable, a man without enemies among his fellow drivers, universally liked, and the seriousness of his injuries cast a particularly gloomy mood over the proceedings. It took a long time to clear the track; the crowd became restless and began to jeer because clearly a debate was going on as to whether the race should be restarted which, against some drivers' wishes, it was. Villeneuve and Andretti made early starts and were penalized one minute each, then Villeneuve led for most of the race. Andretti overtook him on the track to take the flag, followed by Lauda, but once the penalties were applied, Andretti was placed sixth, giving him just one point. With Peterson out of the race Andretti was already Champion. Lauda, the official winner, made his point in his usual pungent way by failing to pick up the trophy. That night, doctors operated on Peterson's legs but there were complications and he died.

Lotus was granted the freedom of the city of Norwich and there were great celebrations at Ketteringham Hall, but just at the height of its new success, Lotus started to lose its way again. John Player was retrenching and after 10 years it

World Champions 1978: Mario Andretti with
Colin Chapman and the Lotus 78, the kit car
teams' answer to turbocharged engines.

decided to stop backing Lotus. Happily, a new sponsor was at hand for 1979, Martini & Rossi. It was also at this time that Chapman met David Thieme of Essex Petroleum, an oil broker who had made a huge fortune out of the growth and volatility of the international oil market. Thieme's main interest was in being part of such an exciting world and using it as a base for corporate hospitality for his oil industry friends. On the technical front, Chapman was determined to stay ahead, but rather than develop the ground effects principle further, he started looking at new revolutionary ways to stay ahead and in doing so he began to lose direction. He also had the opportunity to sign either of the two Ferrari drivers, Reuterman and Villeneuve, and he chose Reuterman to replace Peterson.

Ferrari replaced Reuterman with Jody Scheckter from Wolf, continuing the usual round of musical chairs which had been given an added twist by the death of Ronnie Peterson. Ecclestone replaced John Watson with Nelson Piquet, the son of a former Brazilian Minister for Health who had distinguished himself in Formula 3. Teddy Mayer signed up Watson to replace James Hunt who completed the circle by taking Scheckter's seat at Wolf. Frank Williams took on Clay Regazzoni to partner Alan Jones.

Ferrari took on a new sporting director in 1978, Marco Piccinini, the son of a banking family in Monaco. The family bank, the Principe Société de Banque de Monaco, was widely believed to have financial links with Enzo Ferrari who needed a loyal emissary who could go to races and report on the team's performance. Piccinini was a consummate diplomat and by starting out close to Enzo Ferrari, he got to know how Ferrari wanted matters reported and handled. Piccinini became a courtier, a buffer between the old man and reality, smoothing his master's passage through disputes both internally and in relations with the other branches of the Formula 1 family.

The big manufacturers were stirring again. Alfa Romeo decided to field its own Formula 1 team with Carlo Chiti as boss, although it continued to supply engines to Brabham. Renault was ready for 1978 with its turbocharged engine, and Ferrari, in the doldrums again, also embarked on turbocharging. All three chose to progress with more powerful engines rather than ground effects, believing that the ban on skirts and ground effects by the CSI would hold.

The Lotus 79 was devised as a way of increasing competitiveness over the other Cosworth teams, as well as over Ferrari, Renault and Alfa Romeo engine power, but it suddenly became the underlying theme of the survival of the kit car teams. Ground effects was nothing less than a revolution in racing car design, and it would be copied widely on both sides of the Atlantic. But of the huge number of Formula 1 teams in 1978, only a few had the resources and skills to copy it and at the small end of the scale, some of the more hopeful teams gave up the struggle against rising costs and power politics. A number of well-known drivers including Surtees, Kauhsen, Merzario, Kojima and Lec, all decided to call it a day at the end of the 1978 season.

The Lotus 79 was one of those periodic step changes in the development of Formula 1 which made all other designs look very old fashioned in a single season. McLaren had been pushed off its position as the leading kit car team, first by Lauda and Ferrari, then by the Lotus 79. Marlboro was concerned. Gordon Coppuck's version of Colin Chapman's wing car, the M28, turned out to be very poor indeed. At Williams, Patrick Head started work on his first ground effects car, the FW07, in December 1978 and it was very close to the Lotus 79, although Head had done all the research himself in the same wind tunnel at Imperial College in London. Ken Tyrell ordered Maurice Philippe to build a ground effects car, the 009, based on the Lotus 79. Gordon Murray's first ground effects car, BT48, was rolled out at Christmas 1978 and at Shadow, ATS, Wolf,

Fittipaldi, Arrows, Ensign and RAM, the designers all went down the same route.

The two sides in the power struggle were crystallizing. Jean-Marie Balestre, who was elected President of the CSI in October 1978, had felt the power of the F1CA teams over their unequivocal statement to ignore the ban on skirts and he gave in, preferring to keep his powder dry for the struggles to come. To recover some of what he saw as the legitimate power of the FIA, he began to impose himself on the organization of the sport by introducing new rules and tightening regulations. One of his first actions, as if to signal a new era in which he intended to exert far more influence, was to change the name of the CSI to the Fédération Internationale Sportiv de l'Automobile (FISA), signifying greater autonomy from the FIA.

Recovering the power to regulate and set the rules was one thing, but the F1CA teams believed that what Balestre really wanted was to smash the lucrative package deals which Bernie Ecclestone had arranged with track owners. These deals concerned the amounts track owners paid in starting money and prize money which, combined with television coverage fees, provided much of the teams' income. After several years of hard work, the team bosses believed they owned the right to negotiate over money, and the FIA, with its old-guard stance, had lost it by default.

The Formula 1 Constructors' Association also changed its name, slightly, in 1978. F1CA, the acronym, was a very rude word in Italian, which some thought might have been deliberate, so it was changed to FOCA. However, far greater changes were going on underneath in response to the appointment of Balestre. Bernie Ecclestone had a clear understanding that there was a power struggle looming and he also set about consolidating his position in the organization. On 6 January 1978 it was announced that Peter Mackintosh would leave and Ecclestone would become president and chief executive of administration of FOCA. Max Mosley was appointed legal advisor and Enzo Ferrari was made president of sport. The General Purposes Committee was dissolved and shortly afterwards, the FOCA offices were moved to a building at Brabham's headquarters in Chessington from which Ecclestone ran not only Brabham but the body which represented all the teams.

The two organizations within motor racing were squaring up to each other for a classic power struggle which nearly brought the World Championship to its knees.

Flying Finn: 1982 World Champion Keke Rosberg gained a reputation for commitment to Williams against McLaren, Ferrari and Renault.

5

SPORTING POWER
VERSUS MONEY POWER

The change in status of top sportsmen and women from amateur to professional was one of the great battles in sport as more top athletes wanted to profit directly from their talent. Amateurism had been the basis of the organization of most sports, but that started breaking down in the 1960s. The process was part of the breaking down of social conventions in the 1960s, but the catalyst was the powerful cocktail of sponsorship and television which increased the value of individual success. One of the inevitable consequences was a creeping commercialism in the organization of all sports, and a shift of power from the governing bodies to the performers.

The performers in the World Championships were the drivers and the teams they drove for, and the money which came from the deals arranged by Ecclestone was their lifeblood. It also gave them power which was expressed through the negotiating muscle it gave FOCA and they were not about to see the clocks put back without a fight.

In Formula 1, the battle between FISA and FOCA was a bitter internecine, protracted war in which the industry interests and the kit car teams clashed openly for control of the purse strings. In so doing, they threatened the very survival of the two World Championships. FISA operated through national automobile clubs such as the ACF in France and the RAC in Britain, which sanctioned races in their countries under arrangements with governments. The national clubs, although they issued licences and sanctioned races, were increasingly out of touch with the teams and could not represent them. The failure of national and international systems to stay on top of motor racing as it developed in the 1960s and 1970s gave teams the opportunity to seize power through FOCA.

It was control of the purse strings which Jean-Marie Balestre, president of FISA, wanted back in his hands. Having lost the opening skirmish with FOCA over the banning of skirts, Balestre took a longer view, but the weapons in his battles with

Ecclestone remained legal and administrative. Balestre was determined to seize power for FISA directly, not through the clubs, under the banner of what he called 'sporting power'. In doing so, he prompted a split in the sport which occurred along national as well as motor industry lines. The French and Italians saw Formula 1 as a national enterprise while the British saw it as a business based on a sport. Alfa Romeo, Ferrari, Renault, Matra and Ligier backed FISA, which in turn was backed by their paymasters, the manufacturers. Lotus, Brabham, Williams, McLaren, Tyrell and Wolf backed FOCA and Ecclestone. Ligier, although it was more like the kit car teams in composition and size, sided with FISA because of its links to the French establishment and Matra which supplied its V12 engines.

Engine power and car design were also fault lines in the world of Formula 1. The FISA teams had the resources to go down the turbocharged route while the FOCA teams did not. Following Renault's introduction of the RE30 turbo, Ferrari, Alfa and Matra were all determined to abandon their flat 12 and V12 engines with which they had struggled to keep the Cosworth DFV at bay. Ferrari was planning a V6 turbo for 1981, Carlo Chiti at Alfa Romeo was also planning for turbos, but building their own turbos would take time and in the meantime both continued to develop their 12 cylinder engines.

The development of turbo power put the FOCA teams in much the same position as their predecessors had been in 1961 and 1966 when the change in formula had left the kit car teams without a suitable engine. The situation was worse in 1978 because they had no immediate source of turbo engines and could not afford the price of development. Worse, the FISA teams could easily use ground effects while they remained legal, combined with turbo power. The original turbo-powered Renault RS01 had no ground effects, but Michel Tetu introduced them in the RS10 for 1979. Mauro Foghieri introduced some ground effects in the new Ferrari 312T4, and he was working to give the 312T5 for 1980 even more. The Alfa Romeo 177 was flat bottomed, but Chiti was working on a narrower V12 to replace the flat 12 to give the 179 greater flexibility in using ground effects for 1980 until his turbos were ready. Ligier switched from the Matra V12 to the Cosworth DFV for 1979 in the JS11 and continued to hover uncomfortably between the two camps as the regulations governing ground effects and turbo power were turned into weapons.

The FOCA teams continued to refine their aerodynamic advantage based on the Lotus 79. Chapman's two drivers, Mario Andretti and Carlos Reuterman, were unhappy with the Lotus 80. The idea behind it was to extend the undercar wing area right to the rear, dispensing with the conventional rear wing, but there were problems and they reverted to the Lotus 79s for the start of the season. At Brabham, Gordon Murray had tried, like Lotus, to do away with the rear wing but had to fit one on the BT48 Brabham-Alfa.

The 1979 season started unexpectedly well for Ligier with its Cosworth engine. Laffite put in a fantastic qualifying lap to take pole in Buenos Aires, then won. There had been an eight-car pile up at the start which was later blamed on John Watson. Balestre imposed a fine of 10,000 Swiss francs, which did nothing to improve his already strained relations with Ecclestone. Laffite repeated his win in Brazil. The Brazilian Grand Prix showed just how much of a disaster the McLaren M28 was, and Teddy Mayer had to authorize Gordon Coppuck to start a completely new car.

A number of the new cars made their debuts in the Spanish Grand Prix, including the Williams FW07, the McLaren M28B and the Renault RS10, but the newly confident Ligier team under Gerard Ducarouge, managed to overhaul its Ferrari rival with a win for Patrick Depailler. Jody Scheckter then came through at Spa and Monaco for Ferrari. James Hunt retired after this race – he did not like losing and the Wolf was uncompetitive. The French revival was confirmed by a near-perfect result at the French Grand Prix at Dijon where Jean-Pierre Jabouille put the Renault RS11 on pole and won, the first victory for turbo power, by a French driver in an all-French car with French fuel and tyres. The magic of a Renault 1-2 win was only stopped because the two Ferrari drivers, Scheckter and Villeneuve, had a great fight for second place which took Villeneuve up into second place ahead of René Arnoux. It was a great day for the Renault team, its first Grand Prix victory for over 73 years.

The FISA teams were on top, and it fell to Williams, Jones, Regazzoni and the FW07 to fight back for FOCA at the British Grand Prix. Jones wiped five seconds off the Silverstone lap record but his water pump failed and Regazzoni won, giving Williams its first Grand Prix victory. Frank Williams even received a congratulatory telegram from Enzo Ferrari. The Williams run continued at the German Grand Prix which Alan Jones won with Regazzoni second, a 1-2 for Williams, and following that race, Mansour Ojjeh sent his private Boeing airliner to take the team to Austria for the next Grand Prix, which Jones won again, following it up with victory in Holland.

Williams' four victories put Jones third in the title race behind Laffite and Scheckter, two points ahead of Villeneuve. Scheckter could clinch both World Championships by winning at Monza, and while Regazzoni did his best to stop them, Scheckter won with Villeneuve second, a Ferrari 1-2, as well as the two title wins.

Hunt's retirement after the French Grand Prix had been a surprise, but an even greater surprise came in Canada when his great friend and rival Niki Lauda also quit. He had started out in practice for the Canadian Grand Prix in the BT49 which had been awaited with great anticipation, but after practice he told Bernie Ecclestone he wanted to retire. Ecclestone made no attempt to stop him, he knew that a driver in that frame of mind could make a fatal mistake. Ecclestone had

Entre nous: Bernie Ecclestone and FIA president Jean-Marie Balestre at Monza in 1979 during the phoney part of the FOCA/FISA war.

been close to a number of drivers who had died and, decisive as ever, when Lauda wanted to go, he made no fuss; the two men parted with mutual respect. Lauda wanted to spend more time with his airline, a business which he had built up on earnings from his driving.

With five victories in the ground effects FW07 Williams had shown that the FOCA teams could fight back. TAG was a major source of funds, but to meet the £2m budget, Williams needed more, and this time a sponsor came to him. Leyland, the British truck and bus company which was keen to do business in Saudi Arabia, approached Williams who was happy to take £1m for the season and associate Leyland with his host of Saudi sponsors. The FW07B was named Saudia-Leyland and

Carlos Reuterman replaced Clay Regazzoni for the 1980 season.

As one relationship was flourishing and producing results, another was souring. At the end of 1979 the relationship between Brabham and Alfa Romeo, a relationship across the FOCA/FISA divide, was no longer tenable. Alfa was planning its own Formula 1 team and would naturally align itself with Ferrari and Renault. At the end of the year Gordon Murray was back on the drawing board to put together a new car for 1980 based on the Cosworth engine.

The relationship between McLaren and Marlboro was also souring. The man at Marlboro was Paddy McNally, who had joined after a career as a journalist, racing driver and *bon-viveur* in James

It's good to talk: Ecclestone and Brazilian World Champion Nelson Piquet, who won 2 World Championships together in 1981 and 1983.

Hunt's World Championship year. He counselled keeping John Watson in the team whose performances were undeniably good on the track. He also advised that Patrick Tambay be let go while introducing Mayer to another young French driver, Alain Prost. McNally also suggested that Mayer take on John Barnard, who had been part of the design team which had built the highly successful McLaren M23.

Barnard was a perfectionist, uncompromising in his demands for everything to be just right. One of the reasons he had parted company with McLaren earlier was that he was unhappy with the rather free-wheeling, informal atmosphere. He preferred more discipline, and he found it working for Jim Hall in Texas, designing the Chaparral 2K Indy Car which won the 1980 PPG World Series. He left Chaparral because he felt he had not been given sufficient credit for the 2K. Barnard would have gone back to McLaren, but he refused to join unless Gordon Coppuck went, and despite pressure from McNally, Mayer refused. Instead, Barnard joined that other perfectionist, Ron Dennis, at his Project Four team based at Wokingham in Surrey.

Project Four was also the beneficiary of Marlboro sponsorship. Its great success in 1979 had been in ProCar racing, a series of races using identical BMW M1 cars. Niki Lauda was backed by Marlboro in the ProCar series and Marlboro contracted Project Four to prepare and look after the BMW in which he won the 1979 ProCar title which strengthened Dennis's relationship with Marlboro and Niki Lauda.

Dennis was determined to move into Formula 1. He had approached Patrick Head at Williams to join Project Four but Head remained with Williams; he then tried Gordon Murray at Brabham with the same result. So when Barnard was introduced via Marlboro, Dennis took him on. By mid-1980 there was a revolutionary Formula 1 car on the drawing board at Project Four, revolutionary because carbon fibre was used to build it. Ron Dennis had used carbon to make the

wings on Niki Lauda's BMW and he showed it to Barnard who then started thinking about making the whole monocoque out of the very light and strong material. They knew it would be very expensive, but if it worked, it would lighten the car appreciably, a step as revolutionary as undercar aerodynamics and turbocharging.

At the heart of the tangled web of relationships in Formula 1 was that between Jean-Marie Balestre and Bernie Ecclestone. The gulf between them on the issues was as wide as that between their personalities. Ecclestone was a quiet, private man with a neat, tidy mind, for whom everything had to be in order, with clear practical rules, no mess, no fudges in decision-making. Choices should be made, preferably out of the limelight with maximum profit. He wanted stronger representation in FISA debates, he wanted higher purses and lower costs, and saw turbos as hugely expensive. He thought things through very carefully before acting, planning his tactics to suit the ground, then taking up a very firm stand and sticking to it come what may.

By contrast, Balestre was loud, pompous, public and prone to taking arbitrary decisions such as imposing sudden fines or changing rules. He would try to bully his way through problems and disagreements, relying on the presumed power of his office rather than the reality of power on the ground. He was, as a consequence, often treated with ridicule in the press.

The nasty side of politics bubbled to the surface at Kyalami. Just two weeks before the South African race, Balestre had introduced, via an Extraordinary Meeting of the FISA Executive Committee, a ban on skirts from 1981. This ignored the rule that two years' notice had to be given of any technical change unless it was on grounds of safety; there was a feeling that it was a decision to demonstrate his power and decisiveness. Balestre had a reputation for being indecisive and he also had a reputation as a jingoistic patriot; with three Frenchmen from three French teams on the podium he could not resist attempting to mount the victory rostrum and was physically thrown off for his trouble. He was also developing a reputation for arbitrariness. The drivers, always interested in safety, had presented a package of measures to improve safety, but at that time the one and only suggestion that Balestre concentrated on was the banning of skirts, which seemed to be a ploy to break the power of the FOCA teams. The teams had invested huge amounts of money in the technology and were not going to see their advantage removed by a man who was not directly involved in racing and who had little technical understanding of it. After the South African race, Balestre did propose more safety measures including the reinforcement of footwells and cockpits, a reduction of wheel widths and, most controversially, obligatory briefings for drivers before races.

The US (West) Grand Prix was next. Nelson Piquet took pole position for Brabham with René Arnoux second and Patrick Depailler third for Alfa Romeo. Piquet won, his first Grand Prix victory, and the first for Brabham in the new Cosworth car. Sadly, it was Clay Regazzoni's last race – he crashed at 180 mph and was trapped in the car for 25 minutes. Spinal injuries confined him to a wheelchair. Once again, the politics of safety bubbled over when Balestre announced within 24 hours of the race that FISA would conduct an investigation into safety to see if design could be improved, which was accepted as right and proper. He then went on to pronounce that any accelerated timetable to increase safety was as a result of safety being 'sacrificed by certain constructors for the benefit of speed'. In the statement, he included Alain Prost's crash at Kyalami in which he had broken his wrist. The FOCA teams were outraged. Teddy Mayer wrote him a blistering letter, pointing out that not only were his comments potentially libellous, but that Prost had survived a far more serious accident in his McLaren unscathed. He accused Balestre of

lacking the technical understanding to make any such statement, of making 'cheap political points', and that it was impossible to build a car which was safe in a 150-mph crash and that Regazzoni had been lucky to escape alive from such an accident. Balestre backed down a month later, although he did not retract his remarks. The Safety Committee stated that it did not feel that any of the cars were unsafe and that Regazzoni's survival said a great deal for the safety of Formula 1 cars.

The political row deepened. At the FIA World Congress in Rio, a FISA Plenary Conference ratified Balestre's banning of skirts and suspended the result of the South African Grand Prix pending the outcome of an inquiry into the incident when Balestre had been prevented from mounting the podium. FOCA was also outlawed from taking any part in the organization of World Championship races, in a clear attempt to weaken its arrangements with the track owners over money and television. In the aftermath, the legality of the process by which the new rules had been introduced was challenged and the FIA was asked to judge. Balestre announced that he would resign unless it found in his favour.

The next World Championship race should have been the Spanish Grand Prix, but Jarama, near Madrid became the scene of a showdown between FOCA and FISA. Eighteen drivers had not attended the compulsory FISA briefings before the Belgian and Monaco Grands Prix and been fined by Balestre, but their fines had not been paid. Balestre promptly suspended their licences until the fines were paid. Ecclestone responded by saying that unless the fines were withdrawn, the FOCA teams would not race. It was a trial of strength. The Spanish Automobile Club (RACE) offered to deposit a sum equivalent to the fines but Balestre was adamant, they had to be paid by the drivers, or they could not race. After a great deal of fruitless negotiation between RACE, FOCA and FISA, the Spanish Grand Prix was cancelled. RACE, which had delegated its powers to the

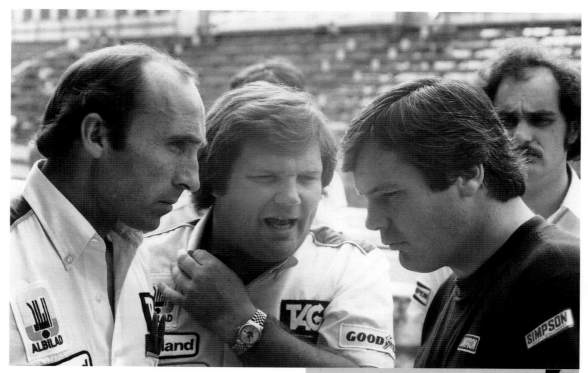

Tête-à-tête: Frank Williams, Patrick Head and Alan Jones, Champion in 1980, the core talent at Williams, the 6th kit car team to take the title.

Federation Espagnol de Automovilismo (FEA), took its powers back and sanctioned the race under FIA regulations, circumventing Balestre, supported by Ecclestone and the FOCA teams. Renault, Ferrari and Alfa Romeo pulled out. The split between the two was now out in the open.

The race took place, and Alan Jones won for Williams, but the following day, the FIA announced its support for Balestre, that the only proper authority in Spain was the FEA, and that therefore the race was not only illegal but the points did not count towards the World Championship. The FIA also endorsed Balestre's position over the introduction of new rules. The cancellation of the Jarama result was doubly frustrating for Jones because the win would have put him into the lead in the Championship

whereas he stayed in third place behind Piquet and Arnoux. Prost had another accident when the McLaren M29's suspension broke.

In response, FOCA threatened to boycott the French Grand Prix and as part of the fallout, Goodyear announced that unless the FOCA/FISA matters were sorted out, it would pull out, an indication that the sponsors were fed up with the battle. They called a meeting in Lausanne to find a compromise, which was agreed by the FISA representatives at the meeting but rejected by Balestre. Ecclestone responded by announcing that unless the compromise was accepted, they would break away and run their own series. Balestre saw Bernie Ecclestone as the problem. Two weeks before the French Grand Prix, he tried to topple Ecclestone from the presidency of FOCA. He did

Engines: Jean-Pierre Jabouille's turbo Renault RS22, Gilles Villeneuve's flat-12 Ferrari 312T and Didier Pironi's V8 Ligier-Cosworth JS/11.

it by approaching Colin Chapman at the Le Mans 24-hour race where Chapman was visiting for the first time since 1962 when he had fallen out with the organizers. He met Balestre in the FISA caravan where a deal was hammered out which involved Chapman flying to Maranello to meet Enzo Ferrari who would come to a deal acceptable to him and the FOCA teams which involved lifting the ban on skirts and replacing it with a ban on slick tyres instead. The plan was for Chapman to then unseat Ecclestone, following which the proposals would be made to FISA and there would be a grand reconciliation between the opposing parties. When Chapman returned to Britain he swiftly dropped the idea of taking on Ecclestone

and flew to Maranello with Max Mosley at his side to do the negotiating. The result was another big meeting at Heathrow Airport at which a compromise was reached: treaded tyres were agreed as an alternative to the banning of skirts and this time Ecclestone backed off a little, agreeing to pay the fines. It was enough to reprieve the French Grand Prix with Ecclestone looking to the longer term benefit rather than the short term high profile victory. He had made his point, he and FOCA could bring Grand Prix racing to a halt if they wished to.

The French press built up the Grand Prix as an all-French affair, a view endorsed by three French drivers taking up their positions on the front of the grid: Laffite for Ligier, Arnoux for Renault, then Pironi for Ligier. After that came Alan Jones and Carlos Reuterman for Williams, then the second Renault of Jabouille. Laffite took the lead while Pironi and Jones fought for second place after Jabouille's transmission failed on the first lap. Alan Jones won the battle for second place behind Laffite and closed on him, finally getting inside on a corner to snatch the lead on lap 35 and win. It was a great win for Williams and a timely one for FOCA, reinforcing its position as providers of grand spectacle on the track. Jones rubbed in the political as well as sporting victory by taking a Union Jack and parading it on his lap of honour.

Jones then won the British Grand Prix for Williams, still leading the Championship despite having lost the points gained in Spain. Alain Prost came sixth for McLaren, a lap behind the winner, and following the race Renault approached him with the offer of a job, aware that he was doing wonders in an uncompetitive car.

At the end of July the FISA Executive Council met and announced that the grooved tyre compromise agreed at Heathrow was unworkable, so the whole package agreed would be dropped, meaning that the ban on skirts would be re-introduced from 1 January 1981. It was another low point. FISA said it would consider technical proposals from FOCA only on the basis of unanimous agreement between the teams. A week later FOCA issued a statement which included the ironic sentence, 'FOCA does not wish to believe that M. Balestre gave his word only to avoid problems at the French Grand Prix'.

The fortunes of the FISA teams were ebbing. In the Italian Grand Prix at Imola, Ferrari came nowhere and kit car teams took all the points, Piquet winning for Brabham followed by the two Williams. The result gave Williams the Constructors' title but lost Alan Jones the lead in the Driver's title. Piquet moved ahead by a point with two races to go. With no Ferrari in the points at Imola, the *scuderia* was in tenth place in the

Constructors' title, Villeneuve joint fifteenth in the Driver's title and Scheckter nineteenth.

Brabham and Williams each took four cars to Montreal for a possible showdown. Piquet took pole by 0.8 of a second from Jones, but at the start it was Didier Pironi for Ferrari who came through from the second row, putting Piquet in the middle with Jones abreast of him on the outside as they went into the first corner. Jones was pulling ahead as Piquet cut across the front of Pironi, then Jones and Piquet touched and Piquet finished up in the wall in a spectacular crash. The debris took an hour to clear. At the restart everybody was very circumspect and Jones led followed by Pironi, then Piquet passed both Pironi and Jones to go into the lead. Piquet's engine blew on lap 23 and if Jones could finish the race in the lead he would take the Championship, while coming second would mean that Piquet would have another chance in the US. Jones held on carefully to finish second behind Pironi, but Pironi had been given a penalty of 1 minute for jumping the start, so Jones and Williams won the Championship.

It was a great year for Williams: Alan Jones won the US Grand Prix, giving him five Grands Prix, making it a top team. Instead of seeking out sponsors, they came to Williams which was useful because oil prices were falling and Middle East producers were feeling the economic downturn.

It was a disastrous year for McLaren: Watson on six points and Prost on five, and Prost had another suspension failure during practice at Watkins Glen, putting the M29 into the wall and leaving him unconscious. Prost was clearly a major talent and he deserved better than the string of mechanical and structural failures, so he decided to quit and go to Renault. Marlboro now turned up the heat on Teddy Mayer and insisted on a merger with Project Four, threatening to remove the sponsorship unless Mayer agreed. Mayer, the realist did agree and Gordon Coppuck left McLaren after 15 years. In September 1980, a new company, McLaren International, was formed with Mayer holding 45

Marlboro man: John Watson's best result in
5 years at McLaren was second in both 1982
Championships alongside Niki Lauda.

percent of the stock, and Ron Dennis and Teddy
Mayer as joint managing directors.

After the triumphs of 1979, the contrast for
Ferrari was stark, and it was nothing to do with the
quality of the drivers. Didier Pironi had ably filled
Jody Scheckter's shoes. Ferrari had been unable to
take full advantage of ground effects technology
which had shown its race-winning qualities and
Ferrari's own turbo engine, the 126, was still in
development. The politics had become intense and
after 20 years it was even beginning to get to
Mauro Foghieri.

It was nothing compared with the politics at the
top of the sport. In September, Jean-Marie
Balestre had given an interview to *L'Equipe*, the
influential French sports magazine, in which he
made clear his intention of taking control, not just
of the sporting power but of the financial side of
Grand Prix racing, to FISA as well. FOCA
submitted alternative technical proposals in late
September, but the showdown came on 7 October
when the FISA Plenary Conference in Paris threw
them out because they did not have support from
all the teams, which was impossible given the split.
It also ruled that all entrants would have to register
by 1 December and that they would be subject to
all FISA regulations including Standard Financial
Regulations which governed all Grands Prix. The
cat was out of the bag – it was about money.

The sponsors threatened to pull out if there
were two Championships and they urged
compromise, suggesting that FISA make the rules
while FOCA ran the finances, but to no avail. By
the end of the month FOCA published a separate

race calendar through a new body, the World Federation of Motor Sport. The WFMS had support from all the FOCA kit car teams and listed 18 races; Ecclestone announced that he had agreements with 15 circuits. Balestre disputed this claim, saying that Ecclestone was disseminating false information. The FOCA teams registered with FISA for 1981, but the row continued over the winter; the FISA teams tested without skirts, Renault and Ferrari with their turbo engines while Alfa Romeo continued with its V12 configuration and Ligier used the Talbot Matra V12.

The prospect of skirts being banned had spurred the FOCA teams to come up with some even more ingenious ways of improving their performance, largely based on reducing weight, to make the most of Cosworth power. FISA raised the minimum weight limit from 580kg to 585kg, which gave an advantage to the FISA teams. At Brabham, Gordon Murray used a hydro-pneumatic suspension system which provided the regulation 6mm clearance between the bottom of the skirts and the track, then lowered the car out on the track to below the minimum ground clearance, then in the pits, the car would rise again for inspection. If anything, this was more dangerous than the skirts. At Lotus Colin Chapman produced the Lotus 88 with two chassis, one which included the monocoque, suspension, engine and gearbox, the other the bodywork and sidepods. When joined at the suspension uprights, the second chassis effectively became a huge aerodynamic wing, acting on the suspension.

The McLaren MP4 took shape over the winter of 1980–81. It was a beautifully finished car with traditional Cosworth engine and Hewland gearbox combination bolted on to a carbon-composite monocoque which cost around $100,000 and was made by the Hercules Corporation in Salt Lake City. The MP4 was the first Formula 1 car to use carbon-composite which was much lighter than aluminium with greater rigidity. Ron Dennis had promised Marlboro that he would win at least one

Grand Prix in 1981 with John Watson and Andrea de Cesaris who had replaced Prost.

There were two other turbo engines on the market by 1981, one from BMW, which had a deal with Bernie Ecclestone to power the BT50 planned for 1981. There was also a British turbo designed and built by Brian Hart, a one-time Cosworth man who had set up on his own. An early customer was a new Formula 1 team, Toleman. Ted Toleman owned the largest vehicle delivery business in Britain. The managing director was Alex Hawkridge, who had started sponsoring club and lower formula races in the 1960s, moved into Formula 2 in the 1970s and been very successful. In 1980 Brian Henton had dominated British Formula 2 in a Toleman car designed by Rory Byrne and Hawkridge decided to move into Formula 1 in 1981 with Byrne's TG181 using a Hart turbo. He arranged sponsorship with an Italian household goods manufacturer, Candy.

The turmoil at the heart of Formula 1 went on behind closed doors, but occasionally the conflict became public: the Argentinian Grand Prix scheduled for January, was postponed, then to put pressure on the FOCA teams, Goodyear withdrew its support. On 7 February, the date set for the South African Grand Prix, Ecclestone went ahead with a World Federation of Motor Sport (WFMS) sanctioned race at Kyalami with an all-FOCA grid: Williams, Tyrell, Brabham, McLaren, Lotus, Ensign, March, Fittipaldi, Arrows and Theodore. The race was won by Carlos Reuterman for Williams. Ecclestone had made his point forcefully. He may be quiet but he was not to be taken lightly; he was a formidable forward thinker who was prepared to act on what he said he would do. Behind closed doors, the point was not lost on Ferrari, Alfa, Talbot-Ligier, and above all Renault, which was in motor racing to promote its cars. Looming ahead was the US (West) Grand Prix at Long Beach, gateway to the huge US market and the threat of cancellation softened their position; Balestre's support started slipping.

Peace was beginning to break out just as the South African race was taking place. The teams had been meeting at the Ferrari headquarters at Maranello in January and produced proposals which were presented to FISA for consideration, while FOCA went ahead with its pirate race at Kylami. A week before the US Grand Prix, FOCA and FISA signed an armistice, the Concorde Agreement, named after Le Place de la Concorde near the FIA headquarters in Paris. Publicly, FISA won the power struggle, but it was a pyrrhic victory for Balestre. The ban on skirts stood and FISA continued to write the rules. Balestre was acknowledged as head of FISA with all the opportunities he wanted to bestride it and make pronouncements, but FOCA got what Ecclestone had always wanted, which was control of the television revenues and the all-important flow of money from the circuit owners, the real prize. He could wait for full control.

The first Grand Prix was the US (West) at Long Beach and there was an air of confidence about the FISA teams which had plenty of testing behind them without skirts, while the FOCA teams had been racing with them as recently as Kylami. Not only that, they had used Goodyear tyres and now everybody would be on Michelins. Frank Williams caused a minor split in the FOCA ranks when he announced that he would retire his cars if the Lotus 88 passed scrutineering. McLaren chose to take the MP4 to Long Beach even though it was not yet ready to race; it was there for the sponsors. It made the M29s look obsolete.

Surprisingly, Riccardo Patrese took pole position for Arrows and made a superb start, leading for 24 laps until a fuel filter blocked and Reuterman took over. Six laps later, Jones overtook Reuterman and led to the end, with Reuterman second, a Williams 1-2 giving the team maximum points in both Championships. Nelson Piquet was third for Brabham. Ferrari and Renault, for all the help the regulations gave them, were not even in the points, all four drivers having retired.

Nigel Mansell, the Lotus test driver who had recently been promoted to the Formula 1 team, and Elio de Angelis drove Lotus 81s in America. For Brazil, Colin Chapman brought the Lotus 88 out to a chorus of protests from six teams including Williams and Ferrari. The Brazilian scrutineers passed it in the morning, then re-examined it and banned it in the afternoon, to the fury of Colin Chapman. To great local enthusiasm, Carlos Reuterman won for Williams, but in doing so he caused a rift with Alan Jones who came second. Reuterman should have given way to Jones under his contract but he did not do so, claiming he did not think Jones was close enough to make the clause in the contract stick, although the pits had held out boards telling him to give way. The two drivers did not get on well after that and Jones decided to leave at the end of the season.

The Argentinian Grand Prix was reinstated on April 12 where the McLaren MP4 made its racing debut with just one car for John Watson. He ran as high as sixth before retiring, his performance putting the other teams on notice that the MP4 was special. Piquet won from Reuterman with Alain Prost third in the turbocharged Renault and Jones fourth, opening up a three-point lead between the two Williams drivers. When Piquet stood on the podium, another little piece of history in the commercialization of the sport was made. On Ecclestone's orders, he removed the traditional laurel wreath from around his neck because it would obscure the name of the team's sponsor, Parmalat, which was across his chest.

The Lotus 88 had been banned again and Colin Chapman issued a statement saying that he believed that there had been collusion against Lotus. Jean-Marie Balestre immediately fined him $100,000 for the comment. The FOCA teams issued a statement criticising Balestre for his heavy-handed approach and in due course, the FIA overturned the fine. The Lotus 88 affair ended in the courts where Colin Chapman lost, which made him very bitter and he withdrew Lotus from the

Parking lot: when Watkins Glen became too small for the US Grand Prix, it moved to the car park at Caesar's Palace in Las Vegas.

San Marino Grand Prix. There were other problems at Lotus. In April, David Thieme, the oilman whose Essex company had supported Lotus in royal style, was arrested in Switzerland and held for fourteen days before being released on bail without charge. His business collapsed and his relationship with Lotus collapsed too. Chapman turned to John Player for sponsorship instead, which was agreed in June.

The Imola scrutineers were ultra efficient, especially over the clearances of the skirts, checking and re-checking clearances as cars came in from practice and taking so much time that a queue formed and drivers became so frustrated that fighting broke out at one point. Gilles Villeneuve put the new Ferrari on pole position,

much to the delight of the *tifosi* for whom the San Marino Grand Prix was effectively a second Italian Grand Prix, the first Ferrari pole position for two years. Villeneuve drove a superb race for Ferrari, stirring the hearts of the *tifosi* who saw a Ferrari revival on the horizon, but Piquet won and Villeneuve finished just outside the points, five of the six places going to FOCA teams.

The personal feud between Jones and Piquet continued at Monaco but with Gilles Villeneuve now part of the struggle at the front. Piquet led for the first 54 laps, then tried to go inside Eddie Cheever's Theodore at Tabac, had to brake hard, and went into the barrier opposite with his brakes locked; Reuterman had already retired. Alan Jones then took the lead, only for his engine to start

Desert heat: the 1980 US Grand Prix saw Alan Jones win the title in Las Vegas in circumstances far away from Grand Prix tradition.

hesitating which he took to be lack of fuel and went in for a quick pit stop, getting out ahead of Villeneuve. The problem continued and Villeneuve steadily gained on Jones, passing him with just four laps to go, giving Ferrari its first victory since 1979. Villeneuve repeated his success in the Spanish Grand Prix at Jarama in a great battle with Jones for the first few laps until Jones spun off, then with Reuterman until he did the same. The Ferrari had no business winning against the opposition on hand. It was Villeneuve who won the race against better cars, the hallmark of a truly great driver.

Goodyear returned to racing to supply Williams and Brabham, but as it did, the World Championship headed for more controversy at the British Grand Prix at Silverstone where Colin Chapman presented the Lotus 88B for scrutineering. It was passed by the RAC scrutineers, but when Nigel Mansell drove it in practice he was disqualified by the FISA representative who overruled the RAC. Balestre had simply banned it because it was derived from the Lotus 88s which had already been banned. In the inevitable row which followed, Balestre threatened the status of the British Grand Prix as a World Championship event if the Lotus 88B was allowed to take part. The RAC gave way. In the race Villeneuve spun off on lap 4 nearly taking both McLarens with him, but Watson got through to give McLaren and the MP4 its first victory.

It was a season without a clear leader: Piquet won in Germany for Brabham; Laffite took the Austrian race for Talbot Matra; Prost the Dutch and Italian races for Renault; and Laffite won at

Notre Dame in Montreal for Talbot Matra again. Then came the second US Grand Prix and more controversy. One of the new FISA rules was that a Grand Prix could not be held over a circuit which had not been used before, but it was waived in the case of Caesar's Palace Grand Prix in Las Vegas on 17 October, and held in a car park under a blazing sun, the last race of the season where the Championship would be decided. Jones won Williams' 15th Grand Prix, and clinching its second Constructors' Championship, but Jones packed his bags immediately and left as he had said he would. Nelson Piquet was fifth, but the two points were enough to make him World Champion, Bernie Ecclestone's first World Championship.

It was the end of a great partnership between Frank Williams and Alan Jones. In four seasons they had propelled the team from nowhere to the top in a heady spiral of success based on firm sponsorship support and sheer hard work. This had been at a time when the sport itself was in disarray which had arguably cost Williams a second Driver's Championship, a glorious struggle against the odds. Financially Williams was on a much better footing and now had its own wind tunnel, but the end of the 1981 season marked the end of that pioneering era. After Jones left, Frank Williams signed Keke Rosberg from Fittipaldi which displeased Reuterman. Saudia stayed as a sponsor and TAG increased its support which led to the team being renamed TAG-Williams. But, even as TAG and Mansour Ojjeh were consolidating their position with Williams, there were discussions going on about a move to the revitalized McLaren.

Things were moving fast at McLaren. In 1981, McLaren embarked on discussions with TAG to provide a turbo engine which could be matched with the MP4's carbon fibre monocoque to create the ultimate combination of lightness and power available at the time. The investment would come from Marlboro, as would the money for the third

part of the package – Niki Lauda, who was in touch with Ron Dennis about joining up again for 1982. He was feeling the attraction of driving again and his airline needed the money.

The BBC had covered the whole of the 1981 season, just the kind of sustained television coverage which suited the sponsors. With the internal conflict seemingly settled, the teams were under great pressure from their sponsors to keep it that way in 1982; but before a wheel was turned, the season started with a drivers' strike. The issue was superlicences which had been issued earlier in the year, tying drivers to teams for the whole year. The drivers saw this as the first step to creating a market in which they could be transferred for a fee between teams, like footballers. The drivers did not like being treated this way and when they arrived at Kylami for the South African Grand Prix, they locked themselves in a hotel room until a compromise was reached so that the first race could take place. The high altitude of Kylami in South Africa favoured the turbos and Prost won for Renault, but as soon as it was over, Balestre suspended the drivers' licences and issued fines.

The suspensions were lifted and the licence issue settled in time for the Brazilian Grand Prix, but no sooner had one dispute been settled than another erupted. Piquet won in Rio in the Brabham-Ford BT49D because the BMW turbo-powered BT50 was still not race-worthy; Rosberg was second for Williams, with Villeneuve third for Ferrari and John Watson fourth for McLaren. After the race Ferrari and Renault lodged complaints over Brabham and Williams' water-cooled brake system. Piquet and Rosberg were disqualified, opening up the old split between the FOCA and FISA teams. The substance of the complaint was that water carried to cool the brakes, was in fact ballast which could be jettisoned, lightening the car to make it faster. The complaint was upheld by FISA, giving Prost the race.

Just before the US Grand Prix at Long Beach, at the start of his eleventh season, Carlos Reuterman

Low point: the last 3-litre Ferrari, the 312T5 was known as a 'dog of a car', its poor handling confounding even the talented Gilles Villeneuve.

announced his retirement, the delayed effect of his disappointment the previous year at Las Vegas. Frank Williams took on Mario Andretti on a one-race deal for the race but Lauda was on form and won, putting him second behind Prost in the Driver's Championship.

The FOCA teams' response to the disqualification of Piquet and Rosberg was to boycott the San Marino Grand Prix, and despite threats from Marlboro and Elf to cut their sponsorship, the only team to break ranks was Ken Tyrell who took part because of his Italian sponsor, Candy. Tyrell used his presence at Imola to mount an attack on turbo power, protesting that the turbine constituted a secondary source of power and was therefore illegal. He started a campaign to ban turbos as part of the power struggle between the FOCA and FISA teams, a way for the kit car teams to show that they could and would fight back. After going through every process in the FIA's rule book, the dispute finished up in the court of the International Chamber of Commerce in Lausanne, the last resort permitted under the Concorde Agreement, where it was unsuccessful.

In the race, Villeneuve and Pironi swapped the lead back and forth, then one lap from the end Villeneuve took the lead as was his right under the team orders. Pironi had other ideas, and completely against the spirit of the team position that no two Ferrari drivers should contest the last few laps of a race they have in the bag, overtook Villeneuve to win. Neither driver had any points in the Championship but Villeneuve was No.1 driver, aiming at the title, and he was furious because he had stuck to the team orders. The Ferrari political machine swung behind Pironi, suggesting that there were no such team orders and that Pironi was within his rights, which most knew to be nonsense, but knowing that the politics were against him only made Villeneuve feel more betrayed.

At the Belgian Grand Prix two weeks later, the atmosphere between the teams and Balestre was deeply suspicious, and the water bottle controversy simmered on. In the Ferrari camp it was even worse, with Pironi and Villeneuve not even on speaking terms. In the last session of qualifying Pironi went a tenth of a second ahead of Villeneuve who went out immediately, determined to do better. Villeneuve was a charger and he was flying when he came up behind Jochen Mass, clipping Mass's rear wheel with his front wheel. The Ferrari was catapulted into the air, landing nose first in a sand pit before tumbling along and breaking up, throwing Villeneuve out into the catch fencing, his neck broken. As with the death of any great popular hero, a number of theories grew up around what caused his death: the Ferrari monocoque was not strong enough; or the restriction to two sets of qualifying tyres, a rule which Balestre had introduced at Zolder, suggested that Villeneuve was trying too hard to make the best use of them. Whatever the technical reason, behind it lay the rivalry with Pironi, fuelled by bitterness at the Imola result and Ferrari's response to it. Villeneuve was 32, handsome, gifted and immensely popular for his geniality, youth and vibrancy; his death left a another huge gap in the driver line up; it also left a widow with an eleven-year old son, Jacques. Ferrari withdrew from the Belgian Grand Prix out of respect. John Watson won for McLaren with Rosberg second and Lauda third, only to be disqualified because his car was found to be underweight.

The last few laps of the Monaco Grand Prix were among the most exciting in its history. Alain Prost had led for most of the race and was in the lead with three laps to go when he spun off in the wet, handing the lead to Patrese for Brabham, with what should have been a cruise to the end. Instead, Patrese slid off and stalled in front of the Loews Hotel. Pironi took the lead on the last lap only to suffer an electrical failure, handing the lead to Andrea de Cesaris who was within yards of giving Alfa Romeo its first victory for 30 years, when he ran out of fuel and burst into tears. Back at the Loews Hotel, marshals had started to push Patrese

Racer: Gilles Villeneuve never really had a car to match his talents before he was killed in 1982.

out of the way but he had managed to get going again and came through to take the chequered flag, his first Grand Prix victory.

In Canada, the Notre Dame circuit was renamed Gilles Villeneuve in memory of Canada's great driver. Didier Pironi took pole position and stalled on the grid, and while most of the drivers found their way round him, Riccardo Paletti, a new driver with Osella, came up from the back of the grid and rammed the stationary Ferrari under full power from behind at around 120 mph, catching fire. The fire was put out and Paletti was removed to hospital where he died. Pironi survived unhurt and drove the spare Ferrari in the race, but Arnoux, Prost and Piquet were soon past him. Piquet moved up to second on lap 9 and held the lead to the flag to post the first victory for a FOCA team turbo car, the Brabham-BMW BT50.

At Brands Hatch a horrible reminder of the start of the Canadian Grand Prix occurred when Patrese stalled on the front row of the grid and Arnoux rammed him, putting both of the turbos

Troubled: Colin
Chapman in 1981, the
year before he died.

Exit: Rosberg's 1982 title was the last for the Cosworth DFV.

out of the race. Piquet led from Lauda's McLaren-Cosworth, until his BMW turbo failed on lap 10 and Lauda led the rest of the race from Pironi.

Hockenheim was wet for the German Grand Prix and in practice all the cars were throwing up great rooster tails of spray. Didier Pironi came up behind Derek Daly who was just behind Alain Prost. As Daly moved to overtake Prost, Pironi thought he was moving over to let him through, went for the inside and straight into the back of Prost, clipping the Renault's rear wheel and becoming airborne before hitting the barrier, crushing both his legs. It fell to Tambay to pick up the challenge for Ferrari which he did with verve, winning the race from Arnoux, leaving his injured team-mate in the lead in the Championship. It soon became clear that Pironi would not be driving again that season, dashing Ferrari's hopes of the Championship. With the McLarens of Watson and Lauda less competitive against the turbos, Rosberg and Williams looked more competitive, and Rosberg's hopes of the Championship increased dramatically.

Elio de Angelis won the Austrian Grand Prix for Lotus, his first and Lotus's first for four years. It was also the 150th Grand Prix to be won by a Cosworth-powered car and it seemed appropriate that it was in a Lotus. Motor racing was banned in Switzerland, so the first Swiss Grand Prix for many years took place at Dijon, a second Grand Prix on French soil. Rosberg won the race putting him in the lead in the World Championship and he only had to gain one more point from the two remaining races to be sure of the title. There were no Ferraris because Tambay had a bad back and Ferrari's hopes of either title had been dashed by Pironi's crash. The team was floundering again and there was nobody with the right qualities to hold it together: Enzo Ferrari was 83 and out of touch; Marco Piccinini was at his side; Luca di Montezemolo was a strategist rather than a team leader; and Piero Lardi Ferrari and Mauro Foghieri were endlessly politicking.

In preparation for 1983, Ferrari signed René Arnoux in time for an announcement at the Italian Grand Prix. Mario Andretti had also signed for two races and promptly took pole position. To keep Watson's chances of the title alive he had to win, and Teddy Mayer reduced the downforce on his car considerably to give him power along the straights to compete with the turbos. It was not enough and Arnoux won for Renault with the two Ferraris of Tambay and Andretti next, giving Maranello the Constructors' title. Mayer's shrewd use of downforce enabled Watson to finish fourth after a great drive, just keeping him a contender with Rosberg two laps down and unplaced.

The circus then moved on to Las Vegas, back to the car park at Caesar's Palace for the last race of the season. Watson had to win to take the Championship with Rosberg out of the points. Michele Alboreto won for Tyrell with Watson second and Rosberg fifth, enough to take the Championship, and once he was sure of victory, Frank Williams ordered British and Saudi flags to be waved as he crossed the line to give Williams his second Driver's Championship.

It had been a landmark year, a year of change, a year of arrivals and departures and slow healing of the damaging split between the rival camps. Double World Champion Niki Lauda came back from retirement and World Champion Mario Andretti came and went. The 1980 World Champion Alan Jones, retired as did the moody Carlos Reuterman. Gilles Villeneuve, the great hope as a future World Champion and basis of a Ferrari revival, was dead. Didier Pironi, the mid-season challenger, had numerous operations on his legs but his injuries prevented him from making a comeback. He took up power boat racing and was killed in a race in 1987.

It was the last Championship for the venerable Cosworth DFV engine, which had been the backbone of the kit car teams for 15 years, including the three seasons when they were under pressure from turbo power: 387 engines had been produced which won 152 out of 217 Grands Prix in 16 seasons, a 70 percent record. For 1983 the company moved to a shorter stroke layout for the

DFV and started on a new, normally aspirated engine designated DFY.

It was the first season for the reborn member of the kit car family, McLaren. The old management was swept away in 1982, including Teddy Mayer and Tyler Alexander who had been together since the early 1960s. Mayer sold his McLaren shares to Ron Dennis and John Barnard, a demonstration of the power of tobacco money to effect change.

It was the first year since Ecclestone had won the important power struggle for control over the money which flowed through Formula 1, and his power base was strengthened by victory in the attempt to topple him. He now sat on the Formula 1 Commission, a body formed by FISA to discuss and set the technical regulations. He out-thought, out-manoeuvred and out-threatened Jean-Marie Balestre, publicly and privately and demonstrated a toughness under extreme pressure which those who saw it at close hand were content to see deployed in the general interest of the Formula 1 fraternity. In November the Formula 1 Commission met in Paris and issued the technical specification for 1983: side skirts were finally banned altogether – all cars had to have flat bottoms. Without skirts the huge downforces were reduced by 60 percent and suspension could begin to have some spring in it again, making the ride much more comfortable for the driver while tyres could have thinner sidewalls now that they no longer had to absorb the downforces.

The safety argument against skirts had always been misconceived; cornering speeds had increased dramatically, but straight line speeds had increased dramatically too, through the power of the turbo engine, and its progress was never hindered by the regulations. It had been a power struggle, the battle had gone on long enough, and while the new specifications signalled that FISA was in charge, the kit car teams had retained ground effects long enough and been innovative enough to win the World Championship during three of the four years of the conflict. By the end of 1982 turbo power was on the cards for everybody who could afford it. That was a new problem: the big kit car teams could, but the small teams, who had been part of the FOCA power base in the struggle, could not and once the battle had been won, the division between the haves and the have-nots in FOCA was sharpened.

The end of 1982 was also the end of Lotus under Colin Chapman. The Lotus 88 controversy had weighed heavily on him and he had been profoundly depressed by the battles he had to fight for what he saw as just another piece of inspired innovation. But beneath that controversial surface, darker and murkier events were unfolding. In 1978, the British government had backed the development of an exotic sports car to be built by John DeLorean, an American entrepreneur and former General Motors executive, who was prepared to build it in Northern Ireland. DeLorean took on Lotus as development consultants, for which $17.65m was paid to an intermediary company with which Chapman had a close association. GDP Services was registered in Panama but operated in Switzerland. The money never reached Lotus, which invoiced the DeLorean company separately

for its services to the tune of some $11m.

In February 1982, the DeLorean company was in dire straits with debts of $60m and the British government declined to put in any more money, so it went into receivership. DeLorean tried to save the company but failed and the Northern Ireland factory was wound up.

Two months later, on 16 December 1982, Colin Chapman – engineer, innovator, designer, leader, businessman and finally crooked dealer – died of a heart attack. He had been associated with many major engineering and technical innovations in Grand Prix racing over nearly 30 years. His most recent great success, the 'wing car' concept, brought him and the other kit car teams who followed his engineering lead into open conflict with FISA, but it had also provided the means by which they had ultimately triumphed. He was, and remains, one of the great figures of the World Championship, an inspirational leader whose life was crammed with success. But it ended mired in two seasons of controversy: the legality of his twin-chassis Lotus 88, the separation from David Thieme, and in the DeLorean affair which was to eat away at the heart of the Lotus team in the years which followed his death.

New man: Ayrton
Senna's first victory,
Portugal 1985.

6

IT'S THE TOBACCO

THAT COUNTS

Bernie Ecclestone, FOCA and the kit car teams lost the battle over sliding skirts, water bottles and having turbos outlawed, but they won the war for control of the money. They had managed to stay competitive throughout, and once the dust had cleared, those kit car team bosses who could afford to joined the turbo club themselves. In doing so, the FOCA ranks were split between those who could not afford turbos and those who could – Colin Chapman then his wife Hazel at Lotus, Frank Williams, Bernie Ecclestone at Brabham and Ron Dennis at McLaren.

Ron Dennis had come a long way since starting out as Jochen Rindt's mechanic. He knew that a Formula 1 team was a fairly precarious basis for a business. The fortunes of the team could go up and down very swiftly if it relied on sponsors. Sponsors could and did change their minds and switch allegiances, especially when a team was not doing well which was just the time it needed the greatest amount of investment. He wanted to change the relationship between sponsor and team, to get away from the selling space on a billboard mentality, towards the idea of investing together. It was in furthering this idea that he made a concerted effort to woo Mansour Ojjeh and his TAG company away from Williams, to become part of the McLaren family, an approach which suited Ojjeh. At Williams, TAG had been a conventional sponsor, getting exposure in exchange for much needed cash which was spent on building a winning car. What Ron Dennis was offering was a partnership between two high-tech businesses. McLaren would also get what every Formula 1 team now needed to stay ahead: a turbo engine.

With TAG's support, McLaren was able to finance a turbo itself. TAG and McLaren went to Porsche to build the engine, with Porsche engineers working under contract. The advantage of this arrangement was that it was built to the McLaren-TAG specification, with John Barnard having final say over its development. He wanted it to fit perfectly into the new MP4. The new engine was

unveiled at the Geneva Motor Show in March 1983 with the declared intention that the turbo MP4 would be ready for the team's two drivers, Niki Lauda and John Watson, at the Belgian Grand Prix at the end of May.

Williams could have been a second customer for the TAG-Porsche engine but Frank Williams was not interested in playing second fiddle. As a result TAG sponsorship of Williams ended in 1983. Albilad and Leyland had already departed, but the Saudia relationship continued alongside new sponsor ICI. Frank Williams' extraordinary capacity to start up again after losing his sponsors, and his skill at finding new backers, extended to finding a new engine. In 1981, he had started secret negotiations with Honda for the use of a V6 turbo which it had developed from a Formula 2 engine for the Spirit team. A contract was signed in February 1983.

Ferrari had its own turbo engine, but the *scuderia* had suffered badly from the loss of Villeneuve and Pironi. In spite of the fact that Enzo Ferrari was in his 80s, he simply could not let go; he still wanted to influence everything and everybody. He relied heavily on Marco Piccinini to act as roving ambassador, to keep him informed and to make sure his orders were executed. Piccinini was assisted by Piero Lardi Ferrari, whom Ferrari officially recognized as his son after the death of his wife Laura in 1978.

Renault, the pioneer of turbo power, was very confident for 1983 with Alain Prost as driver. Gerard Ducarouge, who had joined Lotus from Matra, negotiated the use of the Renault engines in the Lotus 93T.

It was a year of transition: Lotus, McLaren and Williams all continued to use Cosworths until their turbos were ready, Toleman used the Hart 415 turbo, BMW continued its relationship with Brabham while also supplying turbos to the German kit car team, ATS. Arrows, Ligier, March, Theodore and Tyrell had no alternative but to stick with the DFV which was on its way out but it was still competitive in the right hands. Keke Rosberg was just such a pair of hands when he put the Williams on pole for the Brazilian Grand Prix. After him came seven turbos, then Lauda in the DFY-powered McLaren. Rosberg led from the start but the BMW power showed and Piquet took the lead on lap five and won for Brabham-BMW, the first turbo victory for a kit car team.

John Watson won at Long Beach for McLaren, another Cosworth victory over turbo power, made all the sweeter with Lauda second, a McLaren 1-2 which left him leading the Championship. It was the last US (West) Grand Prix to be held at Long Beach: FOCA had demanded too much money and CART took over, spreading Indy Car racing beyond Indianapolis. Las Vegas also opted for indigenous American CART races from 1983, pushing the second US Grand Prix on to the streets of Detroit. The next two races went to the turbos: the French Grand Prix was won by Alain Prost for Renault, and San Marino went to Patrick Tambay for Ferrari. Then the Cosworth teams fought back, Rosberg winning at Monaco and Prost coming back again for Renault at Spa. Then came Detroit where Michele Alboreto won in a Tyrell, the last victory for a Cosworth engine, its 155th.

Ken Tyrell's team was sponsored by a newcomer to motor racing, Benetton, a hugely successful Italian clothing manufacturer which had sponsored various sports, including basketball and rugby. Benetton was a family business based in Treviso but it had worldwide markets and was looking for a way of reaching a wider audience. It was particularly strong in the US where Alboreto's victory was reported from coast to coast on US television, delighting the Benetton family which calculated that the cost of buying such coverage would have been $50m, making its sponsorship at a fraction of that sum very worthwhile.

Prost was leading Arnoux in points in the run up to the Italian Grand Prix, with Tambay equal third. With two Ferrari drivers in contention for the title, Renault feared that something untoward might happen to Alain Prost in Italy. It provided the diminutive Frenchman with three bodyguards when he arrived at Monza. Any doubts that for Italian motor racing, it was Ferrari that mattered in national terms, not the drivers, was clear from the silence which greeted Riccardo Patrese after he took pole position for Brabham, beating the Ferraris. Both McLaren drivers were in MP4/1E turbos. Patrese took the lead at the start, then his BMW engine blew up spectacularly. Piquet was just behind, took over and led to the end of the race, winning from Arnoux. Prost had a turbo failure as well, so the position at the top narrowed to Prost on 51, Arnoux on 49 and Piquet on 46 with two races to go.

Piquet won the John Player Grand Prix at Brands Hatch after a straight fight with Prost, who simply could not find the speed. Prost was second, making the South African Grand Prix the showdown. Rosberg made the debut of the turbo-powered Williams-Honda FW09 and Nigel Mansell did the same with the Lotus-Renault 93T. Prost could win the title for Renault but the pressure from the kit car teams was intense – Lauda was fastest in the pre-race warm up in the MP4/1E. Piquet could win the title if he won the race, even if Prost came second, and the Brazilian set a cracking pace to be 12 seconds ahead of his team-mate by lap 13. Prost was third but he was having a hard time keeping Lauda's MP4/1E at bay. Prost's turbo was not up to scratch and when Lauda passed him, he came in for a pit stop and retired. Piquet eased off slightly now that fourth place would be enough for the title. Patrese won, then de Cesaris for Alfa Romeo, then Piquet, a fantastic result for Brabham and Bernie Ecclestone – the first turbo-powered Championship going to a kit car team.

After all Renault's pioneering work on turbos and the struggle to win the Championship for France, it was ironic that the first turbo victory in the World Championship not only went to a FOCA team, but to Ecclestone's Brabham. It was

Debut: the McLaren-TAG MP4/1E V6 turbo's
first outing at the 1983 Italian Grand Prix. It later
won 4 of 6 turbo-powered Championships.

the high tide mark for Renault in Formula 1, and the high tide for hopes of a French revival. Alan Prost had won 9 Grands Prix for them, 4 that year, and he had been the great hope for that French revival in Formula 1; his perceived failure brought a sour note to the end of the season. The French press accused Alan Prost of dropping out and blaming the car, and two days after the race Renault fired him. He was, in fact, tired of Renault with its huge bureaucratic organization and internal politics, the gruelling round of publicity and PR commitments which went with the job. Alan Prost initially spoke to Marlboro about going to Ferrari, but decided that he preferred the smaller, competitive atmosphere of the kit car teams and spoke to Ron Dennis.

Dennis wanted Prost back, so to create a vacancy he did not renew John Watson's contract for 1984. Watson had won four Grands Prix for McLaren but Prost was a proven winner and Dennis took advantage of Prost's position, offering him a knock-down fee for the year. Prost sensibly accepted because McLaren was clearly the team with the package for 1984 – the TAG turbo in the MP4/2, Marlboro money and two of the most talented drivers in Formula 1. There were few Formula 1 seats vacant that late in the season and Watson could not find another drive.

With the internal feud settled and money pouring into Formula 1, a balance between the top kit car teams and the manufacturers formed around the turbo. The turbocharged 1980s became a decade of plenty based on an unholy alliance between the World Championship, a modern gladiatorial spectacle, the tobacco companies, who largely paid for it, and television. By 1983 tobacco and television provided the lifeblood of the sport, ushering in the age of the carbon-fibre, turbocharged cars which created an ever greater spectacle. This completed the virtuous circle by increasing the sense of event which attracted even more money. Formula 1 had been born again on the back of tobacco.

Not all teams had tobacco sponsorship, but all benefitted from the general increase in the amounts of money flowing in. Williams had no tobacco sponsor but it benefitted hugely from the Honda contract which gave it an engine while being sponsored by Denim, Mobil, ICI and its stalwart supporter, Saudia. In June 1984 the team moved to much larger premises in Didcot, Oxfordshire to build the new car, the FW09, with a carbon fibre monocoque.

Two newcomers to Formula 1 arrived in 1984, two stars from Formula 3 who had contested the 1983 title: Martin Brundle and Ayrton Senna. Senna had won 14 of the 21 races in the season, taking 16 pole positions, breaking two lap records and posting 8 fastest laps, a record which had given him the British Formula 3 Championship from Brundle. In the other 7 races, he was second just twice and in the other 5 he had either crashed or spun off trying to win. He took the Championship in the last race of the season, confirming his utter determination to win or bust. Senna had tests with both Williams and McLaren but there were no vacancies. He also spoke to Peter Warr at Lotus, but there were no vacancies there either. Ecclestone tried hard to get him for Brabham but Nelson Piquet and his main sponsor Parmalat, were against it. Piquet and Senna were both Brazilian and there had always been tension between them. Parmalat wanted an Italian driver, so Ecclestone signed Teo Fabi, although he went on trying to get Senna right up to the moment he had to declare who his drivers were for 1984. Senna eventually signed for Toleman with Johnny Cecotto who had been with Theodore. Senna knew his own skill, knew he had tested well and been rejected – as he saw it – by the top teams. He started his Formula 1 career believing that the sport's establishment was against him and he bridled at what he saw as a personal slight. Martin Brundle went to Tyrell.

Ayrton Senna made his first appearance in Formula 1 on home ground in the Brazilian Grand

Prix at Rio. The race was something of a needle match for Prost who was up against his old team. It also produced a few surprises. Elio de Angelis put the new Lotus-Renault on pole, just ahead of Alboreto's Ferrari 126C4, with Warwick in third place in the Renault RE50, just ahead of Prost in the McLaren MP4/2. Alboreto led for Ferrari, followed by Warwick and Mansell. But Lauda charged his way up to fourth place, taking Mansell, then Warwick, to take second, then passed Alboreto and into the lead. Alboreto then spun off with brake failure. Prost was hard on Lauda's heels, passing Warwick on lap 23, when he went in for fuel and tyres, leaving the two McLarens first and second until Lauda retired with an electrical fault. Prost came in on lap 38 for tyres and fuel, rejoining behind Warwick who stayed ahead until a wishbone failed, the result of an earlier incident with Lauda. With Warwick out, what might have been a first win for Warwick at Renault turned out to be a first win for Prost at McLaren, a great moment for Prost.

Alan Prost moved steadily ahead with another, this time controversial victory at Monaco in torrential rain. He had taken pole position, a huge advantage at Monaco where overtaking is difficult. Ayrton Senna then gave the Formula 1 family a demonstration of how good he was in the wet by climbing from thirteenth position on the grid to ninth at the end of lap 1 and seventh at the end of lap 7. Teo Fabi then spun and finished up in the middle of the road; Alan Prost only narrowly missed hitting his car but did hit a marshal who was trying to move it. Prost slowed and Nigel Mansell, lying second, took the lead. Mansell then spun on a piece of road marking and went into the Armco, then Lauda did the same, putting Senna in second place. By lap 30, as the rain increased, Senna was challenging Prost and two laps later, the clerk of the course, Jacky Ickx, put out the red flag to stop the race. However, Senna went on trying and as the McLaren and the Toleman closed on the line, Senna surged past, thinking he had won.

In fact the result was decided on who was leading when the red flag went out, so the race was awarded to Prost. Senna was not pleased with yet another example of what for him was an impossible fight with the establishment.

The two US Grands Prix were held back to back on the streets of Detroit and at Dallas, Texas, on another hastily laid out circuit at the State Fair Park. Piquet won on the roads of Motown, but at Dallas the newly laid asphalt surface melted in the sun and started to come apart. The drivers protested vigorously, but Ecclestone the ringmaster insisted it went on. Even as the rows continued, the air-conditioned executive suites filled up with guests at $25,000 a time and Linda Gray, the actress who played Sue Ellen Ewing in the TV series *Dallas* prepared to award the trophies. It was a money-making exercise and many of the drivers found it hard to take it seriously. Mansell led from pole then had a thrilling fight with Rosberg who finally won it when Mansell went in for tyres. Rosberg managed to hold on to the lead as car after car dropped out; Mansell collapsed from heat stroke having tried to push his Lotus over the line for fifth place.

Lauda put himself back in the running by winning the British Grand Prix with Derek Warwick second and Senna third. By this point Senna had decided to leave Toleman and started talking to Peter Warr at Lotus. Senna's contract was for three years, although he could buy himself out of it. The difficulty was that he was prevented from speaking to any other team without letting Toleman know and he had not told Toleman about his discussions with Lotus.

McLaren was already way in front in the Constructors' Championship at the start of the German Grand Prix at Hockenheim where the internal battle between the two drivers went on. Prost crossed the line just over 3 seconds ahead of Lauda for another McLaren 1-2.

The European Grand Prix was at the new Nurburgring, refashioned since Lauda's near-fatal accident eight years previously. Piquet was on pole again with Prost second and Lauda down in fifteenth place, having made a very poor tyre choice. Prost led from start to finish and Alboreto and Piquet came in ahead of Lauda who had spun while trying to pass a back marker.

The last race of the season was the first Portuguese Grand Prix for 24 years, on a new circuit at Estoril. Prost was on 62½ points and Lauda on 66. Piquet took pole position again, with Prost alongside him and Lauda back in eleventh place, but it was Rosberg who took the lead followed by Mansell and Prost, who passed Mansell on lap 2 and Rosberg on lap 9. Lauda worked his way steadily through the pack to fourth place behind Senna, Mansell and Prost – two places between him and a third World Championship. He passed Senna but Mansell was 30 seconds ahead, a huge task, but one he took on with gusto. Then Mansell's brakes failed and he spun off, handing over second place to Lauda with 18 laps to go, enough to win the Championship by the narrowest of margins in its history, 72 to 71½.

Prost was close to tears at the victory ceremony; it was his seventh victory of the season to Lauda's five, but he insisted on giving up his place on the top of the podium to Lauda, World Champion for the third time, in a gesture of genuine respect and admiration. Commercialism may have taken over motor racing but sportsmanship among the tiny number of men who knew what it was like at the top, was not dead. Apart from taking first and second place in the Driver's title, their joint total of 12 out of the 16 races gave McLaren the Constructors' Championship by a huge margin, 143½ points to Ferrari's 57½ as convincing a demonstration as could be made of McLaren's hold on the high ground of advanced technology.

New technologies, especially carbon fibre monocoques and turbocharged engines, pushed up the price of winning but the sponsors wanted to win and the money was found, even if it meant the sport danced to an ever more commercial tune.

The cost was not only in technology but in driving talent too; having won the Championships for McLaren, Lauda wanted at least $4m for 1985. He opened negotiations with Renault and Gérard Larrousse, Renault team manager settled. However, the Renault board would not sanction the fee, so Lauda was forced back to McLaren where Dennis argued long and hard but eventually agreed $3.8m. It was a huge fee, but the 1984 result enhanced Ron Dennis's growing reputation for thinking long-term and getting the package right.

Enzo Ferrari, who had been at the heart of his *scuderia* for over half a century, was 88 and struggling to stay in control through his front man, Marco Piccinini. The Ferrari 126C3, with its carbon fibre monocoque designed by Harvey Postlethwaite and its V6 turbo engine designed by Mauro Foghieri, had been completely eclipsed by the McLaren MP4. Ferrari won just one race in 1984 and the fallout split Ferrari into two camps: one led by Piero Lardi Ferrari who, with Piccinini, had become increasingly influential; the other led by Foghieri who was threatened by the 'Anglo', Postlethwaite. The search for better technology was hampered by the power struggle, but it was Postlethwaite who gained; eventually the faithful servant Foghieri lost out to the illegitimate son and heir Piero Lardi Ferrari, whom Foghieri despised as a lightweight. Foghieri was given a job far removed from the racing team, looking after advanced projects, while Postlethwaite worked on the new Ferrari for 1985, the 156/85. In the effort to catch up with McLaren, and to match Foghieri's V6 engine to Postlethwaite's aspirations for the new chassis, Ferrari turned to computer-aided design systems developed by Italy's premier aerospace company, Aermacchi.

Ferrari's problem was that the high technology competition was showing the way. After a poor first season with turbo power in the FW09, Frank Williams' deal with Honda started to bear fruit. The FW10 had a carbon-composite monocoque carefully matched to the Honda V6 engine; the

Modern maestro: Alain Prost's four Driver's
titles, made him the most successful Champion
since Juan Manuel Fangio with five.

chassis was shipped to Japan for testing where
Honda had invested a reported $300m to develop
the new engine, more than compensating for the
effort being put in by Williams' erstwhile partner,
TAG. To match the new car, Frank Williams
wanted Ayrton Senna from Toleman, but he
prevaricated too long and Senna went to Lotus
instead, displacing Nigel Mansell. Having lost the
rising star, Williams signed Nigel Mansell to
partner Keke Rosberg.

Ayrton Senna knew his value better than most,
and he knew that Toleman did not have, and might
never have, the resources to match it. There was
enormous change going on at Toleman. Benetton
wanted a global vehicle to promote its products

and though tired of Alfa Romeo's lack of success,
remained determined to use Formula 1. Motor
racing had a global presence and it was rooted in
Italian sporting culture, a combination which the
Benetton family felt perfectly matched their
aspirations. Rather than simply attach its name to
another team, Benetton decided to invest directly,
become a partner with a view to taking it over
completely and renaming it Benetton.

At Lotus, Gerard Ducarouge was steadily
improving the combination of the Renault engines
and carbon fibre chassis. The Lotus 95T benefitted
from having Renault engineer Bruno Maudit
attached to the team and Lotus had finished in
third place in the Constructors' title, well ahead of

the Renault team in fifth place. In between was Brabham, the only team to give McLaren a run for its money in 1984, but Gordon Murray was the only designer among the top teams to have to stick with aluminium skin for the BT54 monocoque.

Michele Alboreto raised *tifosi* spirits by putting the new Ferrari on pole position for the Brazilian Grand Prix, ahead of Keke Rosberg in the Williams-Honda FW10, Ayrton Senna and Elio de Angelis in the two Lotus 95Ts, Mansell's FW10 and Prost's McLaren-TAG MP4/2B. In the dash for the lead going in to the first corner, Mansell collided with Alboreto, spun and went off leaving Alboreto's Ferrari slightly damaged. Rosberg took the lead, then Alboreto, then Prost, until Rosberg's turbo failed on lap 9 and Prost put pressure on. Alboreto led until lap 18 when he made a bad gear change which was just enough to let Prost through into the lead. Lauda was lying third until an electrical failure put him out and Prost won, McLaren's eighth successive victory.

The Portuguese Grand Prix saw an end to McLaren's victorious run. Rain had all but flooded Estoril during qualifying in which Ayrton Senna took his first pole position, over a second faster than his team-mate de Angelis and 2.5 seconds ahead of Piquet in seventh place. There were three World Champions on the grid: Piquet, Rosberg and Lauda, but Senna made them all look very ordinary in the wet. After 30 laps he was 30 seconds ahead of the pack and he kept on drawing away from them until two laps before the end when he was 1 minute 32 seconds ahead of Alboreto, the only driver on the same lap. The clerk of the course then stopped the race, giving Senna his first Formula 1 victory, the first victory for a Renault engine outside a Renault car, and the first Lotus victory since 1982 and the death of Colin Chapman. He had done it in style – took pole position, led from start to finish, drove the fastest lap and won – days do not come better than that for racing drivers, however wet. It also put Senna equal second with Prost in the World Championship on 9 points, 3 behind Alboreto. There were few that day who did not believe that Senna was a future World Champion, particularly at Lotus where his performance had lifted the entire team.

Senna continued his run at Imola, taking pole position and leading for 23 laps until Prost challenged him in what was to be a series of classic duels of the turbo era. Turbo engines were very thirsty when pushed to full power which was used only in overtaking or in a positioning manoeuvre. The regulations stated that only 220 litres of fuel could be used in each race, forcing drivers to be economical and skilful in their use of boost. Turbo battles used fuel at a great rate, and if a driver was tempted into using too much boost to stay ahead, he could finish up running out of fuel. Prost challenged Senna, but Senna skilfully defended his position and Prost was forced to ease off, but as he did so Stefan Johannson for Ferrari, tried to out-run Senna. He fared no better and ran out of fuel. Senna had seen off two challenges but he had no readout for his fuel consumption and he was robbed of what would have been a famous victory two laps from the end when he too ran out of fuel. Prost crossed the line first but was disqualified after post-race scrutineering found his car was 2kg underweight, the result of greater than anticipated use of the brakes; Elio de Angelis who was second was awarded the race.

The Belgian Grand Prix was abandoned after qualifying because the track repair work had been so bad that the surface was ripped up by the cars. For the Canadian Grand Prix at Montreal Lotus and Ferrari filled the first four places on the grid with Prost fifth and Lauda right at the back. This was the age of the high-speed qualifying lap which practically wrecked engines. Lauda could not get used to the idea of ruining a car just for a pole position or to be near the front, and he was consistently far down the grid from his team-mate. Alboreto and Johannson gave Ferrari a wonderful 1-2 in the race, with Prost third and de Angelis fourth. In Detroit, Rosberg worked his magic on the street circuit again and the Ferraris were second and third. This put Alboreto on 31 points, de Angelis on 24 and Prost on 22, giving Ferrari a position from which it could challenge for the title.

In qualifying for the French Grand Prix, Mansell went through the speed trap at over 200 mph when a tyre burst and he crashed into the barrier. A pole from the catch fencing hit him hard on the helmet, causing severe concussion and he was taken to hospital unconscious. Rosberg had no idea what had gone wrong with the Williams, and could not speak to Mansell, but he went out and qualified on pole at 200 mph plus. Nelson Piquet won the race with Rosberg second, and Prost third.

The Ferrari challenge began to peter out at the Austrian Grand Prix where Senna's Lotus was reliable and fast enough to beat Alboreto into third place, but not fast enough to catch Prost, who won, putting Alboreto and Prost both on 50 points. Lauda, who had been having a bad season retired, and announced that he was going to retire from Formula 1 altogether at the end of the season. Prost won the Italian Grand Prix with Piquet second and Senna third. As if to rub salt in the wound, Lauda then went out and won the last Grand Prix of his career, the Dutch, followed by Prost, Senna and Alboreto. The result did not do much for Lauda's position but Prost moved ahead of Alboreto for the first time in the season, by 56 points to 53.

The Williams improvement continued at the European Grand Prix at Brands Hatch where Prost was content to go for the points he needed to win the Championship. Mansell won from Senna, Rosberg and the new World Champion Alain Prost. It was Mansell's first Grand Prix victory in front of a home crowd at Brands Hatch, a demonstration of Williams' new found form.

McLaren had won six races, half the number of the previous year, but took both Championships again. Williams won 4, Lotus 3, Ferrari 2 and Brabham 1. Renault won nothing and pulled out at the end of the season. In the nine years since Renault had come back to racing and launched the turbocharged revolution, the French giant had helped to bring about huge change. But in eight seasons it had failed to take either of the titles; the best it could manage was second in 1983 with Prost, the last year it had won a Grand Prix. It was a great disappointment, especially since Lotus seemed to have made better use of the engine. It was clear that running a Formula 1 team was not really something a large manufacturer could do very well. It could supply the engine, as Honda had shown, and participate as part of a small entrepreneurial team; it could buy into the kit car concept rather than the whole car concept as a way of participating.

Lauda's seat at McLaren was filled by Keke Rosberg who developed a good relationship with Ron Dennis but found it quite hard to settle into the team, a second World Champion with Prost. To fill his spare seat, Frank Williams signed up Nelson Piquet from Brabham and Ecclestone filled Brabham's spare seat with Elio de Angelis from Lotus where the obvious contender for the spare seat was Derek Warwick. Peter Warr approached him and started discussions, but Ayrton Senna was determined that while he was at Lotus nothing would get in the way of his bid to become World Champion. He knew that Lotus needed him more than he needed Lotus, making it clear he would not drive alongside Warwick. Warr capitulated and signed up Johnny Dumfries whom Senna judged would not tax the resources of the team too much. The British motoring press was very hostile to Senna during this affair, so Senna simply stopped speaking to them.

Without Senna, Toleman had not scored a point all season. Peter Collins, an Australian who had started at Lotus in 1978 then moved to Williams, joined the team but there was no improvement and the Benetton family decided to buy the team, renaming it Benetton Formula. The effect was immediate, starting with a change of engine from

Hart to BMW, and keeping the Italian Teo Fabi while signing Gerhard Berger from Arrows. The the most obvious change was painting the Benetton cars in striking bright colours, reflecting their clothing range just as the McLarens reflected the Marlboro cigarette packet. They wanted attention and they got it and were quickly identified as a team with a difference.

At Brabham, Ecclestone continued as the No.1 customer for BMW engines having been unsuccessful in his search for a new, long-term engine partner. Brabham was slipping into the second rank of teams behind McLaren, Williams, Ferrari and Lotus, a process which could only be arrested by winning. Ecclestone was concentrating on FOCA business, seeking to expand the World Championship into other parts of the world, including Mexican and Hungarian Grands Prix in 1986 following the first Australian Grand Prix in 1985, making it into a much bigger business.

In response to the rising power from the turbo engines, the regulations were changed for the 1986 season, reducing the maximum amount of fuel from 220 litres to 195 litres, further limiting the amount of boost drivers could use. Some drivers liked it but others, including Keke Rosberg, hated it; he could not see the merit in producing lots of very expensive power from turbo engines only to restrict their use.

On 8 March 1986 Frank Williams was driving from the Paul Ricard circuit to Nice airport in a Ford Sierra hire car when he lost control near a small village called Meounes. The car went off the road, down a six-foot drop. William's neck was broken on impact and he lost all sensation in his body. He was taken to hospital in Toulon, then moved to a specialist unit in Marseilles for an operation on his back. An air ambulance flew him to London and by the evening he was in intensive care in the London Hospital where he had an operation on his chest. He fought off pneumonia, which put him back in intensive care, but it was soon clear that he would be paralyzed for life.

Frank Williams' leadership and the strength of his team were evident at the Brazilian Grand Prix two weeks later; Patrick Head was in charge. Practice and qualifying were a delight for the Brazilian crowd as Nelson Piquet and Ayrton Senna fought for pole position. Piquet crashed in the process and injured his wrist and Senna managed to take pole. Just before the race, the other team bosses gathered round Piquet's car in a spontaneous gesture of Formula 1 solidarity holding up a banner to the television cameras with a message for Frank Williams: 'Don't worry Frank, we are minding the store'.

The Williams-Honda FW11 was the favourite for the season and Piquet believed that his main opposition would come from Mansell but he had reckoned without Senna. The first lap was a psychological battle between Mansell and Senna which Senna won. On the first corner, Senna held his position even as Mansell came alongside, then the same thing happened as the two cars approached the corner at the end of the straight, Mansell moving out of the slipstream and coming alongside taking the inside line. Senna would not give way and it was Mansell who hesitated, took to the grass, backed off, then crashed into the barrier removing a front wheel. Now it was Senna versus his arch-rival Piquet, and two laps later Piquet moved from Senna's slipstream as Mansell had done, and was ahead as they came to the corner where he simply chopped across Senna's nose into the lead. Piquet won with Senna second, and they stood on the podium together holding the Brazilian flag in a rather distant display of national pride.

The duel between Williams and Lotus was halted at Imola where the race was won on fuel gauges. Senna and Mansell retired early on and the front runners were Prost, Rosberg and Piquet in that order with three laps to go. All three drivers had calculated their fuel consumption down to the last drop, or so they thought, when Rosberg ran out of fuel, then on the last lap Patrese's Brabham rolled to a halt for the same reason. Prost had a lead of nearly half a lap over Piquet going into the final lap and his gauge showed that he had a small, but manageable margin of fuel to complete it, but three-quarters of the way through the lap, the engine began to cough and splutter. With great presence of mind, Prost started weaving violently from side to side to jostle every last drop in the tank into the pump. The engine picked up enough to get him to the next corner where similar tactics brought a final surge of power before the engine died, fortunately having given him just enough speed to coast to the line in silence. Had Piquet known and charged, he could have won. The race showed graphically how the regulations, designed to curb the power of the turbo, had turned Grand Prix into a lottery whose most important piece of technology was the fuel gauge – not what Grand Prix racing was about.

Elio de Angelis retired from the Monaco Grand Prix with mechanical problems, as he had done from the previous two races. On 15 May, in preparation for the Belgian Grand Prix he was testing the Brabham BT55 at Paul Ricard. As the Brabham went through a high speed left/right complex of corners at Verrerie at 180 mph; he hit the barrier, turned over and landed upside down in flames. It took eight minutes to get him out of the car and there was a long wait for the helicopter to arrive to take him to hospital in Marseilles where he died. With all the new safety arrangements which had been brought in under pressure from the drivers and from FOCA, death was no longer as frequent a visitor to Grand Prix racing as it had been in the 1960s and 1970s. Shock went through the Formula 1 family as it closed ranks in a genuine display of grief and conscience. Less surprising was the prepared statement read by Jean-Marie Balestre to journalists which announced that an Extraordinary Meeting of FISA's Executive Committee would consider unspecified ways of reducing engine power to 600 bhp for 1987. The statement also announced that the Verrerie would not be included in the French Grand Prix in July.

Jean-Marie Balestre took no questions, the most pressing of which concerned the lack of proper safety arrangements during testing sessions.

Elio de Angelis' death left Riccardo Patrese alone in the Brabham team for a subdued Belgian Grand Prix which by some proper twist of fate was won by de Angelis' erstwhile team-mate at Lotus and great chum, Nigel Mansell. Mansell was tight-lipped on the podium, apparently holding back tears as he dedicated his victory to Elio de Angelis, aged 28. The sad irony of de Angelis' death and the opening it created at Brabham, was that Ecclestone signed up Derek Warwick in time for the next Grand Prix, the very man who had failed to get de Angelis' seat at Lotus because of Ayrton Senna's objections.

Mansell continued his winning streak in Canada then Senna won in Detroit, and Mansell came back with victory in the French Grand Prix. Then came the British Grand Prix at Brands Hatch where there was a special visitor for practice day. Frank Williams was flown in by helicopter, arranged by Bernie Ecclestone as head of the Formula 1 family. He was in the pits opposite another banner which read, 'Welcome back Frank – from Brands Hatch'.

Williams watched the race on television and saw what was a highly popular win at Brands Hatch for a number of reasons. Williams took first and second place, fastest lap and pole position, as convincing a demonstration of the superiority of the Williams-Honda combination as it was possible to make. It put Mansell in the lead in the Championship with 47 points to Prost's 43 and Senna's 36, and Williams, in what should have been its darkest year, was also leading the Constructors' Championship by 16 points from McLaren. Best of all, however, was that Frank Williams was back and his wife Virginia was on the podium to receive the trophy.

The senior management of Honda made the pilgrimage to Adelaide to see the Australian Grand Prix where they confidently expected Mansell to take the Championship; they had already won the Constructors' Championship. Mansell was 6 points ahead of Alain Prost and 7 ahead of his team-mate Nelson Piquet and provided he could finish anywhere in the top three, he would take the title, while Prost and Piquet both had to win. Mansell took pole position and made a good start, taking the lead from Senna, Piquet and Rosberg but he made room for all three to pass him before the next corner, letting the race settle down with Prost and Rosberg just behind. On lap 20 the order was Rosberg, Piquet, Prost then Mansell which would give Mansell the title. Piquet then spun off and Prost and Mansell went through before he rejoined. Then Prost had a puncture and Mansell was second as Prost rejoined a minute behind Rosberg in fourth place. Rosberg then heard a nasty noise from the rear and pulled off the track, just as Prost passed Mansell. The Goodyear team had seen the tread come off Rosberg's tyres and they advised all the Goodyear customers to bring their cars in immediately. At that moment, Mansell was charging down the pit straight, passing a back marker at around 200 mph when his left rear tyre burst. He started weaving all over the track, fighting for some kind of control as the bare wheel gouged into the surface. The race director, Burdette Martin, nearly ordered out the red flag as Mansell's Williams headed uncontrollably for the first corner, but miraculously it went up an escape road, leaving the track clear. Had Mansell blocked the corner and the race been stopped, he would have been Champion. Piquet was in the lead but had to come in for tyres as Prost took over. With 16 laps to go and 15 seconds between them, either could still take the Championship. Prost had used a lot of fuel and over the last few laps he slowed down as Piquet caught up, breaking the track record in the process. Prost just made it with his fuel gauge showing under zero, to become only the fourth driver to win the Championship in two consecutive seasons, the only one of the modern age, joining the ranks of Alberto Ascari in 1952–3,

Juan Manuel Fangio 1954–5 and 1956–7 and Jack Brabham in 1959–60. Nigel Mansell was almost inconsolable, but he was alive.

The turbocharged era was moving to a close. To curb engine power seemed perverse but if unrestrained, speeds would have risen uncontrollably. The FIA reduction of the 1984 limit of 220 litres of fuel to 195 litres for 1986 had only kept the problem in check at the expense of drivers running out of fuel. As promised, FISA had examined ways of reducing power, including the use of pop-off valves, pre-set to reduce boost at a particular power output. These were introduced for 1987. But the big decision was to permit normally aspirated engines of 3.5 litres for a two-year transitional period leading to a ban on turbocharged engines from 1989.

Two long-standing relationships between designers and team bosses came to an end in the off season. Gordon Murray and Bernie Ecclestone parted company at Brabham, which was just a shadow of its former self. John Barnard left McLaren after growing difficulties in his relationship with Ron Dennis. Murray moved to McLaren. Part of the problem between Dennis and Barnard was that Barnard wanted greater credit for the success of the cars he designed, greater credit that Ron Dennis was prepared to give, and they drifted apart. Barnard had sold his shares in McLaren to Mansour Ojjeh in 1985 to raise some money to buy a substantial house in Surrey and he no longer had the same identification with McLaren since he was now an employee. Steve Nichols, his protégé, took over and started work on the MP4/3 for 1987.

John Barnard moved to Ferrari where Enzo Ferrari was in his 89th year and still exerting day-to-day control over the company's racing. The cars were not competitive and the evidence was there for all to see: it had not won a single World Championship event since the German Grand Prix in 1985. It was Williams and John Barnard's MP4 series which had been largely responsible for putting Ferrari in the shade, and when he heard that Barnard was available, Enzo Ferrari sent Marco Piccinini to negotiate a deal. Barnard said yes, but the condition was that he would not have to move to Maranello. It was a mark of how desperate Enzo Ferrari was that they came to an unprecedented arrangement in which he was to be paid $500,000 a year, would answer directly to Enzo Ferrari and Ferrari would set up a fully equipped design studio in Surrey, close to Barnard's new home, where he could work and visit the factory as required. The arrangement did not go down well at Maranello. He started work on new aerodynamics and an innovative electro-hydraulic gear change for a new car for the 3.5-litre normally aspirated formula in 1989.

One of Barnard's first actions was to recommend scrapping Ferrari's Indianapolis project which was sapping effort away from Formula 1, and Ferrari agreed, something else which did not go down well at Maranello. The vast majority of the old hands at the company simply could not understand why the arrangement had been made, but Ferrari's word was law and they had to live with it. Mauro Foghieri did not, and having already been sidelined, he left, breaking another even longer-standing relationship between designer and team boss which went back 30 years. He went to Lamborghini to design a new 3.5-litre V12 normally aspirated engine. Johansson's contract was not renewed and Gerhard Berger was signed up from Benetton to partner Michele Alboreto.

Barnard had what he wanted but he was later to regret leaving McLaren when he found that it had been a haven of common sense and technical excellence compared with Ferrari. McLaren's relationship with Mansour Ojjeh of TAG, which had assets of $500m and a high-tech base, strengthened, and Ojjeh was able to bring solid backing to McLaren, making a real business out of a Formula 1 team.

As one new long-term relationship was forming,

so another was coming to an end. At the end of 1986, the 20-year association between Lotus and John Player cigarettes finished. This was the heyday of the asset stripper, and Imperial Tobacco, John Player's parent company, was taken over by the Hanson Trust. Geoffrey Kent, with whom Chapman had built up such a strong relationship and who had served on the Lotus board, left and the sponsorship was not renewed, provoking a switch to Camel for sponsorship and from Renault to Honda engines. Lotus was pioneering active suspension in the Lotus 99T, a computer-controlled system to smooth out the ride of the car, changing the settings for the varying conditions, twists and turns of the track. Senna had a new partner, Saturo Nakajima, a Japanese driver who came as part of the Honda deal.

Frank Williams was also developing active suspension, and after its performance in 1986, Williams started as favourites for 1987. Williams was awarded the CBE in recognition of his services to motor sport. He was back at his desk to preside over his squabbling drivers, Nelson Piquet and Nigel Mansell, who continued to live uncomfortably under the same pit roof.

By June, Ferrari was in complete disarray. The factionalization had led Piero Lardi Ferrari and Harvey Postlethwaite to contract French aerodynamicist Gustav Brunner, to start work on a completely new car which they kept secret from Enzo Ferrari. When the old man found out, he was furious and had a massive row with his son. The result of the power struggle inside the Ferrari family was a forgone conclusion: the 89-year-old patriarch won; Piero Lardi Ferrari was sacked from his job as team boss and given a job far away from the racing action; Harvey Postlethwaite was fired.

Lotus was improving with the Honda engine and Senna won at Monaco and in Detroit, moving him into first place in the Championship on 24 points to Prost's 22, Piquet's 18, Johansson's 13 and Mansell's 12. Senna's two victories had not been lost on Ron Dennis. Prost and Dennis had a very

Colour: television coverage of Michele Alboreto's
victory in the 1983 US Grand Prix led to
Benetton buying the Toleman team.

good working relationship, which both men valued, but that did not stop Dennis from looking to the future. He was investing heavily in a new factory and had to stay competitive. That meant having the best drivers and he had been keeping an eye on Senna's progress ever since he had given Senna a test drive in 1983. Dennis also thought about engines. The TAG-Porsche turbo had been a great success but it had been based on the investment which McLaren and TAG could afford at the time. He was mindful of the progress at Williams and now Lotus with Honda power, backed by all the resources of a major manufacturer, which was clearly a huge advantage. Midway through the 1987 season Honda engines had won 6 of the 8

Grands Prix to TAG-Porsche's 2, so Dennis started discussions with Honda and found that they too had been following Senna's progress while providing him with engines at Lotus.

Honda's attitude to Frank Williams changed following his accident. Williams had won 9 Grands Prix and the Constructor's title in 1986 and despite the progress of Senna, it was in with a real chance of both titles in 1987. The contract to supply Williams with engines ran until the end of 1988, but Honda's management decided to end it, for many reasons no doubt, but one of them seemed to be that they simply could not come to terms with doing business with a man in a wheelchair.

During the summer of 1987, an arrangement

which suited everybody was made, everybody except Frank Williams. Johansson would go and Senna would move from Lotus to McLaren for 1988, alongside Prost. Honda would cancel the last year of its contract with Williams and move its support to McLaren. Nelson Piquet had also formed a good relationship with Honda and he was not too happy at Williams because of the fractured relationship with Mansell, and without the Honda engine, he too wanted out. Piquet's relationship with Senna was even worse than with Mansell, especially after comments made by Piquet about Senna's personal life. Piquet could not possibly move to McLaren, even if Dennis had been prepared to ditch Prost, so he took Senna's place at Lotus.

Frank Williams was given the news in July. It was a cruel blow: Honda was cancelling the engine contract at the end of the year, a clear breach of contract; and his driver Piquet would be leaving to go to Lotus which would continue to have Honda engines. Everything Frank Williams had built since losing the support of TAG was taken away again. It was a crisis, but that was all. Frank Williams, ever practical and courteous, decided against legal action, took financial compensation and started out again with the Judd normally-aspirated engine which was far from competitive, and hired Riccardo Patrese to replace Piquet.

Ironically, the news came in a great month for Williams-Honda. Mansell won the French Grand Prix with Piquet second, a feat the team and drivers repeated at Silverstone, putting the two Williams drivers on 30 points each in the Championship, just one behind Senna, and leading the Constructors Championship by 60 points to 39 over Lotus. Piquet won the German Grand Prix, from which Mansell retired, then he won in Hungary with Senna second and Prost third. Mansell won in Austria, his fourth victory, with Piquet second in an extraordinary display of consistency by Williams, which Piquet carried through at Monza, winning his third Grand Prix.

The Williams run was interrupted by Prost who won in Portugal, his twenty-eighth Grand Prix victory, beating Jackie Stewart's all time record of 27, set in 1973. Then Mansell was back with two more victories in Spain and Mexico, with Piquet second. The two Williams drivers were back on top of the Championship table: Piquet on 73 points, Mansell on 61 with just two races to go. It was all decided at Suzuka on Honda's home territory, where the two Williams drivers battled it out for pole position. Mansell crashed in the process, and was badly bruised and shaken. He was taken to hospital with fluid on his chest and though he recovered quickly, he was declared unfit to race and flown home to England, making Piquet World Champion before the race started.

With all the support of the richest sponsor in the sport, the tobacco money from Marlboro, McLaren had been put in the shade but not for long. Ron Dennis was ruthlessly businesslike and practical. He wanted the best and he had got it: the two best drivers in the Championship and the engine which had just cleaned up in 1987. Through the cross shareholding with Mansour Ojjeh he still had the high-tech support of TAG, and a new factory which McLaren occupied at the end of the year. It was the beginning of a two-year saga, a cocktail of different forces, competitive, technical, financial and personal, the likes of which Formula 1 had never seen before.

Senna joined McLaren and Piquet joined Lotus as planned. The new World Champion had the backing of Honda but he was not as happy at Lotus as he expected. There was great hope for the new Honda engine and for the new chassis designed by Gerard Ducarouge. With Camel as a sponsor the financial future looked better than many teams. Satoru Nakajima, the second driver, was there at the behest of the Japanese engine supplier and was not the fastest but he fitted in well. But there was clearly a gaping hole in the company, the hole where Colin Chapman had been. The aftermath of the DeLorean affair continued to rumble on in the background, the reputation suffered and the spark was never quite ignited again. Some observers felt that the company would not last long following Chapman's death, so there was some surprise at how effectively Hazel Chapman and her son Clive had taken over, but planning for the future was mortgaged to dealing with the problems of the present. Lotus was a company and a team which had thrived for 25 years on the central energy of Chapman, a reliance that he would come up with something which would keep Lotus ahead, and that could never be replaced. Lotus needed a wind tunnel and the kind of investment which McLaren and Williams were building up, but it was not done.

A complex range of issues brought the Brabham team to the end of its association with Bernie Ecclestone. He had not kept pace with the way that Formula 1 was developing at team level and had also been overtaken by McLaren and Williams with their high technology and their engine deals. The death of Elio de Angelis the previous year and the increasing concentration of Ecclestone on FOCA business also had their effect. He sold the team to a Swiss financier at the end of 1987. The sale came at the same time as the final settlement of the FOCA-FISA war with the Grande Concorde, an agreement which opened the way for him to move upwards now that Jean-Marie Balestre's power had been eroded. Freed from running a team, Ecclestone concentrated even more on doing deals with track owners and television companies, expanding Formula 1 and consolidating his own position at the heart of it.

Before the season got under way, Enzo Ferrari celebrated his 90th birthday on 18 February 1988. His party was held in part of the Ferrari factory all decked out in red, yellow and black. Over 1800 people attended and there was an outward show of affection between Enzo and his son Piero Lardi, but in private relations were strained. Ferrari's health was failing and he could not walk without assistance but his mind remained alert. He was an

increasingly lonely old man who spent most of his time in bed on the telephone. Even at 90, his attention was tuned to running the racing team which bore his name.

Sadly for Enzo Ferrari, what turned out to be his last season saw the most convincing performance by the kit car teams he had fought for 30 years. McLaren was in a class of its own with Ayrton Senna driving a car which matched his abilities. He put his McLaren-Honda MP4/4 on pole position at Rio for the Brazilian Grand Prix, just ahead of Mansell who had driven the Judd-powered Williams into an heroic second place on the grid ahead of Prost. Senna's car jammed in first gear on the parade lap and when he reached pole position again he put up his hands and the car was whisked away. Mansell completed a second parade lap to cool his engine then took up effective pole position as Senna went for the spare car and joined at the back. Prost and Gerhard Berger went past Mansell before the first corner. Meanwhile Senna was disqualified for using the spare car after the green flag had been given. Ron Dennis was arguing behind the scenes but to no avail and on lap 30 Senna was black flagged. Berger challenged as well as he could for Ferrari, but Prost led for the rest of the race, finishing 10 seconds ahead of Berger with Nelson Piquet third.

The McLarens got better and only Gerhard Berger and Piquet were able to make any impression on them: at Imola, Senna took pole again, and won with Prost second. At Monaco, Senna was on pole again but had an accident and walked home to his apartment without going to the pits, leaving Prost to win with Berger second. Senna then posted his fourth pole position of the season in the Mexican Grand Prix but Prost was on form and although Senna challenged all the way, Prost kept him in second place. Senna maintained his record of pole positions and won the Canadian Grand Prix with Prost second. McLaren had taken every pole position, won all five races and come second in three. The prospect of a clean sweep was probably in Ron Dennis's mind when he said to journalists with the tactlessness that has sometimes characterized his dealings with the press: 'We are trying to make history; you are only reporting it'. History continued to be made and reported when Senna posted his sixth pole position in a row at Detroit, and won again from Prost, narrowing the gap between the two McLaren drivers: Prost 45, Senna 33, with Berger stuck on 18. Once again, the Ferrari challenge appeared to have petered out.

Prost broke Senna's run of pole positions in the French Grand Prix, then won with Senna second, opening up the gap with 54 points to Senna's 39. Berger then broke McLaren's run of pole positions at Silverstone, but Senna won after Prost pulled out because of the wet, leaving Nigel Mansell to take second place to huge applause. In stark contrast, the French press tore into Prost whose lead was down to six points: 54 to 48. At Hockenheim, Senna was on pole again, his seventh of the season, then he won from Prost. Senna took pole position and won the Hungarian Grand Prix, with Prost second, bringing them together in the title race on 66 points, putting huge psychological pressure on Prost. McLaren had already won the Constructors' Championship by 132 points to Ferrari on 44.

On 14 August 1988 Enzo Anselmo Ferrari died in bed, with Piero Lardi Ferrari at his side. His funeral and burial beside his own father in the family crypt were all carried out in secret. When the news was announced there were outpourings of grief in the press as Italy came to terms with the death of one of its great post-war national heroes. A huge public funeral mass was held in the Duomo in Maranello a month later. Cars had been Enzo Ferrari's whole life for nearly 70 years, cars which bore his name, which carried the Prancing Horse badge, cars which won races. They were his life but they never pleased him as they did other people. Even those Ferraris which did his bidding, winning races, were either destroyed or neglected soon afterwards as he moved on to new cars and new ways of promoting the mystique of the name

Ferrari. When work started on a Ferrari museum in Maranello, close to the end of his life, the company owned only a handful of his cars to put in it. Privately, he despised the rich men who bought his sports cars and few Ferraris were true engineering masterpieces. Ferrari was no innovator; he was deeply conservative and most of the gifted engineers who passed through his factory – Vittorio Jano, Aurelio Lampredi, Giaochino Colombo, Carlo Chiti and Mauro Foghieri – saw their ideas and expertise stifled.

Ferrari prided himself on being an 'agitator of men', providing leadership by ruthless manipulation. Drivers came, did his bidding, or they went. Seven men won nine Driver's World Championships for him: Alberto Ascari; Juan Manuel Fangio; Mike Hawthorn; Phil Hill; John Surtees; Niki Lauda; and Jody Scheckter. They contributed to six Constructors' titles, both records at the time of his death. Most left after a row because they could not stand being part of the factionalized, paranoid team over which he presided. With the exception of Scheckter who retired from Ferrari, they all went on to drive for other constructors. Nine top drivers died in pursuit of Ferrari's ambitions: Alberto Ascari; Eugenio Castellotti; Alfonso de Portago; Luigi Musso; Peter Collins; Wolfgang von Trips; Lorenzo Bandini; Ignazio Giunti; and Gilles Villeneuve.

Enzo Ferrari succeeded through sheer force of personality and autocratic style of management. He managed to bludgeon together just enough engineering, enough money and more than enough driver commitment to win. In the end it was not enough: for the last nine years of his life he knew only the bitter taste of failure as the men he had once dismissed as mere *assemblatore*, took the field. Cooper, Chapman, Brabham, Tyrell, Williams, Dennis and Ecclestone all used innovative engineering and finesse to beat him fair and square. They changed the course of Formula 1 history, not Ferrari, who looked back to history for his inspiration. Although history may judge Enzo

Danger: greater safety
means that big
accidents such as
Mauricio Gugelmin's
in the 1989 French
Grand Prix are
rarely fatal.

Ferrari harshly, long after many of the other names of the last 50 years have been forgotten, the single word Ferrari will linger, standing for power, speed, romance and even excellence.

The extended Formula 1 family paused to mourn the passing of its oldest member, then the battle for the Championship between the two McLaren drivers resumed. Senna took pole position at Spa and won the Belgian Grand Prix, putting him ahead in the World Championship for the first time on 75 points to Prost's 72. Prost was crushed. Then came the Italian Grand Prix on 11 September. Senna was on pole again and led from the start with Prost putting him under pressure in what seemed like a rerun of many a Grand Prix that year. Then Prost's engine started overheating under the strain and he had to retire on lap 35. Berger took up the challenge and put Senna under more pressure. With two laps to go, Senna came up on back marker Jean-Louis Schlesser, who made a tiny error; Senna clipped Schlesser and spun off, dashing any hopes Ron Dennis had of a clean sweep in the 1988 Championship. It left the field clear for Berger to win with Alboreto second in an extraordinary, some said providentially inspired and miraculous Ferrari 1-2. The *tifosi* roared their approval of Berger, the new hero; many in Italy wept into the night and Marco Piccinini hailed the victory as the start of a new Ferrari revival.

The only real competition was between the two McLaren drivers. Prost was determined to claw back the lead in the Championship at Estoril, taking pole position and starting a big battle with Senna for the lead on lap 1. At the end of the lap, as they came down the finishing straight past the pits, they were nose to nose and wheel to wheel, with Prost on the pit wall side of the track. Senna moved sharply across, pushing Prost to within inches of the wall and sending the mechanics scuttling for cover. Sandwiched between Senna and the wall, Prost held on and in the end it was Senna who had to give way or lose the line into the next corner. Prost took the lead. Senna later spun and fell back and Prost won with Senna sixth, putting Prost on 81 points and Senna on 76. Prost said of Senna's intimidating driving, 'If he wants the title that badly he can have it'.

Prost won again in Spain, bringing his total to six victories to Senna's seven. On gross points this put Prost on 90 and Senna on 79, but now the scoring system punished Prost for his success. Only the best 11 results counted, and while Senna could drop his sixth place, Prost had to drop a second place which was the worst finish in the points that he had. This meant that as they went into the Japanese Grand Prix all Senna had to do was win to take the title.

Tension was high between the two and there was the inevitable paranoia on both sides, that the team or the engine supplier might be favouring one or the other driver. It was well known that Senna and Honda had been part of the deal to bring him to McLaren. Paranoia bubbled over into an extraordinary exchange of letters between Jean-Marie Balestre who wrote, as president of FISA, to the president of Honda, Tadushi Kume, demanding that there be complete parity in the engines supplied to the two McLaren drivers. Considering the implied insult, Mr Kume was restrained in his response, simply pointing out that Honda had always been fair.

Senna took pole position at Suzuka, his thirteenth of the season, but he nearly stalled at the start and Prost went off into the lead. Senna started right at the back but immediately started on a charge, and by the first corner he was up to 14th place; by the end of lap 1 he was lying eighth and by lap 20 he was lying second. On lap 27 he took the lead in a daring manoeuvre and though Prost stayed with him, when it rained lightly Prost backed off and Senna won. With the chequered flag came his eighth win, a record for a single season, and the thing he cherished more than anything, the Driver's World Championship.

There is a strong theme which runs through the career of Ayrton Senna: he always tried to harness the full resources of the team around him alone, as the Warwick incident had shown. He was very close to Honda, antipathetic at best to his countryman Piquet and fiercely competitive with Prost, whom he saw as a competitor, not only on the track, but also in the quest for resources and backing inside the team.

Frank Williams had a dreadful season and all that Nigel Mansell could manage was two second places in the Judd powered FW12, retiring from every other race. Mansell departed to join Berger at Ferrari where Michele Alboreto was moved out to accommodate him. Patrese stayed at Williams and Mansell was replaced by Thierry Boutsen to drive the new Williams car. The FW13B was the first with the Renault V-10 engine which Frank Williams had negotiated long and hard to get, the Judd having only ever been an interim measure.

Honda had looked at the competition in 1989 and decided it could only support one team at the level required to be competitive. It dropped Lotus, casting it aside not quite in the same way it had Williams the previous year, but with the same effect; Lotus turned to Judd. Even with the Honda turbo engine, the Lotus 100T had not been very successful, and Gerard Ducarouge went at the end of 1988 to make way for Frank Dernie from Williams. It was clear that in his three years at Lotus, Ayrton Senna had managed to make Lotus look better than it was, to punch above its weight, and with his departure the cracks had begun to show. In 1987, when Williams had lost the Honda engine contract, Frank Williams had responded with a determination which transmitted itself through the team and through the Formula 1 family. When Lotus lost it, the team looked to be floundering. Tony Rudd was brought in but he was from another era, having started out with Rolls-Royce and BRM and he was no replacement for Colin Chapman. Eventually Camel demanded and got the head of Peter Warr as well.

The engine deal was what now divided the teams. The resources which a large manufacturer could put behind developing an engine led to the emergence of a premier league of the top three or four teams which had such deals, setting up a virtuous circle for those teams: a winning engine would get the podium finish which brought greater support and more victories. The Honda RA109E V10-powered McLaren MP4 and the Renault RS01 V10-powered Williams FW13 were out on their own. Then came Ferrari with its engine, the Tipo 034 V12, then Benetton which moved from the Cosworth DFR to the Cosworth-designed but Ford-badged V8 during 1989.

After a year in the doldrums, Brabham was back under new management, with the new BT58 powered by the Judd V8 which also powered Lotus, Euro Brun, Leyton House and March. For the once-glorious names, Brabham and Lotus, to be bracketed with also-rans at the back of the grid was an indication of how far they had slipped since the death of Colin Chapman and the sale of Brabham by Bernie Ecclestone. Cosworth had also slipped from its heyday: AGS, Coloni, Arrows, Dallara, Minardi, Onyx, Osella, Rial, Tyrell and Ligier all used the new Cosworth but once again, the tables had been turned on Cosworth by big manufacturers who could spend millions on development. Lamborghini's V12s powered the Lolas and Yamaha powered the Zakspeed with its V8. Alfa Romeo had finally disappeared.

McLaren was on top, but the internal tensions increased. Ayrton Senna was fiercely committed to winning, chillingly so, and Prost, though competitive could not accept as reasonable the lengths to which Senna went. Senna knew it, was unconcerned, showed it and used it to take over the top position in McLaren for himself, starting with his thirtieth pole position in his native Brazil. Senna not only had Prost ranged against him, there was also Nigel Mansell driving John Barnard's new Ferrari 639 with its electro-hydraulic gearbox. Williams was also looking competitive again with the Renault engine and on the grid behind Senna at Rio was Riccardo Patrese

Landmark: Benetton's colourful entry to the 1986 Grand Prix, was the first by a constructor completely outside the motor racing industry.

for Williams, Gerhard Berger for Ferrari, Thierry Boutsen for Williams, Prost for McLaren, then Mansell whose car had been playing up in qualifying. Senna made a poor start and Patrese pulled slightly ahead of him going into the first corner and Berger also pulled alongside. Senna suddenly found himself sandwiched between the two, but rather than give way he stuck with it and Berger's rear wheel tore Senna's nosecone off. Berger spun off and retired but Senna continued. The race leaders were now Patrese, Boutsen and Mansell. Senna went in and had a new nosecone fitted. Three laps later Boutsen's engine expired and Prost was on Mansell's tail. Mansell got past Patrese on lap 16 and led for most of the rest of the race, showing that McLaren had a challenger and that he had a place at the top table of drivers.

At Imola, renamed Autodromo Enzo e Dino Ferrari, Senna and Prost had an agreement that whoever reached the first corner first, the other would give way on that corner. This would avoid the possibility of the two McLaren drivers taking each other out before the race was even under way. Senna was cleanly away so the agreement was academic. Senna led for four laps until Berger had a terrific accident at Tamburello corner and caught fire. Berger was not seriously injured but the race was stopped and restarted and this time it was Prost who made the better start and was ahead at the first corner, but Senna did not honour the agreement and slipstreamed past Prost before the first corner, going on to win the race with a very angry Prost second. Alain Prost always spoke his mind and after the race he told Senna, plainly to his face, that he was clearly a man whose word could not be taken. The fragile relationship between the two team-mates, which had been under growing strain, started to crack. Ron Dennis tried to mediate and succeeded in getting Senna to make an apology in private, but Prost would not leave it alone. He told the French sports magazine *L'Equipe* that he 'no longer wished to have any business with [Senna]; I appreciate honesty and he is not honest'.

Prost used the occasion of the French Grand Prix to announce that he would be leaving McLaren at the end of the year. He had had enough of Senna and his endless efforts to undermine him. Having made his decision, Prost's performance suddenly improved: he won in France and Britain with Senna out of the points in both races, putting Prost on 47 points to Senna's 27. Senna won in Germany with Prost second but in Hungary, Mansell beat Senna in a straight fight with Prost fourth.

Having announced his departure from McLaren in France, Prost chose Monza to announce that he would drive for Ferrari in 1990, going on to win his 34th Grand Prix victory, giving him 71 points with Senna retiring and remaining on 51. Prost's 9 points clinched the Constructors' title for McLaren. On the podium, Prost dropped the trophy to the *tifosi* below, who roared approval of their new hero's gesture. An angry Ron Dennis then placed the Constructors' trophy at Prost's feet, their six-year partnership ending with pointless gestures and a very sour note.

Senna was on pole again in Portugal, battling with Mansell who showed that Ferrari was increasingly competitive, until they spun off together. Berger won for Ferrari and Prost was fourth. In Spain, Senna won from Berger and Prost, leaving Prost 16 points ahead in the World Championship with two races to go. Senna had to win both the remaining races to have any hope of retaining the Championship, and even then Prost could win by gathering sufficient points with lower finishes. In Japan, Senna was on pole but Prost made the better start and went into the lead and so it continued for 47 of the 53 laps. Coming to the chicane Prost had the line and Senna went up the inside as Prost closed in on the corner. Senna never gave way on the track, that was part of his style, so the two McLarens collided and slid off the circuit. Prost gave up, but Senna got going again and by lap 50 overtook Alessandro Nannini's Benetton which was in the lead. He won on the track only to be disqualified for missing part of the circuit, ending his Championship hopes and making Alain Prost World Champion for the third time.

Senna's appeal was heard the following Friday. When the McLaren team turned up they heard that FISA felt the stewards at Suzuka had been too lenient and asked the court to suspend Senna for a year. The court gave its verdict the following Tuesday, fining Senna $100,000 and a six-month suspended ban. Senna was outraged and at the next Grand Prix at Adelaide he held a press conference calling the decision 'unacceptable'. It rained very hard during the race, and Prost drove one lap then retired. In the murk, Senna drove into the back of Martin Brundle and retired. Thierry Boutsen won, the first victory for Williams and the new alliance with Renault.

At McLaren, Steve Nichols left with Prost for Ferrari and Neil Oatley took over design of the MP4/5B while Gordon Murray was put in charge of designing a new McLaren sports car. Like Ferrari and Lotus before him, Ron Dennis was looking to capitalize on the name by building a glamorous sports car.

At Benetton, Nannini had managed just one controversial victory and only because Prost and Senna had handed it to him on a plate. Benetton's second driver, Johnny Herbert, had been dropped by Benetton in mid-season and replaced by Emmanuele Pirro, an Italian driver who was dropped in turn at the end of 1989 to make room for Nelson Piquet from Lotus. Peter Collins went to Lotus at the same time and Herbert went with him.

The vacancy created by the departure of Peter Collins from Benetton was filled in a most unusual way for the Formula 1 community; it was an unusual company. Flavio Briatore, who knew nothing at all about Formula 1 and had only been to his first race, the 1988 Australian Grand Prix, was appointed to take over. His background was purely Italian business, insurance, stock broking and a spell as right-hand man to the Benetton

patriarch, Luciano. In 1977 he had gone to the US where he had worked in property development while setting up a marketing operation with 750 Benetton outlets across the US. He had no technical background and his appointment was clearly to maximize the marketing impact of the Benetton investment in Formula 1. He was very conscious of the Italian dimension in motor racing but he was the complete opposite of Enzo Ferrari. Briatore was colourful with a real sense of style and the Benetton team was once again leading Formula 1 into new pastures. He provided a gust, if not a wind of change through the sport. Briatore was not the usual sort of member of the Formula 1 family, but he had the formidable personality to make things happen. He formed a friendship with Bernie Ecclestone, and reportedly bought Ecclestone's apartment overlooking the Thames in London. He learned the ropes when it came to swapping people around, replacing Rory Byrne with John Barnard who had left Ferrari.

Barnard's departure from Ferrari after three years came from pressure to either move to Maranello or quit. He quit and was replaced by Argentine Enrique Scalabroni and Steve Nichols from McLaren. To make way for Prost at Ferrari, Gerhard Berger had been ousted and took the spare seat at McLaren. Prost, three times and reigning World Champion and Nigel Mansell were driving Barnard's Ferrari 640 which looked like the challenger in 1990.

Shortly after the close of the 1989 season, Ayrton Senna held a press conference in São Paulo which amounted to an attack on Jean-Marie Balestre and his impartiality, the accusation being that Balestre had manipulated the Championship in favour of Prost. This naturally outraged Balestre and the highly public row between McLaren and Senna, and Balestre and FISA, blared on into early 1990. Senna's appeal to the FIA regarding the collision at Suzuka was unsuccessful and the governing body went further, giving its opinion that Senna was a fundamentally dangerous driver.

Peace: after the FOCA/FISA wars Balestre
and Eccleston worked together in Formula 1
until Max Mosley ousted Balestre in 1991.

Senna saw this as a witch hunt and his stubborn streak triumphed. There was a meeting at FIA headquarters between Balestre, Senna and Ron Dennis, then Senna appeared the following day before the World Motor Sports Council to explain himself. The Council ordered Senna to withdraw his accusations or it would refuse to grant him his superlicence, and Balestre demanded payment of the $100,000 fine imposed after Suzuka, all by 11 January 1990. McLaren paid the fine. The team was required to enter two drivers for the season and on 11 January it nominated Gerhard Berger and Jonathan Palmer, McLaren's test driver. An hour later, Senna's name was substituted, there having been a series of faxes in which honour was at least partly satisfied on both sides, although privately both sides fumed. It was almost too much for Bernie Ecclestone, now a vice president at FISA, who got the season off to a good start by commenting on the Senna-Prost battles that 'drivers are no more than light bulbs, take one out, put another in'.

His comment came just before the US Grand Prix at Phoenix, Arizona and did not get the season off to the most harmonious of starts. The circuit was laid out on the streets of Phoenix, very conveniently for the local population, but they stayed away in droves and it was a complete flop for the promotors. Moving the US Grad Prix from one city to another was clearly not a strategy which

Family matters: Enzo Ferrari with his illegitimate
son Piero Lardi Ferrari, who came into the
business after the death of Ferrari's wife in 1978.

consolidated the idea of a great US motor race.

Ayrton Senna won in Phoenix, then the Championship moved to Brazil. He had never won his home Grand Prix in Brazil, and in 1990 it was at Interlagos in his home town of São Paolo. This was the one that Senna really wanted to win. Once again there was a drama played out by Balestre in the run-up to the race, in which he would not confirm that it would take place, because improvements to the circuit had not been finished. He finally announced that it could take place having had favourable reports from Ecclestone and the teams, who might well have run it without his sanction. He then arrived on race day looking like a character out of *Reservoir Dogs* with bodyguards,

rumoured to be heavily armed, in attendance. He blew provocative kisses to the crowd, then addressed them in Spanish, to be drowned out by catcalls in Portuguese. The outpouring of hatred by Brazilians against Balestre was given full vent in T-shirts with 'Fuck You Balestre' printed on them, and the crowd roared its approval as Senna led from pole.

All went well for Brazil with Senna leading Berger, then Boutsen took second place while Prost moved up steadily until lap 40 when Prost was still over 12 seconds behind Senna. Then Senna came on Nakajima in a Tyrell, who moved over but then came back on to the line and his wheel tore Senna's nose off. Prost took the lead and Senna rejoined more than half a minute behind. Prost won, with Berger second and Senna third. Senna and the Paulista crowd went home mortified; Prost went home delighted as did the Ferrari team and Balestre had his flight home delayed by seven hours due to a bomb scare.

Senna and Prost dominated the season again, arriving in Japan with Senna on 78 points and Prost on 69. Senna was on pole and he asked for it to be changed to the other side of the track. Prost agreed, but the officials did not. The two went into the first corner together, Prost just ahead but leaving some room on the inside line which Senna took, gaining on Prost. When Prost turned into the corner, Senna's nosecone was alongside the middle of Prost's Ferrari. Neither would back off, they collided and went off together. With Prost out, Senna had his second title. The sight of the Championship being decided by what most saw as a cynical and unsporting move by Senna shocked many people at the top of Formula 1. Senna believed that Balestre had been behind the decision not to move pole, so once again propelled by that sense that the world was against him, he tried to defend himself, but to little effect, and the affair descended into a ritual of insults and threats.

Benetton, the main beneficiary of the Senna-Prost battle, had improved from the changes brought in by Briatore. Nelson Piquet won at Suzuka and at Adelaide and formed a very good working relationship with Barnard in developing the B190. Benetton also benefitted from the decline of Lotus as Camel switched its sponsorship to Benetton to take advantage of the huge profile, higher possibly than its success on the track would justify thanks to the marketing skills of Briatore and the Benetton family. The new car, the B191, with a completely new carbon fibre monocoque, was designed to use active suspension and a semi-automatic gearbox.

It was not a happy time at Lotus: Peter Collins had bought shares in the company and signed up Johnny Herbert. During 1989, the DeLorean affair

finally caught up with the company and Colin Chapman's involvement in its downfall was fully revealed when charges were brought against Fred Bushell, the chairman of Team Lotus. Bushell went into the dock to answer charges of conspiracy to defraud the DeLorean company 'together with the late Colin Chapman'. Bushell was eventually jailed.

Brabham was hanging on; its new owners turned to financier Ted Ball whose company, Landhurst Leasing, put up £6m against the assets of the team to keep it going with drivers Martin Brundle and Mark Blundell in the BT60Y powered by a Yamaha V12 engine.

As two once great teams were going through a painful decline, so another was arriving: Jordan Grand Prix. Eddie Jordan had been successful in the lower formulae and decided that the time was right to move to Formula 1. He was 43, born in Dublin in 1948 and had worked at the Bank of Ireland after leaving school, studying accountancy in the evenings. He discovered karting, becoming Irish National Champion in 1972, then rose through the formulae to drive for Team Ireland in Formula 3. He realized that he was not going to make it to the top rank of drivers but loved the lifestyle. He turned to team management, starting Eddie Jordan Racing in 1981 from a lock-up near Silverstone, fielding Martin Brundle in 1983, the year of his classic battles with Senna. In 1985 he gave Damon Hill an outing and had another poor season with Mika Sala, but in 1987 he won the British Formula 3 Championship with Johnny Herbert and met Trevor Foster who came to work for him in 1988. In 1989, he moved to Formula 3000 with Jean Alesi and they won the European Championship.

Eddie Jordan's first attempt to get into Formula 1 was to buy the ailing Lotus, with the help of R.J. Reynolds and Camel. Foiled in this, Jordan decided to go out on his own, believing that he still had the backing of R.J. Reynolds and Camel. Having started out, he discovered that Reynolds was shifting its sponsorship from Lotus to Benetton and

Williams. Sadder and wiser, but undaunted, Jordan turned to 7UP whose livery was emerald green, the colour of Ireland, and did a deal which made 7UP a major sponsor for just over $1m. Jordan did a deal with Ford to use the Cosworth HB engine for the Jordan 191 designed by Gary Anderson and driven by Frenchman Bernard Gachot, who lived in Belgium, and Andrea de Cesaris.

With Prost out of the way, Senna was completely dominant at McLaren and got his own way in most things, including a fee of $12m for 1991. The MP4/6, designed by Neil Oatley, had a new V12 Honda engine, the RA121E which produced 720 bhp but was heavier and thirstier than earlier Honda engines.

Nigel Mansell had announced his retirement, but Frank Williams offered him a place back at Williams to drive what was looking increasingly like the most competitive car and he accepted, driving alongside Patrese for 1992. To replace Mansell, Ferrari signed Jean Alesi from Tyrell. The atmosphere in the team was still appalling, the old ways dying hard. The *tifosi* wanted results, Piccinini hovered around, engineers changed engine settings without telling the driver and though Prost complained bitterly to the team manager, Cesare Fiorio, it was to no avail.

As the 1980s drew to a close, two great names from the past – Cosworth and March – passed landmarks in their history. Both had been sidelined in the World Championship in that extraordinary decade; both had spent the 1980s operating in America where they had provided the backbone to Indy Car racing. Cosworth started supplying DFX turbo engines to Indianapolis drivers in 1975, and by 1978 there were ten Cosworth-powered cars on the grid; by 1980, 30 of the 33 starters were powered by DFXs.

The March experience was similar. In 1981, March built an Indy Car for Tom Sneva and he was fastest in qualifying at over 200 mph. Word spread, and in 1982, 17 of the 33 starters were Marches. By 1984, 31 of the 33 cars were Marches,

and they filled the first 15 places in the race. March's 1000th car was for the greatest of all Indianapolis legends, A.J. Foyt.

From its cash-strapped beginnings, Robin Herd's March had over £1m in the bank in 1984, and by 1986, profits had risen to £1.6m and the business was valued at over £14m, not bad from the £10,000 put in by the four dreamers in 1970. In 1987, March was floated on the stock market, making Herd a wealthy man, though he reserved a large block of shares for the staff who had been there since the beginning.

In the same year, Herd started out in Formula 1 again with sponsorship from a Korean businessman in Japan, Akiri Akagi, who also started a Formula 3000 team based on March cars. The designer of the Formula 1 cars was Adrian Newey, who had made his reputation designing Indy Cars, and the drivers were Italian Ivan Capelli and Brazilian Mauricio Gugelmin. The team grew in stature during 1988, Capelli coming second in Portugal, but just as everything started to look rosy, and even more swiftly than Indianapolis teams had flocked to March in the first place, they deserted March for Lola who was providing more competitive cars at keener prices.

Production for 1988 fell to 56 cars from a high 103 in 1986, while the Formula 1 project was absorbing both money and expertise. In July 1988, profits had collapsed and the auditors recommended that a new chairman be appointed; John Cowen, an extremely experienced industrialist was brought in. Cowen used his skills and his contacts to keep March going while he sold Akagi the parts of the business he wanted, the Formula 3000 team, the Formula 1 team and the wind tunnel for £6.25m. This made March solvent again, but as an engineering company rather than as a racing team. Robin Herd left in April 1989. In sorting out the finances, John Cowen expressed the view that he doubted whether a publicly quoted company should be involved in an activity such as Formula 1 racing.

Personality: Nigel Mansell was voted BBC
Sports Personality of the Year twice, in 1986,
and in 1992 when he won the Championship.

Outsider: Flavio
Briatore, who took
Benetton to the top.

Cosworth, that other entrepreneurial mother lode from which all the kit car teams had derived their start in life, faired better. In April 1990, was sold to Vickers for £163.5m.

The 1991 season started with Ayrton Senna winning the first four Grands Prix, in the US, Brazil, San Marino and Monaco, with second place going to Alain Prost in the first two, Berger in the third and Mansell in the fourth. Senna had 40 points to Alain Prost's 11. Prost had leapt out of the McLaren frying pan into the Ferrari fire. Following Monaco, Cesare Fiorio was sacked and a trio of Piero Lardi Ferrari, Marco Piccinini and Claudio Lombardi took over. Gianni Agnelli, the boss of Fiat, suggested that they approach Senna to restore the team's confidence and talks were opened, which annoyed Prost. It was the same

thinking that had prevailed under Enzo Ferrari: it could not be the car so it must be the driver, so change the driver and everything will be fine. Senna knew enough to stay away.

In Canada, Patrese and Mansell gave Williams-Renault a 1-2 on the grid and Mansell led until his engine failed on the last but one lap, handing the race to Piquet in the Benetton-Ford, another John Barnard car. The B191 had been late for the new season and missed the first two races, but now it had won a Grand Prix and Ford announced that Cosworth would build a new V12 engine for 1992. But the mutual frustration between Briatore and Barnard came to a head just days later, and Barnard was ousted. He was immediately replaced by Gordon Kimball who had worked with him in the days of the Chaparral Indy Car in the 1970s, which surprised him. Two weeks later there was even greater change when Tom Walkinshaw of TWR racing, took a 35 percent stake in Benetton and became technical director. Walkinshaw had been very successful in leading the Jaguar team to four victories in the Le Mans 24-hour endurance race and he had been looking for a way into Formula 1 for some time. He brought with him his own design staff, including Ross Brawn who had designed the XJR-14 Jaguars. Rory Byrne and Pat Symonds also returned from Reynard. Walkinshaw had been keeping an eye on a young German driver, Michael Schumacher, whom he had seen during his time with the Mercedes Junior team in the Sports Car World Championship.

The Williams revival continued with Patrese winning in Mexico and in the French Grand Prix where Prost was driving the new Ferrari 643; Prost had a close battle with Mansell which Mansell won for Williams-Renault, going on to win the British and German Grands Prix too. Mansell's run of victories put him just 8 points behind Senna and 1 point ahead of McLaren in the Constructors' Championship. This was the revival to be proud of; just two seasons after losing his engine and his driver, Frank Williams was getting back on top. It was telling on Senna too; McLaren-Honda was not doing well. Honda made a huge effort to give Senna more power and in Hungary he led from start to finish with Mansell second. Senna could see the writing on the wall and at the Belgian Grand Prix, he started talking to Williams about moving. Williams listened but said no and announced that he would be sticking with Nigel Mansell and Ricardo Patrese for 1992.

Jordan was hit hard when Bernard Gachot, who had given Jordan his first Championship points with fifth place in Canada, was jailed for an incident which had taken place in London the previous December. He had an altercation with a London cabbie which ended with the Frenchman spraying CS gas at him. Following the Hungarian Grand Prix, Gachot appeared in court and the

judge jailed him with immediate effect. To replace him Eddie Jordan swiftly tested a young German driver at Silverstone, Michael Schumacher. Jordan signed him up and in practice and qualifying at Spa Schumacher showed what he could do by putting the Jordan in seventh place on the grid and those who watched knew immediately that a new Formula 1 star had been found.

There was great excitement at Jordan, Eddie had spotted the next Senna in Michael Schumacher, and he was signed to Jordan. However, Tom Walkinshaw had seen Schumacher's potential too and immediately spoke to Schumacher's management who agreed a deal, cancelling the Jordan drive. Eddie Jordan was furious. So was Roberto Moreno whom Benetton then dumped to make room for Schumacher. Moreno started legal proceedings and with the Italian Grand Prix looming, both Jordan and Benetton laid claim to Schumacher's services. Enter the Ringmaster. To stop the unseemly wrangle, Bernie Ecclestone stepped in and the power struggle was fought out with him as moderator. Schumacher finished up at Benetton and the circus rolled on. Ecclestone had both used and enhanced his reputation as the power broker in Formula 1. With one driver in jail and another having jumped ship Jordan took on Moreno. Ron Dennis sought out Eddie Jordan to commiserate, reportedly ending his chat with a famous epithet, 'welcome to the piranha club'.

The Williams-Renault run then continued with Mansell winning in Italy and Patrese winning in Portugal. Mansell won again in Spain where he had a wheel-to-wheel in the rain with Senna at 180 mph; Prost was second; Senna was fifth. The Japanese Grand Prix was set to be the denouement again: Mansell needed to win to have any hope of taking the title. Berger led while Senna blocked Mansell, who spun off on lap 10, making Senna World Champion.

Piquet quit Benetton at the end of the season and retired to be replaced by Martin Brundle.

Benetton looked very strong for 1992 with Flavio Briatore, Benetton family support and plans to move to a single factory the following year. It had Camel as a main sponsor, Ford as an engine supplier committed to a new V12, Goodyear tyres, Tom Walkinshaw, Ross Brawn, Rory Byrne and the hottest young driver in the business, Michael Schumacher.

As the world cantered towards recession in the winter of 1991–2, many of the smaller teams were under threat. The season had started well for Jordan – 13 points and fifth place in the Constructors' Championship – but it left him a wiser man and £4.5m in debt, much of it owed to Cosworth for the supply of the engines. To provide security, he put up his own personal property, everything, in fact, that his working life had achieved. It was widely speculated that Jordan

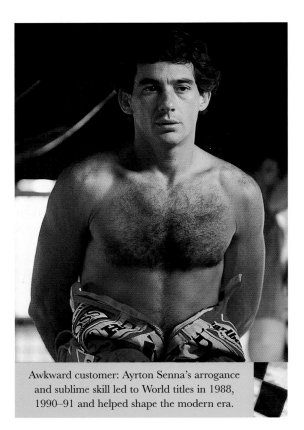

Awkward customer: Ayrton Senna's arrogance and sublime skill led to World titles in 1988, 1990–91 and helped shape the modern era.

approached Ecclestone who arranged to provide finance as part of the 1992 fees, to keep Jordan going. Jordan was unique: it was like the teams which had started out in the 1960s and 1970s, based on an individual with acumen and drive, working in a lock-up with a band of mechanics, designers and fixers all dedicated and held closely together by the sheer force of the personality behind it. Eddie Jordan showed his powers of leadership that year. He held it together, making sure wages were paid first. That January Sasol, the South African oil company, stepped in and, largely on the personal bond he was able to establish with individuals, he secured sponsorship of $8m. He and Trevor Foster wanted to stay with Ford and the car had been designed around it but they knew they could not afford to go on with the Cosworth, so turned to Yamaha which would provide their rather lumpy V12; he had to take it.

In the closing stages of 1991 there was much speculation that Mercedes Benz would come back into Formula 1 after an absence of 35 years through its relationship with Swiss racing entrepreneur Peter Sauber. Sauber had managed the Mercedes Benz challenge for the World Sports Car Championship in 1989 as the official entrant and as Sauber-Mercedes it had won the Le Mans 24-hour race and the Championship in 1989. In October 1990, Mercedes appointed a motor sport manager, Norbert Haug, a motor racing journalist, as part of a policy of edging back into motor racing. Mercedes also supported a junior sports car team and among its members in 1990–91 were two young German drivers, Heinz-Harald Frentzen and Michael Schumacher. In 1991, Sauber wanted to get into Formula 1 and Mercedes had tentatively backed the idea, then backed off while continuing to provide technical and financial support.

Sauber needed an engine. In August 1991 he approached a British engine manufacturer, Ilmor, which had been in business in Northampton since 1983. Ilmor was founded by two ex-Cosworth employees, Mario Ilien and Paul Morgan. They

No quarter: Senna gave Prost no room in the 1991 Japanese Grand Prix, taking his third title when both retired after the incident.

had been approached by Roger Penske to build engines for his Indy Car team and Penske was so impressed he backed them, taking 25 percent of the company and bringing in General Motors for another 25 percent in return for 'badging' the engines with the Chevrolet name. By 1991, Ilmor-Chevy engines had eclipsed everything in sight in the PPG CART Indy Car series: 17 wins from 17 races with 17 pole positions. Ilmor had a V10 Formula 1 engine on the stocks which they had designed in 1989 for Leyton House and its owner, Akiri Akagi. Akagi owned the rights to the engine which had taken over from Judd in his Formula 1 team in 1991, but by the middle of that year it was clear that there was much wrong at Leyton House and Ilmor was having difficulty getting paid. The

reasons were evident when Mr Akagi was arrested for fraud. Leyton House folded soon afterwards. Ilmor then negotiated to buy back the rights to the V10 so that it could supply it to Sauber, but when Mercedes backed off Formula 1, Ilmor developed it and supplied it to Tyrell and March instead.

A combination of recession and the quest for greater driver safety by reducing speeds brought the turbocharged era to a close. Recession also started to thin out the ranks of the smaller Formula 1 teams but the spectacle of wheel to wheel racing by the best drivers in the world, the only link with the heady days in the 1950s, continued to attract huge audiences at circuits and on television, and despite the recession, money continued to flow into Formula 1 racing.

Hard man: Giancarlo
Fisichella takes off
during qualifying.

7

THE HIGH-TECH
GLOBAL RACE TRACK

In October 1991, Max Mosley was elected president of FISA, ousting Jean-Marie Balestre in a victory for common sense. This was the final act in the long saga of the FOCA teams' struggle for the commanding heights of motor sport. It removed a second-rate figure from the top of the sport and began to address the vacuum of respect for Formula 1 which had characterized his presidency. Ten days later, the new World Champion, Ayrton Senna, launched into one of his all-too-familiar attacks on the Frenchman, harking back again to the 1989 and 1990 Championships about which he still felt aggrieved, his language sinking into the gutter in the process. The public rows between Senna and Balestre were damaging to Formula 1 and Senna's obsessive behaviour was unpardonable, but he got away with it because there was little or no respect for Balestre. Four days after Senna's outburst, Mosley asserted his position wisely, and very firmly arranged for Senna to make a contrite statement, describing his remarks about Balestre as 'inappropriate'.

Mosley's election came as the world went into recession, thinning the ranks in Formula 1 as it did. AGS had folded in 1991 and Larrousse, Minardi, Coloni and Tyrell were in poor financial shape. Arrows was sold to a Japanese company, Footwork. The challenge facing Mosley and Ecclestone, as they saw it, was to put Formula 1 on a sounder commercial footing by making it cheaper to run and more interesting to sponsors and television. The problem with making it cheaper was that this challenged the World Championship's status as the pinnacle of motor racing.

The economic model was in America, on which Mosley's mind was fixed for a variety of reasons. US racing was burgeoning, both Indy Car and NASCAR, and it was doing so by giving the audiences what they wanted – close racing between highly competitive teams, with no single team consistently ahead. It was doing it on a fraction of the costs involved in running a Formula 1 team. American racing was based on a huge home market while Grand Prix racing was based on an international calendar, and by 1991 the terminal lack of interest on the part of American fans to watch foreign racing on street circuits was evident in the empty stands. They were unsustainable commercially for the cities of Detroit, Dallas, and Las Vegas and finally Phoenix where the last US Grand Prix was held in March 1991, a parody of the idea of excellence behind Grand Prix racing, ending a 32-year association between America and the World Championship. Mosley campaigned for the presidency, in part on a pledge to seek ways to bring Formula 1 and Indy Car racing back together. Ultimately, Mosley believed that Formula 1 and Indy Car racing could be brought together into a single World Series for open wheel racing, fusing the two traditions, bringing some of the pragmatism and commercialism found in America, to the World Championship. The first step, though would be to re-establish a US Grand Prix, because a World Championship that did not include the US was not really seen as a World Championship worth the name.

The team which more than any other exemplified the difference between the US and road racing traditions was McLaren. Under Ron Dennis, McLaren had won seven World Championships in the eight seasons between 1984 and 1991, taking its total to nine, equalling Ferrari's record which had taken 41 years. The tradition of excellence and constant technical evolution ran deep at McLaren, and in 1991, *Management Week* magazine posed the question of Dennis, 'Is this the Best Manager in Britain?'.

Ron Dennis had become, after Colin Chapman's demise, the sport's leading innovator, bringing in the first carbon fibre monocoque, building his own wind tunnel and developing a turbo engine from scratch to match the manufacturer-based teams. He had also developed as a manager, and although he brought in other talent throughout the years of dominance, he was the boss at McLaren, the man at the centre, who took decisions. While winning four double World Championships in a row, he had also built a highly successful electronics business in TAG with Mansour Ojjeh which carried out work for other Formula 1 teams and 60 other high-tech customers. McLaren also had a marketing company, and was building a racing sports car, the McLaren F1, which sold at around $600,000. In 1991 he even added the idea of breaking the world land speed record, which he abandoned once he heard that Richard Noble, the holder of the LSR, was going to attempt a supersonic record. The downside of Dennis's drive for diversification was that his eye wandered off the Formula 1 ball, and in 1991 it became evident that McLaren could be knocked off its perch at the top of the World Championship. The Honda engine was down on performance compared with the Renault, and Honda had indicated that it would withdraw at the end of the season; Dennis may have believed that he could persuade them to stay.

McLaren's nemesis in 1992 was not Ferrari but a completely transformed Williams which had built a great partnership with Renault and came close to unseating McLaren-Honda in 1991 when McLaren still had Senna, the best driver in the world. Mansell had been second, 24 points behind Senna, but in 1992 Frank Williams, Patrick Head and Adrian Newey were back with the FW14B. Williams was just as convinced of the benefits of high technolgy, but he was not tempted down the diversification route favoured by Ron Dennis, though he did lend the Williams name to a sporty version of the Renault Clio as part of the relationship with his engine supplier.

Ferrari was in a mess. It had not won a single race in 1991, the first time that had happened since 1986. Prost finished fifth in the Driver's Championship and third in the Constructors' title. Prost had been outspoken in his criticism of Ferrari and the management trio fired him, disposing of their greatest asset just when they needed him most. The mystique which Enzo Ferrari had created had not died with him and the roller coaster relationship with the Italian press continued – plaudits for minor successes and calling for heads to roll the minute anything went wrong. What was needed was a dose of reality which would have to come at the expense of some of the mystique. The new Ferrari, the F92A, was sleek, like a guided missile, having been designed using Ferrari's own wind tunnel, a legacy of the John Barnard years. Unfortunately, like Barnard before him, Steve Nichols, who had designed the F92A, had had enough of Ferrari just as his car was ready and left to join Sauber. To fill the gap, Harvey Postlethwaite was brought back as technical director with the aerodynamicist Jean-Claude Migeot. Gianni Agnelli believed that the only man who could put things right was Luca di Montezemolo, who had got it spectacularly right in the 1970s then pursued a glittering career as a senior corporate executive. He had also successfully masterminded Italy's hosting of the 1990 Football World Cup. To help him, he turned to the man with whom he had collaborated in the 1970s – Niki Lauda.

At the start of the season Benetton, the fourth top team, had still not moved to its new 17-acre factory just outside Oxford. Compared with the incipient problems at McLaren, the continuing sclerosis at Ferrari, the setbacks at Jordan, the excruciatingly slow progress at Lotus and the terminal decline at Brabham, Benetton was on the way up thanks to a mixture of Flavio Briatore and Tom Walkinshaw. Ross Brawn and Rory Byrne had a completely new car, the B192, which was relatively simple because there had not been time to include the active suspension and new gearbox which had been planned. The B191 was used for the first part of the season but when the B192 did arrive it proved very reliable.

Nigel Mansell started the season looking like a champion, winning the first five Grands Prix in South Africa, Mexico, Brazil, Spain and San Marino – a record. This rekindled the debate about whether such dominance was bad for

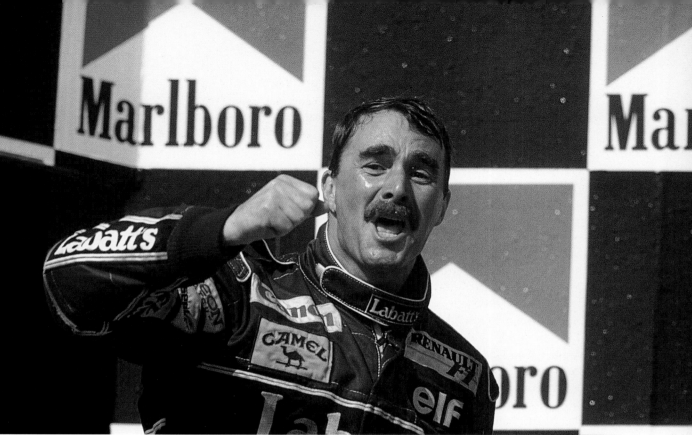

Triumph: Nigel Mansell's second place in the 1992 Hungarian Grand Prix gave him the World Championship after 13 seasons of trying.

Formula 1, making it predictable. To counter it, Ecclestone and Mosley proposed banning electronic driver aids such as active suspension. Senna drove with his usual skill and determination at Monaco but the McLaren was clearly inferior. Mansell led from pole position until seven laps from the end when he had a puncture and had to go in for a wheel change, giving Senna the lead. Mansell caught up with him but could not pass him and had to settle for second place. Then Mansell won the French, British and German Grands Prix and came second in Hungary behind Senna, enough to make him the first British World

Champion since James Hunt in 1976.

Mansell announced that he was retiring, a sad ending to what should have been a fairy story for British motor racing, a British driver and team winning both Championships in style. Instead there was squabbling over money. Shortly afterwards Mansell announced that he was moving to Indy Car racing in the US. He cited that one of the reasons for going was the way that Williams had conducted negotiations after Ayrton Senna had offered to drive for Williams in 1993 for nothing, so keen was he to drive the best car. Senna was not alone; the top drivers were queueing up to drive for

Skill: Senna's finest drive, passing 5 rivals in an obsolete McLaren to take the lead on lap 1 in the wet 1993 European Grand Prix.

Williams. Frank Williams had wanted Senna for years, but even Senna's offer to drive for nothing did him no good because with more than a little help from Renault, Prost took Mansell's place. For No. 2 driver, Frank Williams opened negotiations with Keke Rosberg who was now managing a young Finnish driver, Mika Hakkinen, but he broke off those negotiations and took on Damon Hill who was struggling at Brabham instead.

It was the end of the McLaren-Honda partnership. McLaren was second in the Constructors' Championship and the team had won five Grands Prix, but for the first time in its

history it had been put firmly in the shade by Williams. As he faced 1993, Ron Dennis was wrong-footed over engines as Honda stuck to its decision to leave. Senna also wanted to leave, but the only place worth leaving for was Williams, and that was barred by his old sparring partner Prost. Berger was not that happy at McLaren either; he believed that Senna exerted far too much influence over the team and when the call came, he went back to Ferrari. As second driver, Dennis took on Michael Andretti, like Damon Hill the son of a World Champion. For an engine, Dennis's first instinct was to go for the best, but Renault was already committed to Williams and Ligier. Dennis offered a deal; he would buy the whole Ligier team and take over the contract, use the Renault engines in the MP4/8, then find another engine for Ligier. The one stipulation Dennis made was that the engines must run on Shell fuel and oil under his existing contracts. Initially Renault agreed, then its industrial collaborator, Elf, said no unless its fuel and oil was used as per its contracts. Dennis could not break the impasse, so there was no deal and turned to Ford as second customer for the Cosworth HB V8, after Benetton, which he then uprated using TAG electronics. TAG had also developed a very advanced active suspension system for the MP4/8, to leap ahead of Williams.

Luca di Montezemolo worked hard on the revitalization of Ferrari, including trying to tempt Senna to Maranello, but when that was unsuccessful, he found a willing candidate in Gerhard Berger. He also opened discussions with Peugeot's sporting director, Jean Todt, a man of great energy and a great planner, who had masterminded Peugeot's rally operations and was preparing a challenge for the Le Mans 24-hour race in 1993. Todt agreed to join but not until after Le Mans. Di Montezemolo's boldest move was to bring back John Barnard following his ousting from Benetton. Barnard had not had a good relationship with Cesare Fiorio and now that he was gone the door was open to start on a completely new car, working from the Ferrari premises near his house in Guildford.

Benetton had a far better season. Michael Schumacher had improved greatly during the season: one victory and a place in the points in every other race he finished, putting him third in the World Championship, behind the two Williams drivers, but ahead of Ayrton Senna. His performance put Benetton third in the Constructors' Championship, 70 points ahead of Ferrari, and only 8 points behind McLaren. Benetton had moved into its new factory in October 1992, from which the B193 emerged with

active suspension, traction control and an automatic gearbox, catching up with Williams and McLaren as a high-tech team.

It was precisely this high technology which made for winning teams, but the high cost base which went with it further split the Formula 1 teams in to the haves and the have-nots. It was also against the policies of Max Mosley and Bernie Ecclestone who were determined to bring costs down, something which the sponsors certainly supported. Walter Thoma of Marlboro made a speech in which he warned that motor sport could not defy the logic of the market place: 'the message about world recession seems to have taken a great deal of time to penetrate the world of Formula 1'.

The recession did not stop the tobacco companies from beating a path to the doors of Formula 1's top teams: for 1993 Camel sponsored Williams and Benetton; Marlboro sponsored McLaren and Ferrari; Chesterfield sponsored Lola, and Gitanes sponsored Ligier. The other ironic twist was that Bernie Ecclestone, who saw Formula 1 as a business which needed to reduce its costs in a recession, had a salary reported to be £29.7m in 1993, the highest in Britain. With a decent engine deal, a team could be run very handsomely on such a sum. Indeed, Eddie Jordan was probably running his team on less. Jordan had scored just one point in the Constructors' Championship, coming joint 11th and last. He had a number of problems, the greatest of which was the heavy and uncompetitive Yamaha engine; its only advantage being that it was effectively free. Strapped for cash, Jordan took a bold decision, signing up Rubens Barrichello and Eddie Irvine and ordering engines from Brian Hart in a two-year deal.

The evidence that Formula 1 was not recession proof was not far away and teams balanced on the edge found it hard to continue, three great names from the past in particular. The Hungarian Grand Prix was Brabham's 399th, but it was clearly a team in the throes of disintegration. Frank Warren, the boxing promoter had visited Monaco amid

Taste of victory: Michael Schumacher's gesture in the 1994 Pacific Grand Prix was to celebrate maximum points in the Championship.

rumours that he was interested in supporting it, but nothing came of it. Damon Hill had failed to qualify for the British Grand Prix and he wrote off one BT60 in practice at the Hungaroring, qualified in another and finished eleventh. Ted Ball, who had kept Brabham afloat by lending money against the assets of the team, was at the Hungarian Grand Prix, but by the time he returned to England, Landhurst Leasing had been put into receivership with debts of £44m; Brabham's assets were frozen.

Landhurst Leasing had also provided finance to Lotus which was struggling to survive under Peter Collins and Peter Wright, with Johnny Herbert and Mika Hakkinen as drivers. There was sponsorship from Castrol and a string of Japanese companies but the financial situation was dire. In a completely unconnected event from the past, and ten years after Colin Chapman's death and the DeLorean collapse, Fred Bushell, who had been Colin Chapman's financial right hand for nearly 25 years, pleaded guilty to taking part in a conpsiracy to defraud DeLorean of $17.65m with Chapman, and went to jail.

It was the arrest of Akiri Akagi in September 1991, following an alleged scandal at the Fuji Bank in Japan which threw the third great name, March, into its final throes. Following his arrest, the team had abandoned the name Leyton House in favour of March and started preparing for 1993, but its debts were mounting and the end was in sight.

Prost won the South African Grand Prix for Williams-Renault with Senna second, despite an active suspension malfunction. The Brazilian Grand Prix was at Interlagos again, the race Senna wanted to win more than any other, which he achieved when it started to rain and Prost aquaplaned off. Two weeks later, at Donington Park for the European Grand Prix, Senna did it again. Diana, Princess of Wales was there for the race with the two princes and King Hussein of Jordan. Prost was on pole with Hill second, then Michael Schumacher and Ayrton Senna. Race day

was wet, which did not suit Prost but the two Williams made a good start, as did Schumacher, who briefly got ahead of Senna, elbowing him back to fifth place. Senna then passed Schumacher to take fourth place, then Karl Wendliger, who had slipped though with Schumacher, then Damon Hill, to take third place. He started eating into Prost's lead, taking his old adversary before the end of the first lap, emerging in front of the grandstand in the lead. It was a hectic race of many tyre changes, but Senna moved inexorably ahead in a display of skill and determination which even by his standards was special. Prost dropped to third behind Hill who was the only driver on the same lap when Senna took the chequered flag. Prost was visibly depressed at the press conference afterwards.

Senna won in Monaco, Prost won in Spain, Canada, France, Britain and Germany, then in Hungary, Prost started on pole but stalled, leaving Damon Hill to take the lead and win his first Grand Prix, the first time the son of a World Champion had ever done so. Hill's run continued at Spa, where he held off a strong challenge from Schumacher. Prost led the Italian Grand Prix which would have clinched the Championship had he won, but with just five laps to go his engine failed and Hill inherited the lead to win his third Grand Prix in a row.

Prost clinched his fourth World Championship with second place in Portugal, but had already announced his retirement. Behind the scenes, a major move had been agreed. Prost had initially signed for two years, but he had always made it plain that he would not serve in the same team as Ayrton Senna. Senna was the best driver around and he announced at Estoril that he would not be driving for McLaren the following year. Williams' sponsor, Rothmans, wanted him and so did Frank Williams who had failed to sign him twice before, so Prost had to resign and he chose to retire. In doing so, he passed on the opportunity to go for a fifth title, to equal the all-time record set by Fangio;

that opportunity now fell to his great rival Ayrton Senna who would have to win two Championships to do so. Senna won in Australia, his last race for McLaren after six years.

Michael Andretti, who had come third at Monza, his best result yet, was clearly not making much of an impression in Formula 1, and within days he left to go back to Indy Car racing. He was replaced by McLaren's test driver, Mika Hakkinen.

Ron Dennis's plan to buy Ligier in order to get the Renault engine contract had not gone unnoticed. In early 1993, Guy Ligier had sold 85 percent of the team to French businessman Cyril de Rouvre, who had previously been involved in AGS. Williams, who was keen to keep Ligier in business and out of the hands of rivals, particularly McLaren, supplied the team with a semi-automatic gearbox to make it more competitive.

Ron Dennis wanted Senna to stay at McLaren and in trying to convince him, had opened up conversations with Peugeot, which had decided to get into Formula 1. A deal was done by October 1993, but by then Senna had gone to Williams, so Dennis tried to tempt Prost out of retirement. Prost tested the MP4/9, but decided that he had truly had enough and with the prospect of Senna driving the best car on the grid, stayed in retirement. It was a low point for McLaren. The 1992–3 seasons had been disastrous and at the end of 1993 Philip Morris, owners of Marlboro whose livery the team had carried for 20 years, decided to pull out at the end of the rolling three-year contract. Dennis was starting out for the first time since 1981 without a World Champion, and like Frank Williams before him, Ron Dennis took up the challenge and started rebuilding.

The two previous seasons had seen Nigel Mansell and Alain Prost virtually walk away with the title for Williams, adding fuel to the debate over the use of electronic driver aids which rumbled on throughout 1993 among the top teams, Bernie Ecclestone, increasingly part of the new establishment with FISA, Max Mosley and the

sponsors. The debate centred on whether a ban would produce more exciting racing or whether it would remove the true competitive backbone from Grand Prix racing. The high-tech teams saw it as an attempt to take away their advantage in much the same way that FISA under Balestre had tried in the late 1970s with ground effects. Ferrari had clearly not mastered the high-tech route, but both Benetton and Jordan had without the benefit of the huge backers of McLaren, Williams and Ferrari. It was precisely that type of competitiveness, the relentless pursuit of excellence, on which Formula 1 had always thrived.

Ecclestone and Mosley won the power struggle, and for 1994 all electronic driver aids were banned: – active suspension, anti-lock and power braking, traction control, 'fly-by-wire' throttle control and continuously variable transmission. At the same time pit stops, which had been banned ten years on grounds of safety, were once again introduced to increase excitement on the track. The ban on electronic driver aids was introduced to reduce costs but behind the scenes Ferrari was in favour of the ban because the Williams and McLaren teams were way ahead on the high-tech front. In its editorial that year, *Autocourse* more than hinted that the move was for Ferrari's benefit, saying: 'it seems as though the FIA was determined to spoon-feed Ferrari its first title [for fifteen years]'.

If costs were the issue, then the tobacco industry showed no signs of backing away in 1994. Williams was sponsored by Rothmans, Benetton and Tyrell by Mild Seven, McLaren and Ferrari by Marlboro, with a shift towards Ferrari following its decision to pull out of backing McLaren; Marlboro also backed Arrows in a small way. In France, Larrousse was sponsored by Gauloises Blondes and Ligier by Gitanes Blondes.

At the end of 1993, the arrangement between Chevrolet and Ilmor came to an end. But now, under Helmut Werner, Mercedes decided to get back into Formula 1. It bought General Motors' shares in Ilmor and the V10 Formula 1 engine was

Not forgotten: tributes to Ayrton Senna are paid at Imola every year since his death, ranging from simple messages to a bronze statue.

re-badged Mercedes and supplied to Peter Sauber's team which was renamed Sauber-Mercedes. Karl Wendliger stayed while Heinz Harald Frentzen took over from J.J. Lehto.

Ayrton Senna started the season under a three-race ban, suspended, for hitting Eddie Irvine following an altercation on the track at Suzuka the previous year. The Brazilian Grand Prix was a head-to-head confrontation between Senna and Schumacher, both regarded as natural talents in a class of their own. Senna was on home ground at a packed Interlagos, the fans willing him towards

the Championship. Senna took pole and led from the start with Schumacher right behind him, and that is how it stayed until the first pit stop. They came in together and the Benetton pit crew got Schumacher out in the lead. Schumacher stayed ahead through the second pit stop, then just as Senna seemed about to make a challenge, he spun off and stalled. Schumacher eased off and won, but long before he crossed the line the Brazilian fans were streaming out of the exits. Senna, their hero had been beaten fair and square – at home.

Despite being banned, electronic driver aids

remained an issue because many in the teams were concerned that the FIA did not have the technical means to police infringements. At the Pacific Grand Prix, the FIA technical delegate, Charlie Whiting, an ex-Brabham mechanic, was alerted to just such a possibility when he listened to Nicola Larini's Ferrari engine note fluttering. When he investigated he found the car was fitted with a rev limiter which might be interpreted as a traction control device. He suggested that the device be disconnnected for the race while its legality was investigated and Ferrari completely cleared, however the incident left a nasty taste again, that Ferrari was being treated with kid gloves and that other teams would have been treated more harshly. Senna was on pole again, with Schumacher second again, but Senna spun off on the first lap, giving Benetton its second straight victory, ahead of Gerhard Berger for Ferrari and Rubens Barrichello who gave Jordan its first podium finish.

The Formula 1 circus moved on to San Marino. Schumacher was on maximum points with Barrichello second. Senna had yet to open his score. The first session of qualifying was stopped when Barrichello had a spectacular 140 mph accident at the Variante complex which put him in hospital. In the next session, Roland Ratzenberger, an Austrian driver with Simtek, came through the Tamburello corner on to the straight when it seems the right front wing came off. He lost control, hitting the concrete wall hard, then bounced back on to the track. He was rushed to hospital with head injuries from which he died later that day. It was the first fatality in Formula 1 since Elio de Angelis died testing at Paul Ricard eight years previously and the first on race weekend since 1982 when Riccardo Paletti hit Didier Pironi's Ferrari. Roland Ratzenberger's death was all the more shocking because death had been absent for so many years and because so much effort had been put into making cars and circuits safer. In a rather insensitive move, the session was restarted, although Sauber, Williams and Benetton did not take part out of respect. Gerhard Berger did, visibly upset by the death of his countryman, putting his Ferrari in third place on the grid behind Schumacher with Senna on pole.

The tone of the day was all wrong: J. J. Lehto stalled at the start and Pedro Lamy's Lotus ploughed straight into it, scattering debris across the grid and into the crowd where several spectators were injured. With Senna leading, the safety car came out and stayed out for three laps. When the safety car went in, Senna made a superb restart down the pit straight, closely followed by Schumacher. As Senna went into Tamburello, Schumacher was close behind, close enough to see Senna's Williams twitch as it went over a bump, then go straight ahead into the concrete wall, hitting it head on then bouncing back across the track. The race was stopped and Senna was taken out of the car by Professor Sid Watkins and taken straight to Bologna hospital by helicopter.

The race was restarted. Gerhard Berger took the lead, which had to be adjusted for the time lost by the accident. The race continued with an air of unreality. Schumacher and Hill challenged Berger, but he felt the Ferrari was behaving oddly and he retired on lap 11, crushed by the events of the two days. Before the appalling weekend was over, it was once again marred when a wheel came off Michele Alboreto's Minardi after a pit stop, hitting four mechanics who were all taken to hospital. Schumacher won with Nicola Larini second for Ferrari and Mika Hakkinen third for McLaren.

Ayrton Senna died in hospital at 18.40 that evening. The Italian police impounded the remains of his Williams and looked for somebody to blame. The Formula 1 family went into mourning in its own way, with tributes from Alain Prost, Niki Lauda, Emerson Fittipaldi and Stirling Moss, and pledges of greater safety in the future. There was a political price to pay; politicians expressed alarm and for those few who could remember it, there was an atmosphere not unlike that which followed the crash at Le Mans in 1955.

Ayrton Senna's funeral in São Paolo was a state event in all but name. Jet fighters of the Brazilian Air Force escorted the aircraft carrying his body as it approached Brazil, a million people lined the route to the Legislative Assembly where his coffin lay in state. The Senna family led the funeral cortège to the open grave where soldiers fired a volley of shots witnessed by the whole Formula 1 family gathered round it. There were two notable absentees, Nelson Piquet and Bernie Ecclestone, who had flown to Brazil but had not attended the funeral after the family let it be known that his presence would not be appropriate following what they saw as the insensitivity of restarting the race.

The death of Ayrton Senna removed one of the greatest and most controversial drivers in the history of the World Championship. Coupled with Prost's retirement, the sport was shorn of two of the greatest talents of the modern age; inevitably, all eyes turned to Michael Schumacher.

Political pressure for new safety measures was intense, particularly from France and Italy, and Max Mosley, who had been firm in resisting the hasty introduction of new regulations, had to act. At Monaco he announced that downforce would have to be reduced by the Spanish Grand Prix, increased cockpit protection would be required from the Canadian Grand Prix, and from the German Grand Prix, cars would have to have a stepped bottom to further reduce cornering speeds. From 1995, engine power would be reduced. Monaco was subdued as preparations for the Grand Prix went ahead, and the already frayed nerves came close to breaking point when Karl Wendlger crashed his Sauber-Mercedes and was taken to hospital in a coma. There were more muted calls for the race to be cancelled but motor racing is a tough, competitive business, and those who reach the top need more than hand wringing to stop them; the sport's leadership and the drivers remained firm. There was a minute's silence followed by a start which left the two front places on the grid symbolically empty. Once the race started, competitive instinct took over and Schumacher won, drawing Senna's mantle more tightly around him as the man to beat.

Senna's death was widely felt, but it was particularly intense inside the Williams team where Damon Hill was faced with exactly the task which had faced his father in 1968 when Jim Clark had been killed. Senna's replacement was Williams' test driver, David Coulthard, but it was Damon Hill who had to shoulder the burden which only a driver could – that of restoring morale by winning. That is what he did, in Spain, from Schumacher. The gloom was beginning to lift, especially when news came through that Karl Wendliger was talking to his family.

Schumacher won in Canada and France where Nigel Mansell made a 'guest' appearance in a Williams. Bernie Ecclestone had negotiated the deal directly between Carl Haas, for whom Mansell was driving in the Indy Car series, and Williams, all in the interests of boosting television audiences, which it did. The two Williams were side by side on the grid with Hill on pole and Schumacher third. Schumacher made an outstanding start, sweeping between the two Williams in such style that it provoked speculation that he was using some sort of traction control. Schumacher led most of the race, only giving way to Hill once for six laps; Hill was second.

Hill was on pole again for the British Grand Prix, three thousandths of a second ahead of Schumacher. On the parade lap, Schumacher overtook him which was strictly against the rules. Hill made the best start and was leading at the end of the first lap when Schumacher was given a five second stop-go penalty for overtaking on the parade lap. Briatore and Walkinshaw kept him out while they argued with race officials until he was black flagged, but still he stayed out, infuriating officials who then forced him to come in and he rejoined second. That is how the race finished, with Hill parading the Union Jack around Silverstone. Benetton was fined $25,000 for the

Generations: Damon Hill and Jacques Villeneuve,
World Champions in 1996 and 1997 respectively,
are both sons of Formula 1 stars.

infringement, but after the race the FIA convened a special meeting of the World Motor Sports Council and Schumacher was excluded from the results of the British Grand Prix, given a two-race ban and Benetton had its fine increased to $500,000. The FIA also announced enigmatically that Benetton was one of three teams which had computer systems which were capable of breaching the regulations.

McLaren and Benetton were both fined $100,000 that week for not making certain aspects of their software available, then the FIA released a

dossier about its concerns regarding Benetton's launch control system, saying that 'on the best evidence' Benetton had not used the system at Imola. Releasing the dossier may have been a warning, but Benetton was robust in its rebuttal, denying any action against regulations.

The build-up to the German Grand Prix was ugly: German fans threatened to set fire to the forests around Hockenheim if Schumacher did not race, and Damon Hill received death threats and was given a police escort to and from the circuit. Schumacher had appealed against his fine and his ban, mainly so that he could take part. Berger took pole and led from start to finish, giving Ferrari a great boost, its first win since Alain Prost in Spain in 1990, the end of Ferrari's longest fallow period. Benetton was put even more firmly in the dock at Hockenheim when Jos Verstappen's pit stop came close to tragedy. As the mechanics clustered around, a stream of fuel was released under pressure and the car was suddenly engulfed in flames as it came into contact with the hot engine. Fortunately the fire was put out very quickly and nobody was seriously injured, but later examination found that the Benetton refuelling rig had been used without a regulation filter and its absence had the effect of increasing the speed of refuelling.

Schumacher won the Hungarian and Belgian Grands Prix, but following the Belgian race he was disqualified, giving maximum points to Hill who was second on the track. The reason for the disqualification was the wear on the skid block which had to be fitted to the underside of the car to guarantee the minimum 10mm clearance. It had been worn down to 7.4mm at the front, outside the tolerances. Benetton claimed that the wear had been caused by a spin but the stewards disagreed and the disqualification stood. The FIA also upheld the two-race ban on Schumacher following the British Grand Prix infringement so he missed the Italian and Portuguese Grands Prix. Damon Hill won both. In the days before the European Grand Prix at Jerez, Schumacher chose to say that Hill was not a world-class driver, comments which Hill brushed aside and set fastest time in the first qualifying session. Schumacher took pole and won the race with Hill second. Hill then won the Japanese Grand Prix from Schumacher, leaving Hill just one point behind Schumacher with one race to go, the Australian Grand Prix, a race which both needed to win to take the title.

On lap 36 Schumacher was in the lead with Hill challenging hard by going wide into a left hander. Hill saw a gap on the inside and went for it, then Schumacher 'closed the door' by pulling right across Hill's bows; they came together and both retired making Schumacher World Champion by 1 point, the first German driver to win the World Championship. He immediately dedicated it to Ayrton Senna.

The death of Ayrton Senna was tragic and it set the tone for a very uncomfortable year in the Championship. The view that danger was one of the attractions of motor racing was endorsed by the increased television audiences which followed, left a bad taste. The endless wrangling over the regulations, the paddock gossip, the sense that the many disputes involving both Benetton and Schumacher had to have some substance were also part of the uncomfortable atmosphere. In correspondence with Max Mosley, Flavio Briatore even questioned whether the FIA was competent to run Formula 1. For many it was a tainted Championship and there was a determination that the act would have to be cleaned up in 1995.

On 12 September 1994, the day after the Italian Grand Prix, accountants Robson Rhodes were called in as administrators at Lotus. The business owed around £7m to Landhurst Leasing, itself in receivership. Peter Collins and Johnny Herbert, who had started out as mentor and protégé, were barely speaking to each other at the end. By January 1995 it was all over, the business sold to American Sam Brown. Herbert, who had been with Lotus since 1991, went to Ligier, then to Benetton.

McLaren was having a bad year, the first year it had failed to win a single Grand Prix since 1981, the year Dennis joined. The Peugeot engine had not delivered what had been expected, and although it had improved during the year, McLaren announced a five-year partnership with Mercedes. Norbert Haug had decided that if Mercedes was going to be in Formula 1 it was better to be in with a top team rather than starting out with a relative unknown. During the year, one of Sauber's other sponsors had not been able to pay and Mercedes had stepped in, a reminder of how precarious Formula 1 finances are at the back of the grid. Ron Dennis was doing with Mercedes in the 1990s what he had done with TAG in the 1980s – getting a major partner with a shared company culture of excellence, high-quality engineering and technology and building a long-term platform for awareness through investment, rather than short-term publicity. Less far-sighted was Dennis's decision to bring back Nigel Mansell.

McLaren's switch to Mercedes left Peugeot without a car for its engine, so they approached Eddie Jordan. Jordan had a fairly good year, the high point being Barrichello's third place in the Pacific Grand Prix. Jordan had none of the high technology of the big four, relying instead on the way the old kit car teams had done business, by buying in from others; even that was difficult while still paying off debts from its first season.

Ron Dennis's dream of bringing Nigel Mansell back to Formula 1 turned out to be a nightmare, then a farce, when it emerged that the MP4/10 was not wide enough for him to be able to steer properly. It had to be redesigned so he missed the first two races of the season. Mansell was highly critical of the team and this lapse of standards had a profound effect on Marlboro who wanted to cut the $45m annual payment to McLaren by half. It was rock bottom for McLaren, the result of the loss of the attention of that single-minded and relentless figure at the centre of the team, checking detail, looking at strategy, motivating by raw, personal leadership which is so essential to winning the World Championship.

The season was a rematch of the previous year: Schumacher and Benetton versus Hill and Williams, both cars using the Renault engine. The controversy was also the same: Schumacher won the Brazilian Grand Prix with David Coulthard second but the fuel samples from both cars were then found not to match those submitted before the race. Schumacher was back in controversy in Argentina when he weighed in before the race

weekend at 77kg but afterwards could only manage 71.5kg, raising a few eyebrows. Hill won in Buenos Aires, then again in San Marino. Hakkinen was faster than Mansell in qualifying in Spain, and after spinning off twice, Mansell did not start. Schumacher won. At Monaco, Marlboro had a huge promotion prepared featuring Mansell, but he had already left the team and been replaced by Mark Blundell, deepening the rift between McLaren and Marlboro. Schumacher won again, putting him on 34 points to Damon Hill's 29.

The Canadian Grand Prix saw an upset of the form book when Jean Alesi won for Ferrari, his first victory in 91 races. It was not much good in terms of the World Championship, but it did put Ferrari back on top in the record for all-time number of Grand Prix victories, 105 to McLaren's 104.

It was Renault-engined teams versus the rest. In the British Grand Prix, Mika Hakkinen was fastest in practice with the Mercedes V10 but Hill pulled ahead by over a second on the first lap, increasing his lead by around a second a lap. After pit stops, Hill rejoined just behind Schumacher and narrowed the already small time between them to less than a car's length, and on lap 45 he decided to have a go as they braked for Priory corner. Schumacher would not give ground and they came together as he turned in and both cars spun off out of the race. Schumacher's team-mate, Johnny Herbert won, leaving Schumacher on 46 points and Hill on 35.

David Coulthard won the Portuguese Grand Prix, his first, in a tough race with both Hill and Schumacher challenging for a place at the top. He took pole position at the Nurburgring for the European Grand Prix and after a great race between six drivers – Coulthard, Schumacher, Hill, Irvine, Berger and Alesi – Schumacher won, taking his second Championship.

Schumacher won the Pacific and Japanese Grands Prix, giving Benetton the Constructors' title too. Hill won in Australia but the race was remembered more for Mika Hakkinen's accident.

His left rear tyre suddenly deflated after running over debris and he spun off over a high kerb and into a tyre wall in front of a concrete wall. Rescue was swift; he was given a tracheotomy at the trackside to help him breathe and was taken to hospital where he was close to death for some time.

Jordan finished sixth in the Constructors' title but the political upheaval in South Africa brought an end to the Sasol sponsorship, reluctantly on both sides. The team's performance had attracted Benson & Hedges sponsorship for 1996, tobacco money giving it the funds to challenge the big four more assiduously. In another move, Coulthard moved from Williams to McLaren, a move sparked off by pressure from Ecclestone who wanted to bring Jacques Villeneuve, the 25-year-old son of Gilles Villeneuve, who had just won the Indy Car PPG World Series, into Formula 1 with Williams.

Ferrari won one race in 1995, its first since 1990, and that only because Schumacher had an electrical fault. Luca di Montezemolo was clear that he would not be swayed by short-term considerations and certainly not by a hostile press. The influx of foreigners continued: John Barnard continued to work away at the drawing board in Surrey; Paulo Martinelli was in charge of engine development, but he was assisted by two specialist engineers, Gustav Brunner from Austria and Osamu Goto, a highly regarded ex-Honda engineer who came by way of McLaren. Stefano Domencicali was team manager with Nigel Stepney as chief mechanic looking after the F310 with a new V10 engine and carbon fibre gearbox. But the big change was in the drivers: at the end of the season, di Montezemolo fired Berger and Alesi, much to the surprise of the *tifosi*, then to their even greater horror, replaced them with Michael Schumacher, the reigning World Champion, from Benetton and Eddie Irvine from Jordan. Eddie Irvine's contract made it very plain he was the No.2 driver and expected to play a supporting role. This was a team making a serious bid for the Championship. The budget was around $60m,

The Boss: Mika Hakkinen, 1998 World Champion, modelling for Hugo Boss, one of the non-motoring brands attracted to Formula 1.

roughly twice that of any of its opponents, plus a reported $25m fee for Schumacher. Gianni Agnelli, the head of Fiat, endorsed the shift in attitude from the old days where cars were supreme and drivers dispensable with his injunction to the team: 'If Ferrari does not win with Schumacher, then it will be Ferrari's fault'.

Schumacher, the size of the budget and the assembled talent did give the British-based teams something to worry about. Schumacher had won nine races in 1995, equalling Nigel Mansell's record of 1992, and Benetton had taken both titles. When Ferrari approached Schumacher to sign for them, it appeared he might be leaving a team with a winning combination of people, technology and sponsors, but when the fee of $25m was put into the equation, things looked different. Flavio Briatore was on a high, he had broken through the economic and technical barriers to join the top teams and he wanted to show the world, and the *tifosi*, that Benetton was a match for Ferrari. As part of making the team more Italian, he changed the address from which the entries were made to Italy, dropped Johnny Herbert and hired the two discarded Ferrari drivers, Jean Alesi and Gerhard Berger. When the B196 was ready, he held a massive two day launch party on a hill top town in Sicily to which hundreds of journalists were flown. This was the point in Benetton's history when style completely triumphed over substance. It was all a ghastly mistake: the *tifosi* were not best pleased by the driver moves because Alesi and Berger were both immensely popular, but their loyalty was to Ferrari and the Prancing Horse, its history and its standing in motor racing, not to individual drivers.

Williams had substance. The relationship with Renault had endured for eight years and seen the team back to the top. With Patrick Head and Adrian Newey behind them, Frank William's cars really were the best, and in Damon Hill he had a driver of proven ability. While Jacques Villeneuve had yet to show he could make the move from Indy Car to Formula 1, the team felt confident they could match what was going on at Maranello.

Television revenues continued to underpin much of the teams' budgets, and Ecclestone was always on the lookout to improve them. He wanted more coverage of qualifying, of the personalities, of pre- and post-race analysis, and as the battle between Hill and Schumacher in 1995 had shown, personality battles did improve ratings but the BBC's prime position in sports coverage was about to receive a double blow. In early December, ITV signed a deal to cover the FA Cup final at Wembley, ending the BBC's dominance of the event for as long as anybody could remember. Then a few days later, Jonathan Martin took a call from Bernie Ecclestone which was brief and to the point: he had been negotiating with ITV for the rights to Formula 1 and the World Championship, they had agreed terms and the ITV contract would start in 1997 and run for five years. It was announced at a press conference the same day to howls of protest from the BBC and from people who did not want to have commercial breaks in their race coverage. No figure was given but the speculation was that ITV had agreed to pay between £65m and £70m for five years, between nine and ten times what the BBC had paid.

The grid for the Australian Grand Prix was predictable but contained a big surprise too: Jacques Villeneuve was on pole for Williams-Renault in his first appearance in Formula 1, ahead of Hill, Irvine, Schumacher, Hakkinen and Jean Alesi for Benetton. Hill won with Jacques Villeneuve second and Irvine third; Schumacher retired with brake problems. Hill was on pole in Brazil with Rubens Barrichello second for Jordan ahead of Villeneuve, then Schumacher and Alesi. Hill won with Alesi second, Schumacher third, then Hakkinen.

There was no doubt about the Williams car, or about Hill: he took pole again in Buenos Aires ahead of Schumacher and won with Villeneuve second, a satisfying Williams 1-2. Hill was on pole at the Nurburgring, with Villeneuve second. The

Silver Arrow: Mercedes has entered Grand Prix
racing four times, in 1914, 1934, 1954 and in the
1990s; the policy is to be on top or out of it.

start was a shambles for Benetton: both cars struggled away from the grid with their parking brakes locked on and Alesi slipped back to eighteenth place, then, in an attempt to make up for the lost time, went inside Mika Salo, collided with him, and was out. At the front, Villeneuve led and held off a challenge from Schumacher while Hill and Coulthard scrapped for third place. Villeneuve drove superbly to win his first Grand Prix, with Schumacher less than a second behind. That was bad enough for the *tifosi*, but there was no respite in San Marino where Hill beat Schumacher by 14 seconds. Williams had won five races and Ferrari had little to show for its challenge.

At Monaco, Schumacher crashed into the barrier, a rare mistake, and Hill seemed to have the race sewn up, leading in majestic style until lap 40 when his oil warning light came on, his engine seized and he was out. Alesi inherited the lead until he retired with a suspension fault which left Olivier Panis in his Ligier-Hart in the lead ahead of Coulthard. Coulthard could not catch him and Panis won, Ligier's first victory since 1981.

In Spain, Michael Schumacher's ability in the wet brought him his first victory for Ferrari, raising Italian hopes, only to have them dashed as the Williams run continued with victories for Hill in Canada and France. The dream team went on, Hill winning in Germany, opening up a 21-point lead over Villeneuve, but as he did, behind-the-scenes negotiations between Hill and Frank Williams had reached stalemate. Hill was reported to be asking for $10m for 1997 and Williams was not prepared to pay that, even for an incipient World Champion.

Ferrari had a new aerodynamics package for the Hungarian Grand Prix and Schumacher managed pole position and the lead for the first eighteen laps until the two Williams drivers got the measure of the Ferrari. Schumacher was lying third with six laps to go when his throttle stuck and Villleneuve won from Hill, deciding the Constructors' Championship. In the five races since

Schumacher's victory in Spain, Ferrari had only one fourth place and one ninth place, the other eight possibilities being all retirements. Jean Todt was lambasted in the Italian press but di Montezemolo stood firm: it had to be the car and not the driver

There was no hope of a Championship, but Schumacher showed how swiftly matters can turn around when he won at Spa, his 21st Grand Prix victory. Just before the Belgian Grand Prix, Williams broke off negotiations with Hill, the third time Frank Williams had let a World Champion or in Hill's case at least the most likely Champion, go. Williams gave no reasons. Hill had his heart set on a place at McLaren and opened discussions with Ron Dennis.

Then came the Italian Grand Prix and Schumacher's first appearance in front of 100,000 *tifosi*. Hill could clinch the Driver's title at Monza and he took a vigorous lead. On lap 6 Hill clipped a tyre wall and spun off under no obvious pressure and Alesi took over the lead, then Schumacher second, a poignant position for Ferrari on home ground. Benetton and Ferrari were both only making one pit stop and Schumacher was eating into Alesi's lead with every lap. Alesi pitted first, leaving Schumacher to put in some very fast laps before he came in for a perfect pit stop and out again into the lead which he held to the end and a hugely emotional greeting from the grandstand. Michael Schumacher had impressed the *tifosi*; the Italian press stopped hounding Jean Todt.

Jacques Villeneuve kept Championship watchers on the edge of their seats by winning the Portuguese Grand Prix in a race-long battle with Hill which he won, leaving Hill with just one point to get from the Japanese Grand Prix to take the title. Villeneuve took pole, but Hill led from start to finish and claimed his Championship, the first son of a World Champion to do so. Hill was World Champion but he was out of a job and Heinz Harald Frentzen replaced him.

From winning two successive Driver's

Championships and one Constructors' title, Benetton had slipped to third place in the top four, at best. Ferrari had improved its position but it had been a disappointing season. Schumacher was third in the Driver's Championship and Ferrari was second in the Constructors' title but 105 points behind Williams, hardly a result. Luca di Montezemolo was now determined to bring design back to Maranello and with Barnard's contract coming up at the end of 1997, when he said no to moving to Maranello the relationship was ended. As part of the separation, Ferrari sold the premises in Guildford to Barnard. Tom Walkinshaw pulled off a coup by signing Barnard for Arrows. To replace him, di Montezemolo pulled off another coup: he poached Benetton's two top men, Ross Brawn and Rory Byrne, the men who had been behind Schumacher's two World Championships, completing his collection of what became known as 'the Benetton Three'. Having Brawn as technical director with Rory Byrne on board brought a sense of calm to Ferrari, but Benetton had been stripped of its primary assets, top people.

At McLaren, Ron Dennis had prepared the ground for Marlboro's departure to Ferrari carefully and was able to announce a deal with West cigarettes, a German brand, for 1997, the cars to be painted silver, reminiscent of the historic Mercedes racing cars of the 1930s and 1950s.

Eddie Jordan had not had much of a season. The final payments had been made on the debt, putting the team on a much sounder financial footing and Peugeot stayed with the team for 1997. Martin Brundle had crashed badly and Jordan dropped him; Rubens Barrichello left to join a new team, Stewart, founded by former World Champion Jackie Stewart and his son Paul. When it became clear that Williams would not be retaining Damon Hill, Jordan tried to secure his services but could not afford him, so Jordan leased Giancarlo Fisichella from Benetton and signed Michael Schumacher's younger brother, Ralf.

The Stewart team had been launched with nationalistic overtones – the Stewart tartan wrapped around a white car with the commercial logos of the Hong Kong & Shanghai Bank, the Malaysian Tourist Board, Ford, its engine supplier, Sanyo electronics., but no tobacco. With equal nationalism another World Champion, Alain Prost, bought Ligier for $8.5m, giving France the dream of an all-French team, run by a multiple French World Champion with talented Frenchman, Olivier Panis, as No.1 driver, alongside Italian Jano Trulli and Shinji Nakano. The prospect of such a team, racing in blue, brought sponsorship from Gauloises, Bic and Canal +, the TV station.

For his 1997 launch, Flavio Briatore moved back from Italy to London for one of the biggest parties yet, at Planet Hollywood with the Spice Girls in attendance. But Benetton was trying to reinvent itself without talent behind the wheel and under the bonnet and it obviously lacked the substance of earlier years.

The 1996 season had been a British television channel's dream: a tremendous battle between two personalities going right down to the wire and culminating with a British Champion, the first since James Hunt had sparked off the BBC's interest 19 years previously. For its last season, the BBC did cover every race live, and the coverage was excellent, increasing the audience.

The problem with Frank Williams' decision to part company with Damon Hill was that Adrian Newey, the talented aerodynamicist behind Williams' recent cars, wanted to leave because he felt that under his contract he should have been consulted. Newey had discussions with Ron Dennis, as did Hill, and Dennis offered Hill $1m retainer plus $1m per victory, which he turned down and went to Arrows instead. Dennis offered Newey a reported $2m to come to McLaren once he had settled with Frank Williams, and Newey announced he would join McLaren on 1 August 1997, in accordance with the settlement.

The season opened on 9 March in Melbourne,

Press pack: Jacques Villeneuve faces the press his
way after changes of engine and main sponsor
were made at Williams for 1998.

Australia. Villeneuve was on pole, 1.7 seconds ahead of Frentzen who took the lead while Schumacher and Coulthard battled it out behind him. Frentzen's brakes failed and Schumacher moved up to second behind Coulthard, who won for McLaren-Mercedes, its first victory for McLaren since Senna's in Adelaide in 1993, 50 Grands Prix previously; Hakkinen was third.

On March 30 at Interlagos, Villeneuve stamped his authority, and that of Williams, on the proceedings by leading all the way except for pit stops, putting him equal with Coulthard in the Driver's title, with Hakkinen in fourth place. Villeneuve won again in Argentina, but retired at Imola with gearbox problems and Frentzen managed to hold off Schumacher for a Williams win, ahead of the two Ferraris. Schumacher won in Monaco, Villeneuve fought back in Spain, then it was Schumacher again in Canada and France. His run faltered at Silverstone where he retired when a wheel bearing went and Villeneuve won. Then Villeneuve faltered on Schumacher's home ground at Hockenheim, where he spun off, but the best that Schumacher could do was second behind Gerhard Berger. After the race, Berger announced that he was leaving Benetton; Briatore had decided to bring back Fisichella whom he had only leased to Jordan for 1998. Fisichella had given Berger a very hard time at Hockenheim until a tyre blew.

Villeneuve won in Hungary, but only just, from Damon Hill, who looked like taking a famous victory for Arrows for most of the race until a throttle linkage malfunctioned, almost within sight of the flag. The performance enhanced his bargaining position but it was not enough to persuade Ron Dennis any further. Schumacher won in Belgium with Fisichella second. Coulthard won at Monza. Coulthard had taken the lead in the pit stops, coming in fourth at the same time as Alesi came in leading, but the McLaren crew had him out again in 7.8 seconds to Alesi's 8.7 and when Schumacher came in on the same lap, Coulthard was in the lead which he held to the end. To cap

McLaren's performance, Hakkinen made fastest lap, set a new lap record and finished 9th. The McLaren team was coming together; it announced that the driver line up would be the same for 1998, even though Mika Hakkinen had yet to win a Grand Prix.

Villeneuve's victory in Austria put him just one point behind Michael Schumacher who was sixth. Then Villeneuve won the Luxembourg Grand Prix and Schumacher the Japanese, leaving the European Grand Prix at Jerez as the decider, with Schumacher on 78 points and Villeneuve on 77. The air was thick with official warnings about confrontational driving as Villeneuve took pole with Schumacher second, but Schumacher made the better start. After the first pit stops Villeneuve was all over the back of Schumacher until, on lap 47, Schumacher left a gap at Dry Sack and Villeneuve went for it. Schumacher saw him and turned in; the two cars collided, but while Schumacher spun off, Villeneuve continued, his car only slightly damaged. Villeneuve did not need the winner's points to take the Championship, so he eased off and the two McLarens started to close on him; they wanted to win. Ron Dennis then instructed Coulthard, who was leading, to give way to Hakkinen, a way of breaking his duck. Coulthard was clearly not pleased but did so and the two McLarens swept by to take a McLaren Mercedes 1-2 with Villeneuve third, giving him the Championship. Ferrari had lost another Championship which it had been desperate to win.

A complaint was made to FISA which sat the following week, stripping Schumacher of his second place in the Championship, an almost meaningless punishment. Many felt that at least a three-race ban would have been appropriate. It all added to the feeling that Ferrari and Schumacher led charmed lives. Ferrari and Michael Schumacher were box office, and the prospect of a start to the following season without Schumacher would have been a disaster for TV audiences, especially in Germany.

In the six seasons between 1992 and 1997,

Williams had won the title four times, split by two years in which Benetton triumphed after the death of Ayrton Senna. But it was the last year of the Renault engine deal and the end to a great partnership with Williams. Once again, the story of Williams was the story of triumph mixed with crisis; losing Hill in 1996, then Newey and Renault in the same year, was a blow, but it was the kind from which Williams had recovered before. As far as the engine was concerned, he had known that Renault was going to leave and he had been preparing for that day and was able to announce that BMW would be its supplier in 2000 amid persistent reports that part of that deal involved BMW getting a stake in the team. The company is still 70 percent owned by Frank Williams and 30 percent by Patrick Head. For the 1998–9 seasons, Williams agreed to pay a reported £13m for Mecachrome engines, effectively the Renault engine built under a franchise. Cigarette advertising continued, but for 1998 the brand changed to Winfield and the cars became red after years of Rothmans blue.

Despite the best efforts of Briatore, Berger and Alesi, Benetton had only one victory in two seasons to show for all the effort. Flavio Briatore had to go; his last race in charge was the Luxembourg Grand Prix. He was replaced by David Richards, an ex-rally co-driver and managing director of his own business, ProDrive with which he had taken the Subaru rally team to great success. British American Tobacco were looking for a way into Formula 1 and it approached David Richards to see if he would put a team together from scratch. He declined but suggested BAT speak to Benetton to see if it was interested. The Benetton family said no but saw in Richards a man to fill Briatore's shoes and they offered him the job. He started with radical moves, sacking Alesi and Berger, replacing them with Giancarlo Fisichella and Alexander Wurz who had deputized for Alesi several times in 1996 when Alesi had sinus problems. Renault had pulled out but like Williams the team would have

the same engines as customers of Mecachrome.

The ITV coverage had been very good, and although audiences were down compared with 1996, it had improved the audience profile for ITV hugely by attracting a young, aspirational audience at a time in the week when it had been finding it hard to attract much of an audience at all. It quadrupled their share of the audience and attracted advertisers back from other channels. The key to ITV's coverage was that it had promised to do it the way Ecclestone wanted it to be done: pre- and post-race coverage, qualifying on the Saturday covered live, a highlights and magazine programme and a new image for the whole event, a weekend in which there was a constant awareness of the event, provoking greater newspaper coverage as well.

Curiously, the huge sums paid by ITV were stark evidence that tobacco sponsorship was not vital to Formula 1. First it provided income which could be used to replace tobacco revenues rather than simply adding to the pile of cash which the sport was generating. Secondly it showed that other businesses and companies could be attracted to the sport, particularly car manufacturers.

Jordan's reputation as a serious team was slowly being enhanced, but it had yet to win a Grand Prix. It had a reputation as something of a Crazy Gang among the afficianados who mistakenly found Eddie Jordan difficult to take seriously. Having failed to get Damon Hill in 1997, Jordan did get him for 1998 and anticipating Peugeot's departure to Prost, had started talks with Mugen Honda as early as the Japanese Grand Prix in 1996. On the back of the two-year Benson & Hedges deal, the team now had a new factory, nothing on the scale of McLaren, Williams, Ferrari, or even Benetton, but it was equipped with wind tunnels, test rigs and computer design systems. Jordan was a serious challenger; he had made the transition and it was tobacco money that had made it possible. The truth was that, as in its first season, it appeared more successful because of its brash image and the sheer charisma of Eddie Jordan, his approachability, his willingness to talk where most team bosses are very buttoned up. Eddie Jordan is a man of the 1990s.

Whatever European politicians and bureaucrats may say or do, the fact remains that money in the right hands can be turned into victory in Formula 1 and the World Championship. The lure of Formula 1 for the tobacco companies and the addiction of Formula 1 teams to that money, has increased. For the 1998 season, Marlboro contributed $50m to Ferrari to finance its revival, West put $32m into McLaren, Winfield put a similar amount into Williams, Mild Seven put $20m into Benetton, Benson & Hedges paid Eddie Jordan $17m, the same as Gauloises paid Prost. British American Tobacco (BAT) made a deal with Ken Tyrell to take over the team and invest $275m over three years with Craig Pollock, Jacques Villeneuve's manager, as team boss. It was the end of the line for Ken Tyrell – with the exception of Ecclestone, the last of the class of the 1950s and well past his 70th birthday. He resigned early in 1998, reportedly over the decision to take on Riccardo Rossett, a genial driver with limited talent but good sponsorship.

In a sad postscript to the demise of Brabham and Lotus, on 20 October 1997 Ted Ball, the managing director of Landhurst Leasing, was jailed for three years for corruption in connection with the receipt of improper payments to keep Brabham afloat.

The 1998 season was extraordinarily competitive, a classic. At its heart was a highly personalized duel between the undisputed best driver in the world, Michael Schumacher, driving the second best car, the Ferrari F300, and arguably the second best driver in the world, Mika Hakkinen in the best car, the McLaren-Mercedes MP4/13. And so it proved. Hakkinen, Coulthard, Schumacher and Irvine usually shared the front of the grid. The subtle differences between the cars, the drivers and the circuits filled the pre-race

debate, and the dominant theme was whether Schumacher's superb driving could make up for any deficiency in the Ferrari. At the Australian Grand Prix McLaren showed that it had more than filled Williams' position as the top high-tech team with Hakkinen on pole and Coulthard second. The two McLaren drivers had a deal that whoever was into the first corner first, the other would not contest it. Hakkinen led and McLaren was completely dominant, easing away as a pair from the rest of the pack for a second McLaren 1-2. It was a great moment for the team, signifying its renaissance since the low point in 1995, but it was immediately surrounded by more controversy. Arrows and Ferrari complained to the FIA over the McLaren's brakes. The system stabilized the car going through the corners by reducing the effect of the braking on the outer wheels, and since it was operated by the driver, the complaint was that it was really a driving aid, a way of steering since it could be used to reposition the front of the car in a corner. The problem was that it had been in use since the middle of the previous season and had been passed by the FIA as conforming with the technical regulations, and Williams and Jordan had similar systems. The FIA rejected the complaint, but pointed out that if a team wanted to protest then it should do so officially.

Before the Brazilian Grand Prix, Ferrari got behind an official protest about the brakes and the stewards upheld it. McLaren, Williams and Jordan agreed to disengage their systems. It appeared to make little difference as Hakkinen took pole again and what were now called the two 'Silver Arrows' pulled away from the rest of the pack. Hakkinen won, a full minute ahead of Schumacher.

Bernie Ecclestone missed the Argentine Grand Prix because he was in Los Angeles meeting with Rupert Murdoch to talk about television and Formula 1 in the US. The previous weekend he had been at Long Beach for the Indy Car race where he had a meeting with the Mayor of San Francisco, Willie Brown, to discuss the possibility of

Over and out: overtaking is so rare today that drivers fight for position early, making first lap crashes, like Wurz's in Canada, common.

staging a Grand Prix in San Francisco. It was seven years since there had been a US Grand Prix, and Ecclestone was considering other alternatives, the front runner being Indianapolis.

Schumacher won in Argentina, but Coulthard won in San Marino and Hakkinen won in Spain and in Monaco, putting him on 46 points to Coulthard on 29 and Schumacher on 24. Schumacher then found new reserves, winning in Canada, France and at Silverstone, then Hakkinen fought back, winning in Austria and Germany. Schumacher made a brilliant counter-attack, winning in Hungary from Coulthard, which brought about a track invasion while some cars were still racing, such was the passion for a Ferrari victory in the Championship. That passion was evident again at the Belgian Grand Prix, the 600th in which Ferrari had participated. It turned out to be one of the most exciting and controversial races to date. It was very wet and a major crash at the start put four cars out of the race. The restart produced another series of incidents which put Hakkinen out when he was touched by Herbert, leaving Hill in the lead for Jordan. Schumacher got past him on lap 7 and led to the pit stops on lap 25, and with Hakkinen out of the running, it looked promising for Schumacher to take the lead in the Championship. With Hill in the lead, Schumacher set off after him in very murky conditions and smashed into the back of Coulthard, removing a wheel from his Ferrari. On the back of the mayhem, Hill won a fabulous victory for Eddie Jordan with Ralf Schumacher making it a Jordan 1-2. Ron Dennis was there to congratulate Eddie Jordan on the pit wall, welcoming him to the small number of people who have done it – won a Grand Prix as a team manager – and done it in such style. The team went into orbit, as did Jordan's growing band of passionate fans in Ireland.

Jordan wanted to retain Ralf Schumacher for 1999 but his contract provided that if Jordan was four points or more behind the fourth placed team after the 13th race of the season, then he was free

to go. Jordan had no option but believed they had agreed he would stay in a series of faxes and was prepared to go to law about it, but dropped it. Ralf Schumacher went to Williams.

Michael Schumacher duly rewarded the *tifosi* with pole position at Monza. Past Ferrari World Champions were there to celebrate Ferrari's 600th Grand Prix and to anticipate a Championship for the first time since 1979: Phil Hill (1961); 'Il Grande John' Surtees, still able to raise a massive cheer from the 125,000 strong crowd, 34 years after his Championship in 1964; and Niki Lauda (1975–7). Schumacher and Irvine managed a perfect result, a Ferrari 1-2; it was a highly emotional weekend, not least because Hakkinen's fourth place put the two title contenders on 80 points each. There was great tension as the teams prepared for the last two races of the season, the Luxembourg Grand Prix at the Nurburgring and the Japanese at Suzuka.

At Luxemburg Mika Hakkinen took the fight to Ferrari and beat Schumacher on the track, earning himself enormous goodwill and support, a 4-point lead, and setting up a fantastic finish to the Championship. Hakkinen could take it by winning or coming second while Schumacher had to win. The tension was palpable: Schumacher was on pole but the first start had to be abandoned when Jarno Trulli's Prost-Peugeot stalled after the parade lap. On the second start, it was Schumacher who stalled and had to make the second restart from the back of the grid. There was still hope; he was the best driver and Hakkinen could retire. It was not to be: Hakkinen led from start to finish with Eddie Irvine second, Coulthard third and Hill fourth.

Of the two teams that had set out to reinvent themselves – Ferrari and McLaren – McLaren had made it first. For McLaren, it signalled a return to the top; for Ron Dennis, it had shown that he could still do it; It was a great season for West and for Mercedes which had backed Dennis. It was particularly rewarding for them all because Ferrari had put everything into winning the Champion-

Rare talent: with Williams, McLaren, Benetton and Ferrari dominating the 1990s, Eddie Jordan's 1–2 at Spa in 1998 was impressive.

ship with backing from Marlboro which had dumped McLaren in 1993 and switched to Ferrari.

It was bitter for Ferrari which had lost again, making it 19 full seasons since the Driver's Championship had gone to Maranello, ten years since the death of Enzo Ferrari; it was bitter because 1998 was Ferrari's third challenge with Michael Schumacher.

There was no escaping the conclusion that it had to be the car. Just as Ayrton Senna had made Lotus look better than it really was between 1985 and 1987, so Schumacher's sheer skill and guts had obscured a far deeper problem at Ferrari, the only name left in the entry lists of the World Championship since 1950. The new management had not been able to rid itself of the legacy of the man who invented the *scuderia*, any more than Lotus had been able to rid itself of the ghost of Colin Chapman. The difference was that Ferrari was not fighting a cash crisis at the same time, indeed it has never been richer. Niki Lauda's valedictory note at the end of the 1998 season was, as ever, to the point. 'In Japan we saw that there was something not quite right with the team. It surprises me that a company such as Fiat continues to invest something like $140m to chase a Championship which Ferrari has not won for 20 years. It is time that those in charge try to get to the bottom of these problems'.

There was much soul-searching at Michael Schumacher's *alma mater* Benetton. Edged out of the top four by Jordan, and finishing just ahead of Sauber was not a comfortable position for the team which had won the Championship twice in the 1990s, and Dave Richards decided to go. It appears that Richards' plans were both too radical and too long-term for the Benetton family. He was replaced by Rocco Benetton, the 29-year-old son of Luciano. If Richards was too radical for some, then maybe he had got to the heart of what it takes to lead a winning team in the World Championship: never be swayed by sentiment, be ruthless in pursuit of any advantage, and have the

vision and the patience to build the whole package over time around real driving talent.

The ingredients to win are easy to describe but very difficult to deliver: a very high calibre leader, a good relationship with one of the top three or four drivers, a corporate structure aimed at winning, not counting the cost, which in turn means a plentiful supply of money, a long-term engine deal with a supplier of the calibre of Honda, Renault, Ford or Mercedes, one that is prepared to put whatever it takes into building a winning engine. The great divide between the top three teams and the rest since the end of the Cosworth era in 1982, has been those who have found a successful marriage with an engine supplier and those who have not. The 17 Championships since 1983 have been won by just four teams, McLaren with 9, Williams with 5, Benetton with 2 and Brabham with 1.

The 1999 World Championship was an extraordinary contest in Formula 1 history. The battle lines were as clearly drawn as in 1998, between McLaren and Ferrari, two teams representing two different cultures and traditions. One was the pinnacle of evolution of the kit car team, the other represented a grand vestige of a glorious past. Of the two top teams' four drivers, Eddie Irvine finished the first Grand Prix in Australia, where both McLarens retired with mechanical problems and his Ferrari team-mate, Michael Schumacher, had a puncture. Irvine won, with Jordan's Heinz-Harald Frentzen second and Ralf Schumacher third for Williams, evidence of two new German talents on the way up and of Jordan's continued progress into the premier league of teams. Mika Hakkinen beat Schumacher into second place in Brazil, but threw his advantage away at Imola by spinning off in a completely unforced error while in the lead, giving the home team a welcome 1–2, a feat the Ferrari pair then repeated at Monaco.

In Canada, it was Schumacher who made the unforced error, crashing into the Armco while in the lead; Hakkinen won. Ferrari slipped even further behind when Frentzen won the French Grand Prix from Hakkinen, with Schumacher fourth. Two weeks later, Ferrari's hopes were set back when Schumacher's rear brakes locked at Silverstone and he speared into a tyre wall, breaking a leg but otherwise unhurt. Hakkinen should have run away with the race from that point, but a wheel came off and he retired too. Eddie Irvine won in Austria, then Mika Salo stood in for the injured Schumacher in Germany, and led before handing the lead to Irvine. Hakkinen crashed when a tyre blew.

As time passed and Schumacher convalesced, speculation grew as to whether he would drive again in 1999. The question was, would he help Irvine take the title? McLaren won in Hungary and at Spa, but in Belgium the stark difference between the two cultures became evident at the first corner when the two McLaren drivers touched and Coulthard went into the lead, clearly upsetting Hakkinen. At Ferrari, the No. 2 driver was expected to sacrifice his position and help the No. 1 garner points. Coulthard, who still had a mathematical chance of winning the title, won, with Hakkinen second, four points behind, crucial points in the Championship since he finished with 60 to Irvine's 59. Hakkinen led in Italy but crashed again. Frentzen won for Jordan with Irvine sixth, putting Hakkinen and Irvine on 60 each. The strain showed when Hakkinen left the curcuit: overcome with stress and emotion he broke down and cried in public. At Nurburgring, it was Ferrari which fell apart, this time leaving Irvine with only three wheels in the pits for valuable seconds, but since Hakkinen could only manage fifth, he only moved ahead by two points.

Schumacher returned unexpectedly for the first Malaysian Grand Prix at Sepang amid strong speculation that he had been subjected to pressure from Ferrari. He could not win the Championship but his effect on the race was profound. He took it by the scruff of the neck in dominant style,

claiming pole position, with Irvine second, then leading, before handing over to Irvine. Schumacher then held Hakkinen back while Irvine forged ahead, and after shrewd use of pit stop strategy, handed Irvine the lead for a second time. Hakkinen could not get past and the race finished with a glorious Ferrari 1–2, putting Irvine four points ahead with one race to go, in Japan. Schumacher's reputation as a driver and as a team motivator was greatly enhanced, but within hours the FIA Technical Delegate ruled that Ferrari's barge boards, air scoops in front of the air intakes for the radiators, were illegal because a 10mm lip along part of the bottom was missing. Both Ferraris were disqualified. Ferrari agreed they were illegal but claimed it was a fabricating error and, on the basis that it gave them no advantage, appealed to the FIA. In the meantime, Hakkinen was declared provisional champion.

The Formula 1 world debated the rights and wrongs of the disqualification for a week, creating tension between those who felt that Ferrari's breach was clear, and those who wanted the Championship to go down to the wire in Japan. The latter group won the day when the FIA court ruled that Ferrari's infringement was within a tolerance and overturned the disqualification.

The last Grand Prix of the twentieth century was a needle match between Ferrari and McLaren. Suzuka was packed. Schumacher was on pole with Hakkinen alongside him, then Coulthard, Frentzen and Irvine who could win the title from behind, provided Hakkinen was no better than third. With Schumacher's grip on the team, confidence was high, but he fluffed the start and Hakkinen went into the lead and held it to the end to win his second title and McLaren's eleventh, a record. Thanks to Schumacher's second place, Ferrari won the Constructors's title, its first title of any kind since 1983, but the real prize, the Driver's title, had eluded Maranello for the twentieth successive season. The bells stayed silent in Maranello and honour was barely satisfied.

Relaunch: Denise van Outen marks BAR's takeover of Tyrell.

POSTSCRIPT:

FORMULA ONE AT FIFTY

The World Championship will be 50 years old on 13 May 2000. In October of the same year, Bernie Ecclestone will be 70. Both have prospered greatly and both have weathered extraordinary change, but as the Golden Jubilee approaches there is a whiff of fundamental change in the air. This time it not just the return of the big manufacturers, nor the continuing controversy over tobacco, the opportunities in the Far East, or the challenge from Indy Car racing. This time the biggest potential for change is the prospect of Bernie Ecclestone's departure from the scene. He is still at the centre of the World Championships, spinning the plates as he always has done, settling disputes inside the Formula 1 family, placing drivers, bringing in big sponsors, looking after politics, furthering globalization and building up the television revenue. However his recent efforts realize his interests in Formula 1 have signalled his departure and the only real question is when. His departure will leave a power vacuum at the top of Formula 1, and various forces are manoeuvring to fill it, both from inside and outside the Formula 1 family.

The power to control the future of the World Championships will come from controlling television coverage. Ecclestone has always kept himself close to television and has concentrated his efforts on making the sport as friendly as possible to the cameras: more overtaking possibilities; pit stops reintroduced; on-board cameras; corners at existing circuits modified; and new circuits such as Sepang in Malaysia were designed especially to slow down the cars and the race.

It seems to work. According to the FIA's own audit of worldwide TV audiences, they are growing dramatically. In 1994, the World Championship was broadcast in 150 countries; in 1997 it was broadcast in 202 countries. The worldwide audience broke through the 10-billion mark in 1981, 20 billion in 1991, 30 billion in 1993, 40 billion in 1994 and 50 billion in 1997. Even allowing for hype, it is still a huge global television audience.

Getting the mixture right for television has been Ecclestone's forte. He understands the needs of television and has laboured hard to shape Formula 1 to fit them. The three-day build-up is all part of it, starting with practice and qualifying, which television channels are obliged to take under their contracts with Ecclestone, creating a sense of anticipation, of wanting to be there as even national weather forecasts carry predictions for the race venue thousands of miles away. The sense of belonging reaches its peak an hour before the race starts, with feature coverage of the drivers, the circuit, the cars and the teams rubbing shoulders with film stars, pop stars, sportsmen, the rich and famous as they loaf around the grid, the pits and the paddock.

Ecclestone understands how this spectacle can be harnessed by television to create a virtuous commercial circle: greater sponsor interest, spinning off into greater publicity in other media, driving up TV audiences, making Formula 1 richer and more closely aligned with international popular culture, which in turn leads to greater demand for national Grands Prix from countries which want to be part of that culture. Globalizing the World Championship has been part of Ecclestone's long-term plan, not only in Europe, South America, Japan and Australia, in 1985, but by forging links in less obvious parts of the world, starting with his coup, the first Grand Prix behind the Iron Curtain, in Hungary in 1986. This prompted the Soviet government to nominate Leningrad as the possible site for a Soviet Grand Prix in 1989 just as the Soviet empire was about to collapse, but contacts continue, and Russia still wants a national Grand Prix. Malaysia had its first national Grand Prix at Sepang in 1999, the US will regain its place in the World Championship at Indianapolis in 2000, the same year that China has been given a slot at Zhuhai, and waiting in the wings are India, Lebanon, Dubai, South Korea and the new South Africa.

Staging a national Grand Prix is a symbol of

McLaren man: Ron Dennis went from racing mechanic in 1966 to Formula 1's most successful team boss, keeping a strong presence in the pits.

modernity and national prestige, and Ecclestone understands how to handle the paradox between nationalism and globalization, balancing the two better than many politicians. He understands the maze of contradictory forces at work, how a multi-national and nationless event can include nationalism, how teams whose chassis, engine, gearbox and a myriad other components can come from different parts of the world. He understands the demands of advertising global consumer brands while still allowing room for the passion of the *tifosi*, for Mika Hakkinen's Finnish followers to feel included, for Eddie Jordan and Eddie Irvine to reach Irish hearts, for Michael Schumacher's German fans to express their support. He understands why French fans root for Prost and his

Italian driver Jarno Trulli, why Brazilian fans follow Rubens Barrichello in Jackie Stewart's Scottish team and why Scottish fans follow David Coulthard in an Anglo-German team.

Every driver has a nationality and a personality, and the impact on that country created by projecting a single successful driver to international prominence on global television stirs interest and goodwill inside that country while promoting the World Championship in places with no tradition in Formula 1. Ecclestone understands the value of nationalistic aspirations in a global structure. Japan has had a Grand Prix since 1976, and has provided Formula 1 with some of its best engineers, but the string of hopeful Japanese drivers has yet to produce a driver capable of troubling the middle positions on the grid. The reason for the lack of success by Japanese drivers is difficult to divine, but it appears that cultural differences may be at the heart of the lack of success, that Asian countries with their long tradition of authoritarian societies and collective endeavour, have yet to produce the individual skills and individual ruthlessness needed to win Grands Prix. The nations which have produced the champions are generally individualistic and competitive.

There is more recent evidence of the impact of a local hero on interest in Formula 1: between 1994, the year that Michael Schumacher won his first World Championship, and 1996, the year he attempted his third Championship with Ferrari, television audiences for the World Championship in Germany went up by over 200 percent. Mercedes knows this and somewhere a calculation has been made about the impact of luring Schumacher to McLaren-Mercedes, strengthening the German brand with Mercedes, West and the world's best driver.

Similar ground has been covered in China as it prepares for its first Grand Prix: the search for a potential Formula 1 driver from its 1 billion people is on through its television audience of 250 million which already covers FIA-sanctioned Formula 3

McLaren-Mercedes: the dominant partnership in Formula 1, so much so that Mercedes may take a stake in McLaren.

races from Zhuhai and the Formula 3 classic from the Portuguese colony of Macau, which will soon be returned to the Chinese fold.

The other region which has all the ingredients to interest Ecclestone is the Middle East: rich enough to afford a Grand Prix, it has money for sponsorship, it has a growing television audience of consumers, aspirational consumers, young consumers, rich consumers with a taste for global products, patriotic consumers who would love to have an Arab driver as a local hero. Lebanon could be the gateway to the Middle East for the World Championship. There have been Formula 3 races on a street circuit in Beirut promoted by a local entrepreneur with hopes that they will lead to

support for a purpose-built circuit, and there is a Pan-Arab Formula Corporation to promote it through the Middle East.

Ecclestone knows that to be global, Formula 1 has to be in the United States, where the last Grand Prix took place in 1991. The two traditions – Formula 1 and CART – have always been very guarded about their relationship and wary of invading each others' territory, but both want to be *the* global series for single-seater, open wheel racing and to be global they will have to invade each other's territory. The World Championship used to be shown on ESPN, America's premier sports cable channel which has 60 million subscribers, but that contract ended in March 1998 and instead of renewing it, Ecclestone transferred coverage to Speedvision, another cable station with only 20 million subscribers projected for the end of 1998. The difference was that while ESPN just showed the races, Speedvision signed up to the Ecclestone package, promising to provide coverage of qualifying, pre- and post-race analysis, the whole race, repeats, highlights and some magazine-type coverage. It also agreed to the race going on the much larger Fox Network, owned by Rupert Murdoch, as a repeat on Monday after the race.

Motor racing in America is split between Indy Car and NASCAR, stock car racing, which is growing steadily in the US, while Indy Car is weakening. The problem for Indy Car is that it too is split, between CART and the Indianapolis Speedway which broke away from the CART's PPG World Series in 1996, forming the Indianapolis Racing League (IRL) with the Indianapolis 500 at the heart of it. Ecclestone had been looking for an opportunity to move Grand Prix racing back to America and he had discussions with the mayor of San Francisco about a street circuit race in that city in 1998. He finally moved into the gap between the two Indy Car series, bringing back the US Grand Prix on a specially built road circuit at the Indianapolis Speedway where the 500 had been part of the World Championship in the 1950s. The IRL series is not a competitor to Formula 1 while the CART PPG World Series could be. CART is looking for a global audience but in doing so it must compete with the World Championship which has the edge in international prestige. CART racing reaches 188 countries and claims just over 60 million viewers per race, but it is weak on the World Championship's heartland, Europe, where there are no races and it is broadcast on Europsport to a tiny audience of 700,000. Formula 1 is equally weak in the US, although it will be back in the year 2000, but it is particularly strong in CART's international venues – Canada, South America, the Far East and Australia – where Formula 1's

image as the top international form of racing is its single biggest asset.

The Grand Prix tradition of excellence comes at a price. Running a Formula 1 team is 20 times more costly than running an Indy Car team, precisely because of the endless quest for excellence in all things, innovating from race to race, challenging the regulations and the formula which is all part of the Grand Prix culture. Fans want to know that McLaren and Ferrari are working all hours between races to find some tiny extra bit of speed, reliability or grip which will give them a slight advantage on a particular circuit, optimizing the car for the number and sharpness of the corners, the length and surface of the straights, the altitude of the circuit or the latest advance in tyres. As things stand, the glue which holds all that together is largely provided by tobacco sponsorship and all tobacco sponsorship will be banned from European television screens from 2006, Grand Prix racing's centenary year. If it goes, it will remove one of the largest and longest-running sources of money which makes possible racing on the scale and the competitiveness of Formula 1. Ecclestone and Mosley have campaigned to bring down the costs of building Grand Prix cars. Ecclestone understands that a balance has to be struck between the cost of maintaining that tradition of innovation and excellence, and simply running out of money. With most decisions vested in him and a tiny circle of advisors and colleagues, the balance can be maintained, but if he was to be replaced by a multinational corporate body, then decisiveness may be replaced by muddle in the search for compromise.

In the 1950s, the glue was provided by multinational fuel, oil and tyre companies – Esso, Shell, Castrol, Dunlop – and the cars were built by national motor manufacturers, particularly sports car manufacturers such as Alfa-Romeo, Maserati, Ferrari, Mercedes, Talbot and offshoots in Britain like BRM and Vanwall, operating through national clubs and the FIA. They produced aesthetically pleasing cars like the Alfa 158, the Ferrari 500, the Lancia D50, the Mercedes W196 and the incomparable Maserati 250F, which were painted in national racing colours, and raced through sleepy villages on road circuits with not a spectator or a sponsor's logo in sight.

That romantic age was unceremoniously swept aside by a band of gritty, small-time entrepreneurs from the British motor trade who provided the glue through their energy while earning their livings as mechanics, running engineering shops, garages and petrol stations, second-hand car lots, motor car and motor cycle dealerships, men like Ecclestone. They changed Formula 1 the hard way, by taking on the factory teams and winning races. It took entrepreneurial flair, guts and staying power to race and win against the established factory teams.

In the 1970s, the glue came from the sponsorship which those kit car teams attracted and from their ability to band together through FOCA and extract a fair price for their talents. The 1980s saw the same group of men sweep all before them with turbos, aerodynamics, carbon fibre monocoques, active suspension, data links and a whole host of other high-tech devices. To pay for it they became addicted to tobacco sponsorship. The successful suspension of the tobacco ban until 2006 has brought about signs of a rethink on this issue. Max Mosley is on record as believing in a tobacco-free future, 'There are a lot of big sponsors who would be more inclined to come into Formula 1 if it weren't for tobacco. I think, the idea that F1 will be worse off without tobacco is nonsense'.

Not quite the theme of his meeting with the Prime Minister in October 1997. Ecclestone's threat, supported by Mosley and the FIA, that the whole kit and caboodle could be taken offshore, was no more than the flexing of muscles in the bigger power game, the expansion of Formula 1 and the World Championship. Taking the lion's share of the global television audience for single-seater, open-wheel motor racing is the prize, and the power game to achieve it is based on Ecclestone's

acute vision of the future and his astute cultivation of political, commercial and other interests, shaping the World Championship as both a global and a national forum. The internal power struggles over the Concorde Agreement, the EU Directive over tobacco sponsorship, the competitiveness of Formula One Holdings' monopoly on TV rights are all necessary family squabbles inside the Formula 1 family as it instinctively prepares for a change of leadership and structure.

The retirement of Ken Tyrell broke one of the last living links between modern Formula 1 and the 1950s, but of the kit car pioneers, Frank Williams, Ron Dennis, Max Mosley and Bernie Ecclestone are still in control of much of the sport, men who have masterminded successful teams, won multiple World Championships, as has Flavio Briatore from Italy, but the youngest of them is now in his fifties and Ecclestone is almost 70.

There is a new group of charismatic and talented individuals like Jackie Stewart from Scotland, Alain Prost from France, Peter Sauber from Switzerland, and particularly Eddie Jordan from Ireland, who have shown ingenuity and staying power but have yet to topple the pioneers from their perch and have yet to show they have the real toughness to survive and win. In staying on top, the really successful team bosses, particularly Ron Dennis at McLaren and Frank Williams at Williams, have consolidated their companies and put in place highly professional management systems, a million miles away from the garages and welding torches where they began. They have stayed competitive while creating real businesses out of their teams, steadily deepening and broadening them. In 1995 Williams moved to a new 32-acre site at Grove in Oxfordshire, and in 1998 McLaren moved into a 120-acre greenfield site with the racing team at the hub of a diversified business. Just as the diehards of the post-war era lamented the passing of the romantic age, so there is sadness for the passing of the small rugged teams of the 1960s, 1970s and 1980s.

Milestone: the celebrations for Ferrari's 600th Grand Prix in 1998 were a mixture of looking backwards and forwards at the same time.

Over the horizon is the return of the big motor manufacturers looking for ways to maximize their positions as part of global Formula 1, either as partners with the best teams or running their own teams. Ferrari, and Mercedes through McLaren, are the top two teams today, the only two who go back to the 1950s, but many names familiar to the World Championship are knocking at the door from Honda, Peugeot, BMW and Ford – all committed to Formula 1 programmes of different shapes and sizes – to General Motors, Toyota, Audi and Renault who all have ambitions to use motor sport to promote their names.

Throughout 1997 and 1998, Honda worked to provide the ingredients of a manufacturer-based team, building a car and an engine. There was confident speculation up to May 1999 that it would join in 2000 but instead it opted to supply engines

to BAR and Jordan, the traditional partnership between the small-team dynamics and industry muscle which has worked in the past.

Mercedes shows no sign of wanting to take the operation in-house and maintains exclusive use of its engines for McLaren despite many lucrative bids to buy them. Ferrari is the only original World Championship team still in business, heroically resisting change and hanging on to its mystique as part of the rationale for the support it receives from Fiat. The Ferrari name is an important part of the tradition and prestige of the World Championship.

Bernie Ecclestone appears to believe in the importance of the Ferrari heritage to Formula 1. Such sentiment is rare, and counter to a rational view of that future, especially the kind of ruthless commerical rationale which Eccelstone usually brings to the business. That future is likely to be dominated by a small number of mega-manufacturers, all with their own brands, their own images and and their own heritage to promote. For these manufacturers, Ferrari will be just another competitor on the track and another comperitor for global attention which will count for more than heritage.

Preserving the balance between the heritage of Formula 1, while constructing a model for that future, remains largely in the hands of Bernie Ecclestone until he decides to go, and until the parting of the ways comes, there is bound to be more instability as the various forces at work try to exert maximum pressure while avoiding a head-on collision. Many of the players remember all too well the last great battle for control of Formula 1 and its purse strings, between 1979 and 1982, which nearly destroyed the Championship. Bernie Ecclestone was the winner then, the main beneficiary of a victory in which sentiment and heritage lost out to commercialism.

Sentiment has been in short supply as another of the great institutions of motor racing faces up to an uncertain future. Silverstone is one of the few bastions of Formula 1 which, like Ferrari, can trace its history beyond the beginning of the World Championship which was born there in May 1950. Silverstone was transformed from a windswept, disused airfield into the spiritual home of British motor racing in a gentlemanly time or a snobbish time, depending on your view, but it was the beginning. Bernie Ecclestone earned his living selling motor cycles at the time, and racing them at Brands Hatch. Today he is one of the richest men in the world because he saw the commerical potential of that World Championship and managed to exploit it to the full.

In July 1999, Silverstone played host to the fiftieth British Grand Prix in the World Championship under a contract to stage the race which runs until 2001. The curcuit is owned by the British Racing Drivers's Club (BRDC) which counts most of the British motor racing

establishment among its 832 members, from Ron Dennis to Martin Brundle, and from World Champions Nigel Mansell, Jackie Stewart and Damon Hill, to its patron, the Duke of Kent, and the Chairman, Lord Hesketh. The 1999 race was held against the background of a hostile bid to acquire a fifty-year lease on Silverstone from Brands Hatch Leisure (BHL), which has been awarded the British Grand Prix from 2002 by Ecclestone for £11m, far higher than the BRDC had paid. Nicola Foulson, BHL's Chief Executive, preferred to use her contract to try and secure Silverstone for her company, and she offered BRDC's members £60,000 each to give her a lease, a move which was successfully rebuffed. It was a clash of cultures on a grand scale. Ecclestone and Foulson were determined to be purely commercial while the BRDC represented part of the British motor racing heritage and had resisted paying the kind of money to stage the race which Foulson was prepared to risk. Whatever the final result of the power struggle for the British Grand Prix, commerical imperatives rather than heritage will decide it.

As with most authoritarian leaders, succession planning has not been Ecclestone's strong suit. Maybe Nicola Foulson is the kind of entrpreneurial spirit who could fill Ecclestone's boots when he does move on; maybe Formula 1 will be too corporate for such individualists by then. Whenever he goes, Ecclestone will leave as he joined, an enigma. He remains secretive about much of his business and private life and despite his imminent departure, there has been no public recognition of his contribution to what has been a singularly British achievement, making this country the centre of the World Championship. Perhaps he does not want it, perhaps it really is the deal alone that motivates him. Perhaps Bernie Ecclestone is just too rich, or too controversial. He is the man, after all, who once expressed the view of Formula 1 drivers, if not himself that, 'first you get on, then you get rich, then you get honest'.

Nice work: Ferrari is
the only Formula 1
team to have
survived 50 years
of racing.

INDEX

BIBLIOGRAPHY

Allsop, Derick, *Formula One Uncovered*, Headline 1998

Autocourse, *Grand Prix Annual, 1969–71, 1978–85, 1986–99* Hazleton

Bellu, Serge, *Blue Blood*, Warne 1978

Boddy, William & Brian Laban, *The History of Motor Racing*, WH Smith 1977

Casucci, Piero, *Enzo Ferrari, 50 Years of Greatness*, Haynes 1980

Cimarosti, Adriano, *Camel Grand Prix Motor Racing*, Motor Racing 1990

Crombac, Gerard (Jabby), *Colin Chapman, The Man And His Cars*, PSL 1986

Collings, Timothy, *The New Villeneuve*, Bloomsbury 1997

Cooper-Evans, Michael, *Private Entrant*, Motoraces Book Club 1965

Court, William, *Power and Glory*, PSL 1988

Drackett, Phil, *Benetton Ford, A Racing Partnership*, Crowood 1990

Drackett, Phil, *Brabham, Story of a Racing Team*, Arthur Barker 1985

Donaldson, Gerald, *Grand Prix People*, Motor Racing 1990

Doodson, Mike, *Nelson Piquet*, Hazleton 1991

Dymock, Eric, *Jim Clark*, Haynes 1997

Edwards, Robert, *Managing A Legend*, Haynes 1997

Ferrari, Enzo, *The Enzo Ferrari Memoirs*, Hamish Hamilton 1963

Francis, Alf, *Racing Mechanic*, Foulis 1966

Frostick, Michael, *Pit & Paddock*, Moorland 1980

Gill, Barrie and Frostick Michael, *Ford's Competition Cars*, Haynes 1976

Gill, Barrie, *Motor Racing, The Grand Prix Greats*, Pelham 1972

Grant-Braham, Bruce, *Williams, the Story of a Racing Team*, Crowood 1990

Grant, Gregor, *World Championship*, Autosport 1959

Hamilton, Frank, *Frank Williams*, Macmillan 1998

Henry, Alan, *Benetton*, Haynes 1998

Henry, Alan, Brabham, *The Grand Prix Cars*, Autocourse 1985

Henry, Alan, *Driving Forces*, PSL 1992

Henry, Alan, *Fifty Famous Motor Races*, PSL 1988

Henry, Alan, *McLaren, The Epic Years*, Haynes 1998

Henry, Alan, *Remembering Aryton Senna*, Weidenfeld & Nicolson 1994

Henry, Alan, *Williams*, Haynes 1998

Henry, Alan, *Williams, Triumph Out Of Tragedy*, PSL 1995

Hill, Damon, *F1 Through The Eyes Of Damon Hill*, Little Brown & Co. 1998

Hill, Graham with Neil Ewart, *Graham*, Haynes 1997

Hilton, Christopher, *Aryton Senna*, PSL 1994

Hilton, Christopher, *Grand Prix Showdown*, PSL 1992

Hilton, Christopher, *Mika Hakkinen*, Haynes 1997

Hodges, David, *Encyclopedia of Grand Prix*, Hamlyn 1988

Hotten, Russell, *Formula 1 The Business of Winning*, Orion 1998

IOTA, *Edited Highlights of F3*, Transport Bookman 1980

Jenkinson, Denis, *A Story of Formula 1*, Grenville 1960

Jenkinson, Denis, *The Racing Driver*, Mass, Bentley 1969

Jenkinson, Denis and Postumus, Cyril, *Vanwall*, PSL 1988

Jones, Bruce, *The Complete Encyclopedia of Formula One*, Carlton 1998

Kapadia, Behram, *The Turbo Decade*, Osprey 1990

Lauda, Niki, *For The Record*, William Kimber 1977

Lauda, Niki, *Second Time Around*, Guild 1984

Lawrence, Mike, *Grand Prix Cars 1945–65*, Aston 1989

Lawrence, Mike, *The Story of March*, Aston 1989

Mansell, Nigel and Derick Allsop, *Mansell and Williams*, Weidenfeld & Nicolson 1992

Matchett, Steve, *Life In The Fast Lane*, Weidenfeld & Nicolson 1995

Mays, Raymond, *BRM*, Cassell 1962

Morrison, Ian, *Motor Racing, Records, Facts and Champions*, Guinness 1989

Morrison, Ian, *The Guinness Book of Formula One*, Guinness 1989

Molter, Gunther, *Juan Manuel Fangio*, Foulis 1958

Moss, Stirling with Nye, Doug, *Stirling Moss, My Cars, My Career*, PSL 1987

Murray, David, *Ecurie Ecosse*, Motoraces Book Club 1962

Nixon, Chris, *Racing the Silver Arrows*, Osprey 1986

Nye, Doug, *Autocourse, History of the Grand Prix Car 1966–85*, Hazleton 1986

Nye, Doug, *Cooper Cars*, Osprey 1983

Nye, Doug, *Famous Racing Cars*, PSL 1989

Nye Doug, *McLaren, The Grand Prix, Can-Am and Indy Cars*, Guild 1988

Nye, Doug, *The British Grand Prix*, Batsford 1977

Nye, Doug, *The Story of Lotus*, Motor Racing, Batsford 1972

Nye, Doug, *The United States Grand Prix*, Batsford 1978

Nye, Doug, *Theme Lotus 1956–86*, Motor Racing 1986

Rendall, Ivan, *Aryton Senna, A Tribute* Pavilion 1994

Rendall, Ivan, *The Chequered Flag*, Weidenfeld & Nicolson 1993

Robson Graham, *Cosworth, The Search for Power*, PSL 1990

Rollo, Alex, *The Monaco Grand Prix*, Ian Allan 1987

Rudd, Tony, *It Was Fun*, PSL 1993

Sheldon, Paul, *A Record of Grand Prix and Voiturette Racing Vols 1–10*, St Leonardís

Small, Steve, *Grand Prix Who's Who*, Guinness 1996

Smith, Ian H, *The Story of Lotus*, Motor Racing 1970

The Motor, *Year Book 1956*, Temple 1956

The Motor, *Year Book 1949*, Temple 1949

Tremayne, David, *Ferrari*, Haynes, 1998

Tremayne, David, *Jordan*, Haynes 1998

Tremayne, David, *Racers Apart*, Motor Racing 1991

Tremayne, David, *The Science of Speed*, PSL 1997

Walker, Murray, *1994 Grand Prix Year*, Hazleton 1994

Williams, Geoffrey, *McLaren, A Racing History*, Crowood 1991

Williams, Richard, *Racers*, Viking, 1997

Yates, Brock, *Enzo Ferrari*, Doubleday, 1991

Young, Eoin S, *Bruce McLaren*, PSL, 1995

Distributed in the United States of America
by Sterling Publishing Co., Inc.
387 Park Avenue South, New York, NY 10016-8810

A CIP catalogue record for this book is available from
the British Library

ISBN 0 304 35399 X

Design Direction by David Rowley
Designed by The Senate
Edited by Marilyn Inglis
Printed and bound in Printer Trento srl, Italy

Cassell & Co
Wellington House
125 Strand
London
WC2R 0BB

ACKNOWLEDGEMENTS

This book has been a labour of love, but without the
professional advice and support of a number of people, it
would have been hard labour. I am indebted, as ever, to my
agent Anthony Shiel, and to Anthony Cheetham of Orion and
Michael Dover of Cassell & Co for their advice and
encouragement. I am particularly grateful to Marilyn Inglis
whose editing skills have improved the text no end, all
achieved with the uncanny ability to balance firmness and
compassion with me. Suzanne Bailey performed miracles in
the picture research and her judgement of images and dogged
persistence in finding them have made a huge contribution to
the finished book. In this she was greatly assisted by Ker
Robertson of Allsport, Doug Nye at The GP Library, Simon
Anning at Sporting Pictures, Nicola Hill at LAT Photographic
and Leo Mason at Split Second. Lastly, I am grateful to my
family: my wife Heather, whose household has been disrupted
by loud and lengthy discussion of World Championships at
mealtimes, and whose television has been hijacked too often to
watch Grand Prix racing; and to my son David, who aided
and abetted me and provided much invaluable research.

PICTURE CREDITS

Hulton Getty: (jacket) 3 portraits on left; pages 3; 46; 48; 58;
63; 66; 86; 88; 92; 99; 101; 112; 127; 138; 142; 156; 185.
The GP Library: pages 20; 23; 30–1; 35; 36; 38; 42; 54–5; 80;
82; 85; 103; 104; 108; 122; 145; 147; 148; 163; 172; 181.
Allsport: (jacket) Williams, Ferrari flag, main image; pages 4;
76; 116; 135; 166; 196–7; 200; 203; 204; 207; 208; 211; 212;
218; 221; 232; 236–7; 239; 242; 244; 245; 250–1; b. endpaper.
Sporting Pictures (UK) Ltd: (jacket) Senna; pages 10–11; 13;
173; 248.
Leo Mason/Split Second: pages: 169; 170; 174; 175; 210; 216;
f. endpaper.
LAT Photographic: pages 6; 50; 53; 73; 96; 107; 118; 124;
129; 131; 132; 136; 151; 153; 159; 160; 164; 178; 192; 214;
224; 229.
The National Motor Museum, Beaulieu: page 26.
Popperfoto/Reuters: (jacket) Ecclestone; page 15.
Photograph: © Hugo Boss, Baldessarini, Spring/Summer
1997: page 227.
Photograph courtesy of Ford Motor Company: page 128.